I Am Bonhoeffer

᷐

I Am Bonhoeffer

A Credible Life—
A Novel

Paul Barz

Translated by Douglas W. Stott

FORTRESS PRESS
Minneapolis

For
Rudolf Herrfahrdt
(1907–2005)
Retired Superintendent and Pastor of the Confessing
Church who actualized love for one's neighbor
in the spirit of Bonhoeffer

I AM BOHNHOEFFER
A Credible Life—A Novel

English translation copyright © 2008 Fortress Press, an imprint of Augsburg Fortress. Translated by Douglas W. Stott from the German *Ich bin Bonhoeffer: Roman eines glaübwurdigen Lebens*, by Paul Barz, copyright © 2006 Gütersloher Verlagshaus, Germany. All rights reserved. Except for brief quotations in critical articles or reviews, no part of this book may be reproduced in any manner without prior written permission from the publisher. Visit http://www.augsburg fortress.org/copyrights/ or write to Permissions, Augsburg Fortress, Box 1209, Minneapolis, MN 55440.

Cover image: Dietrich Bohnhoeffer. Copyright © Gütersloher Verlagshaus. Used by permission
Cover design: Gütersloher Verlagshaus
Book design: Eileen Z. Engebretson

Library of Congress Cataloging-in-Publication Data
Barz, Paul, 1943–
 [Ich bin Bonhoeffer. English]
 I am Bonhoeffer : a credible life : a novel / Paul Barz ; translated by Douglas W. Stott.
  p. cm.
 Includes bibliographical references and index.
 ISBN 978-0-8006-6234-9 (alk. paper)
 1. Barz, Paul, 1943—-Fiction. I. Stott, Douglas W. II. Title.
 PT2662.A734I3513 2008
 833'.92—dc22   2007047324

The paper used in this publication meets the minimum requirements of American National Standard for Information Sciences—Permanence of Paper for Printed Library Materials, ANSI Z329.48-1984.

Manufactured in the U.S.A.

12   11   10   09   08   1   2   3   4   5   6   7   8   9   10

Contents

∾

The Church Must Remain the Church!

Christian—or National Socialist

I Want to Be a Saint

No Time for Saints

Invitation to a Tightrope Act

Silent Witnesses to Evil Deeds

Are We Still of Any Use?

Are You Bonhoeffer?

Who Am I?

Who am I? They often tell me
that I step out of my cell
calmly and cheerfully and firmly
like a manor lord from his mansion.

Who am I? They often tell me
that I speak freely and cordially and
clearly with my guards,
as if I were the one giving orders.

Who am I? They also tell me
that I am bearing these days of misfortune
with equanimity, smiling and proud,
like someone accustomed to victory.

Am I really that which others say I am?
Or am I only that which I know about myself?
Restless, longing, sick, like a bird in a cage,
gasping for breath as if someone were strangling me,
hungry for colors, flowers, for the song of birds,
thirsting for kind words, for human nearness,
trembling in anger at arbitrariness and petty insults,
driven by anticipation of great things,
helplessly worried about friends infinitely removed,
too weary and empty for praying, thinking, creating,
exhausted and ready to say farewell to everything?

Who am I? This one or the other one?
Am I this person today and a different one tomorrow?
Am I both at once? A hypocrite before others
and a despicably pathetic weakling before myself?
Or is what is left within me like a vanquished army
fleeing in disarray before the victory that has already been won?

Who am I? Such lonely questions mock me.
Whoever I am, you know me, and I am yours, O God!
—Dietrich Bonhoeffer (1944)

MARIENBURG ALLEE, APRIL 5, 1943

Dietrich Bonhoeffer goes over to the telephone, dials, waits. Silence. He glances at the person sitting over at the table, eyes down, hands folded as if praying. "No one seems to be there, Eberhard."

Eberhard looks up. "Not Christine either?"

Bonhoeffer shrugs, then continues to listen to the muffled, monotone ringing at the other end of the line. Then a voice, harsh, dry, imperious. "Who's there?" And then immediately again, this time as a curt command: "Tell me who it is you want to speak with."

Bonhoeffer hangs up slowly. "I think it's happened." He fumbles a bit with his left hand in his jacket pocket, anticipating the familiar, *Don't go lighting up another cigarette now, Dietrich.* But Eberhard just looks up at him with wide eyes.

"What's happened? Who was it?"

Bonhoeffer does not answer.

Strangers over at the Dohnanyis, at the home of Bonhoeffer's sister Christine and her husband, Hans. Gestapo. House search. And soon they would be here. In an hour. Perhaps two? Bonhoeffer again reaches for the telephone.

"Ursula?—Tell me, what are you having there for lunch?— Vegetable soup? Then potato pancakes? Seriously? And you could use two more guests at the meal?"

Eberhard vehemently waves him off. Bonhoeffer just laughs. "We'll be right there. I'll bring along a bottle of wine from Father's cellar."

The cellar is cool and dark. Bonhoeffer carefully chooses between several bottles. *It's happened* drones in his brain. A peculiar sense of relief washes over him, as if a burden has been lifted whose real weight he had never before really sensed.

So, a house search. And afterward the arrest. How often have he and his brother-in-law Hans played through this scenario! And now it would indeed soon happen, and yet he feels more curious than fearful.

He climbs back up to the ground floor on his tiptoes, a good Bordeaux under his arm. His parents are resting a bit just now, and he does not want to disturb them. "Come on!" The two of them go to the house next door, the home of his brother-in-law Rüdiger Schleicher and his wife, Bonhoeffer's sister Ursula.

"I have to say, it makes me very uncomfortable just barging in on them at lunch like this. It really seems awkward."

"Awkward?" Bonhoeffer laughs again. "But you're part of the family, Eberhard. Nothing should seem awkward in one's family."

Ursula is already waiting at the door.

"Is something up?"

"They're over at Hans and Christine's right now. They'll probably be here soon."

"Who?"

"You know who."

They sit together in the dining room, Eberhard leaning forward and silent, Bonhoeffer more talkative than almost ever. His laughter is almost too loud, his eyes slightly glazed. It occurs to his sister that usually just the opposite is the case. Usually it's Dietrich who holds back, Eberhard who is effervescent.

"Don't go lighting up another cigarette now, Dietrich."

But Bonhoeffer has already lit a cigarette, his third or fourth since arriving. He inhales deeply, then sculpts an impressive smoke ring in the air. "Ursula, a good meal really is the best thing for one's nerves when things break loose."

"What's going to break loose?"

Bonhoeffer ignores the question. "Keep a cool head. That's what's important. That's also what Hans always says, our clever legal scholar." For a moment he can almost hear his brother-in-law's sharp, slightly nasal voice: *Always remember they have nothing concrete against us.*

"They have nothing concrete against us," Bonhoeffer repeats now, "my military deferral, my trips abroad. All of it quite legal and with blessings from above."

His sister fetches the potato pancakes. "Perhaps you should . . ."

"Perhaps I should what?"

"I mean, if there are any papers in your desk. . . ."

"It's clean."

At the same time, however, he thinks, *Caution can't hurt. After the potato pancakes I'll go over there again and have a good look.*

Over at the house, things are still quiet. *Peculiar*, Bonhoeffer thinks as he goes upstairs to his attic room, again on tiptoes. Peculiar, his parents have only been living here for eight years; there have been other houses as well, previous houses, and the first not even in Berlin, but in Breslau, where he had been born just over thirty-seven years ago, on February 4, 1906, to be exact.

But now, in the film playing in his memory, it seems that for the entire thirty-seven years it was always the same house, the same world with its same dark furniture and the same pictures in the same gold frames, and with all the music, a silver veil of noble transience over everything, a world of slightly minor-key, profoundly reflective harmony.

He stands before the desk, rummages around in the drawers, then shakes his head. Nothing here that could in any way implicate him. In fact, almost too empty. *Let's not leave things too orderly. Otherwise they'll think you were anticipating a search*, his brother-in-law had warned him. Clever Hans! Always clever, always wily, always the tactician. Bonhoeffer himself has never been that way, will never learn how to be that way, and now cannot suppress a laugh.

Bonhoeffer the conspirator! Truth be told, certainly not his best role.

Going back downstairs, he glances at his watch. Already 3:00! He had called the Dohnanyis around 1:00. The visitors there certainly seem to be taking their time.

"Perhaps they won't come at all." Over at the house next door, it's his sister. She has again waited for him at the door.

"They'll come. Of that you can be sure." He marvels at his own certitude.

In the living room, Eberhard casts a glance at him, questioning, anxious. *I should never have drawn him into all this,* Bonhoeffer thinks. Though only three years his junior, Eberhard has always seemed like a little brother who needs to be protected from the ills of this world.

The clock on the wall ticks asthmatically.

"Father!"

His sister has been standing at the window, looking over at their parents' house for a full hour now. She runs to the door.

"Father, what's wrong?"

Karl Bonhoeffer enters the house. "Two gentlemen are over there, Dietrich. For you. They're waiting in your room."

Bonhoeffer is expecting to find the entire room turned upside down and the desk broken open. But everything is just as he had left it. Except that a gentleman is now standing by the desk, slender, quite proper, even slightly smiling. The other gentleman, sitting on the edge of the bed, stands up when Bonhoeffer enters, even giving him a quick bow in greeting.

The other one is still smiling. "Roeder! Supreme High Court military prosecutor." And gesturing toward the other man, "Commissar Sonderegger from the Gestapo. We're conducting the investigation here."

Bonhoeffer nods faintly. *Almost like a tea dance,* he thinks. Only with some effort is he able to suppress a chuckle. To be honest, he had imagined a visit from the Gestapo to be somewhat different.

Nocturnal, murky, threatening. Men in trench coats, hats pulled down low over their faces, perhaps even a gleaming revolver. But in broad daylight? The sharp April sun shining outside? And these men are looking at him so amiably, so expectantly, as if asking him, the pastor, for spiritual counsel.

Quite involuntarily, Bonhoeffer leans forward, slightly tilting his head toward the two visitors, as if he were all ears. "What can I do for you gentlemen?"

"Unfortunately, certain accusations have been raised against you, Herr Pastor."

The man who has introduced himself as the "Supreme High Court military prosecutor"—but where had Bonhoeffer heard the name "Roeder" before?—really did say, "Herr Pastor." That makes it easy for Bonhoeffer to maintain a politely noncommittal tone.

"Accusations?"

"In that regard we have already seen your brother-in-law, Herr von. . . . Pardon me, what is the correct pronunciation of his name?"

"Just as written. Doh–nan–yi."

"Ah, then not 'dokh–nan–yi,' as Commissar Sonderegger thought." He casts a brief, triumphant glance at the other man. "Because it's Hungarian, actually."

Sonderegger clears his throat slightly, and Bonhoeffer knows that the two of them agree in wanting to get to the issue at hand.

"Your military deferral, Herr Pastor. It's always seemed a bit strange to us that the intelligence service requested precisely someone like you—forgive me, but clerics are not exactly viewed as ideal candidates for intelligence work—freeing you from your obligation to serve in the military itself. And then your trips abroad to Switzerland, Sweden, Norway—and aren't you about to embark on yet another as well?"

"Yes, to the Balkans, and another to Rome. I'm waiting for my passport to arrive any day now. There were probably problems of some sort."

"Well, yes, and I'm afraid those problems will remain and you will have to wait a bit longer for that passport. But for now, we must ask you to come along with us."

"I'm being arrested?"

Roeder merely gestures in a fashion almost resembling an invitation.

"And my brother-in-law Hans von Dohnanyi? Have you also arrested him?"

Again a gesture dismissing the question as superfluous.

"And Major General Oster? Admiral Canaris? After all, they were the ones who got my military deferral approved."

The two men now look at each briefly, and as they turn back again to Bonhoeffer, it seems he is now looking at two stone masks without the slightest trace of cordiality or empathy.

They descend the staircase. The stairs creak. Not maliciously, or loudly, but quite properly, just as stairs do. And this creaking, like a gentle admonition to exercise caution when stepping out into the real world—this creaking itself belongs to this world here, just as does the candlelight on the evening dinner table, or the music-making on Saturday evenings, or the rows of gilded book spines in the library, or the faint whiff of eau de cologne in his mother's room.

All that seems to be a fixed part of the world out of which these two gentlemen are now accompanying him. *And really,* Bonhoeffer thinks, *really, up to this very day I have never left this world, not even when I was physically somewhere else. In New York, London, Barcelona, but also in Scandinavia, Italy, Africa. I have seen misery and wealth, splendor and poverty, good and evil. But this world here has always been with me. All-encompassing. Omnipresent.*

A fortress, he thinks. *Yes, that's what this house, my parents' house, has always been, with its precepts and laws such as courtesy, culture, tolerance. But now the walls are crumbling, and the precepts and laws on the outside are likely quite different from those here.*

From the corner of his eye he suddenly sees a man standing next to him, of medium stature, stocky. He starts slightly. Only then does he recognize himself in the full-length mirror next to the stairs. He gazes at himself for some time.

Ash-blond hair, a high forehead. Pale blue gaze behind eyeglasses. Rather flat features, peculiarly without any stronger definition. Hardly any wrinkles around his mouth and eyes. A face anticipating being fully inscribed.

So, that's me, he thinks. *That's Dietrich Bonhoeffer. Pastor. Doctor of theology. Confessing Christian. And now a prisoner. Perhaps not the worst role.*

He hesitates. Roeder grabs his arm as would a young person who wants to help an elderly citizen cross the street, and pushes him gently, almost tenderly toward the door.

I am Bonhoeffer, he thinks once more, *still single, albeit engaged, perhaps a couple of pounds overweight, thirty-seven years old.* "I will not live to be older than thirty-seven, absolutely not," he had once told his friend Eberhard, though he no longer knows why.

Bonhoeffer steps outside the house. A beautiful day. He looks up at the blue sky, and his mouth breaks into his characteristic smile, a smile some call haughty, others yearning.

A Little Prince

1912–1924

People like you have a foundation,
you have ground beneath your feet,
you have a place in the world.
—from the fragment of a play written in Tegel prison, 1943

GOD ALSO LOVES THE CHIMNEY SWEEP

The young boy dies. Lies there, stretched out flat, hands folded over his chest. His bright, youthful voice sinks into the hoarse roughness of an old man, whispering, "And to you, dear Father, let me say. . . ."

"What are you doing in there, Dietrich?"

The boy jumps up, is once again a lad of seven and very much alive. Confused, he looks over at his sister standing in the doorway.

"Are you playing 'dying' again, Dietrich?"

It is precisely this childhood scene—but why this one alone?—that Dietrich Bonhoeffer frequently recalled during his imprisonment, indeed, even during that very first night when they led him into the Tegel military prison.

Ah, but how he had enjoyed pretending he was dead back then, in his childhood home. In his imagination, the entire family used to gather around him as he spoke his last, weighty words. Yet only his sister Sabine was privy to any of this.

It was with her alone that he spoke about things such as dying and death, and she alone knew about the anxiety and fear that seized him each morning anew on his way to school, inexplicably, mysteriously.

He had to pass over a high bridge, and he was always afraid he would slip through the cracks and fall down into the river. Occasionally a dark man would cross his path, with a soot-stained face and a top hat, perhaps Death, or perhaps the devil himself. Dietrich was not consoled by the simple explanation that this was merely the chimney sweep, an utterly harmless fellow.

For the child, the world was full of terrifying things, and only his sister knew about all these fears. The others would merely have laughed at him.

"The others"—those were his elder siblings and his parents and several cousins who, of course, were given accommodations when they came to study at the university in Berlin, and several unmarried relatives as well who had no fixed residence. All these people gathered together at one time or another in this house in the Grunewald section of Berlin with its high-ceilinged rooms, gently creaking floorboards, and spacious surrounding garden.

And what a fine area it was, indeed, almost the finest in Berlin amid the teeming millions, with all the greenery and the white stucco facades of all the fine villas shimmering in the sunlight behind well-manicured hedges of boxwoods. Here lived scholars and physicians and professors, sometimes a theologian like the renowned Professor Harnack or a historian like the equally renowned Professor Delbrück; in a word, Berlin's intellectual elite.

The Bonhoeffers, too, were part of that elite.

Karl Bonhoeffer had come to Berlin from Breslau in 1912. He was now a professor of neurology and psychiatry at the university as well as head of the Clinic for Nervous and Psychological Disorders at the Berlin Charité Hospital. A thinker indebted to the spirit of the nineteenth century with little inclination for the school of thought that had emerged in Vienna and that now bore the name of Sigmund Freud. "Well, I think he's just a charlatan. Don't you think so as well, Paula?"

Paula Bonhoeffer nodded even though she was, as a matter of fact, not entirely of the same opinion at all and indeed found Professor Freud's views on the "mother attachment" and the "father complex" quite interesting. Over the years of their marriage, however, she had given up contradicting her husband and at most quietly pursued her own thoughts in private. Paula Bonhoeffer, née von Hase, was the daughter of a court preacher about whose noble lineage considerably less fuss was made than about the ancestors of the Bonhoeffer line, whose family tree was handsomely rendered in a painting now hanging in the hallway.

She had once wanted to become a teacher, but of a somewhat different sort than the others. She rejected the traditional Prussian principle of education according to which one first broke a young person and only then put him back together in the accepted Prussian fashion. Indeed, she had her own children educated at home until they entered secondary school. And she herself took care of their religious instruction.

To that end, she always used the grand pictorial Bible with the magnificent illustrations by Schnorr von Carolsfeld. "Just look, Dietrich," and Dietrich would move closer, gaze at the illustrations, and always be astonished, his blue eyes growing ever wider.

Here Jacob on the ladder to heaven, there Absalom, his hair caught in the tree branches, and then Samson pulling down the temple pillars, or King Saul hurling the spear at David while the latter sang. And the other as well, the New Testament, Bethlehem, the Sermon on the Mount, Golgotha . . .

"So, you like all this?"

Dietrich merely nodded. And then, turning back a few pages, "Who is that?"

"Our dear Lord God." In the very first picture in the Bible, God could be seen in a flowing garment, with a powerful beard and outstretched arms blessing the waters of chaos beneath him.

"Why is he called 'dear Lord God'?"

"Because we must love him."

"Does he also love us?"

"Certainly he does."

"Me too?"

"Most certainly."

"And even . . . even . . ."

The boy pondered for a moment.

"Even the . . . the . . ."

He pictured the man with the soot-stained face, the one he saw on his way to school, the one whom, dark and grim, it seemed no one could love. The child whispered very softly: "Even the—chimney sweep?"

His mother laughed, then told the story to the rest of the family at lunch, laughing then as well. Even his father raised his dark eyes and chuckled to himself. The others almost roared with laughter. Dietrich, however, just sat there and felt a bit ashamed. The others soon moved on to other topics.

The others. Three older brothers. Two older sisters. Then Dietrich and Sabine, the twins, born ten minutes apart. "You're rich," people sometimes said, prompting a smile from their mother. "Yes, rich in children." Ultimately an eighth child was born as well, Susanne.

Their grandfather also came to her baptism, bringing along imposing camera equipment. "Well, now, let's get all of you lined up nicely in a row." So they all stood one behind the other, looking to the side for the camera lens, the three elder brothers Karl-Friedrich, Walter, and Klaus, the sisters Ursula and Christine, "and you two twins as well."

What a fine picture it was.

"What charming little girls your twins are!" That was the reaction of one of their mother's friends after seeing the photograph, and Paula Bonhoeffer had looked up at her, astonished. "Girls? That one there is a boy, our Dietrich. . . ."

And as a matter of fact, at this time Dietrich did indeed look like a girl, what with his wheat-blond, almost shoulder-length hair. A veritable little prince with radiant blue eyes.

But he did not want to be a prince, and certainly not a girl. He wanted to be like his three older brothers: real boys, angular boys, sturdy, strong boys. And when Christmas approached, he defiantly scribbled on his wish list: "Soldiers. And a pistol."

"I would have thought you wanted some sheet music." His mother looked at him a bit disappointed.

Her Dietrich could play the piano so wonderfully, so charmingly, even sometimes—secretly—composing little pieces. But his gaze drifted over to his brothers, and to his father, who acted so differently toward them, much looser, almost like a pal. His father's critical assessment of his youngest son was quite different: The little one seemed more on the soft, gentle side, almost too tender, too dainty, a mama's boy. And Dietrich, sensing the silent reproach, bit his lip and withdrew, vehemently jerking away from this association with motherly tenderness.

Beware of too much emotion! Never betray who you are inside! And indeed, such would remain the case with Dietrich virtually till the end. And even at this early period, there were those who found this child to be unusually reserved, peculiarly cool, and, frankly, a bit haughty. Only his sister Sabine knew better.

But this was not a time when people gave too much thought to children as children. And the Bonhoeffers did not. Children were simply there, in this large house, which was always full of noise and laughter. The siblings brought their friends over, and their friends often brought their own friends, and so on. It didn't matter; quite to the contrary.

After all, here one was always among friends. In fact, this fine section of Berlin was in reality like one big family. Everyone knew everyone else, everyone liked everyone else, everyone celebrated all of life's little festivities together, balls, masquerades, parties. Everyone made music together, performed little plays together, married someone from among their acquaintances, like the Bonhoeffers with the Delbrücks or the Dohnanyis. Here everything seemed just a bit more free than elsewhere, a bit more merry, indeed almost gypsylike. Then there were the Leibholzes, the wealthiest of all, with a huge villa in the huge park and their own tennis court, owners of a cloth factory. They were Jews.

"Their father is still very much a part of the Jewish community. No, he never goes to the synagogue, but he does still belong to it."

"But not the son, not Gerhard. He sits next to our own Klaus in confirmation instruction, just like Hans from the Dohnanyis as well."

"Indeed. Hans as well. Even though the Dohnanyis are actually Catholic, funny. Oh, well, perhaps Hans is just trying to annoy his father for having left his wife and family. But Gerhard Leibholz was baptized quite early. He's always been a Protestant." And with that, the discussion was over.

Those were good times, rich times, at least for families like those here in Grunewald. "The luxury in which the upper classes live incites the lower classes." That's what Dietrich Bonhoeffer later wrote in a school essay. Here in the stable tranquility of his early childhood, however, precious little could be sensed of any such "incitement of the lower classes "

People did indeed enjoy all this luxury, which was not just for the sake of show. That would have been scorned and viewed as being in poor taste. But one did have money, time, and servants enough, and even a country house. The Bonhoeffers' was in Friedrichsbrunn, in the Upper Harz Mountains, only a hut, really, a bit crooked perhaps, but certainly cozy enough. And they went there every summer, first as far as Thale by train, then on farther with horse-drawns. Once they arrived, the adults first took a deep breath and set about relaxing, while the children stormed forth to all their wild games with the village children, Dietrich leading the way.

There he was certainly no little girl, nor a fine little prince. He ran faster and climbed higher than all the others. No one could throw the dodgeball as fiercely as he, and once he even returned home with a laurel wreath on his blond head. The others laughed at him.

During the summer there were also shooting contests with a big fair, with colorful tents and horses bobbing up and down on carousels. The villagers sat around inside the tents, guzzling beer, clapping along when the small brass band played marches, ending with "Hail to You in the Victory Wreath," the unofficial national anthem. Then everyone would stand up, their gazes exuding fond enthusiasm for the emperor.

But the day always came when the music stopped.

The carousels were dismantled and carted off, the festival tents as well, no more colorful pennants, no more brass bands. And in the Bonhoeffers' country house, Fräulein Horn—Maria Horn, the governess—said: "Quickly, children, get all your things packed up! Time to return to Berlin."

In the neighboring train compartment, men in gray uniforms howled. Soldiers, yelling and waving to people along the way, who themselves waved back enthusiastically and threw flowers to them through the open windows of the train.

"Why are they so happy, Maria?"

"Because war has broken out, Dietrich."

It was August 14, 1914.

"I Must Inform You That Your Son . . ."

So, there was a war. And at the beginning, bells were ringing and proclaiming new victories daily. Children in school assiduously stuck pins on wall maps charting the inexorable advance of the conquering German troops, and at home people conscientiously repeated the words of the departing soldiers: "We'll be back home when the leaves change color . . ."

The leaves changed color. And fell. But no one had returned from the front. And the victory bells rang less and less frequently. Instead, in the Bonhoeffer house Dietrich's parents increasingly looked at each other with concerned faces. "Our nephew Karl . . . he, too . . . and young Goltz . . . his poor mother. . . ."

In the meantime, the family had moved into an even larger house on Wangenheim Street with an even larger garden around it, and now they planted potatoes and vegetables and kept chickens and even a goat for milk, which quickly became part of the family and was even taken along to Friedrichsbrunn during vacation.

The children, and especially the twins, thought all this was grand fun. After all, they did not really have anything against the war and did not really understand the grownups' frequent sighs of "If only we could have peace again!" Particularly as far as Dietrich was concerned, all this could just as well last a bit longer. At least until he himself were old enough to go out into the field with all the other soldiers. That was his most ardent wish.

First, however—it was already 1917—his oldest brothers were in line, Karl-Friedrich and Walter, and once at dinner their mother had quietly asked whether their father might not obtain a somewhat safer position for them at the back lines. The two boys vehemently protested. "Hey, we're not shirkers!" And now their little brother looked up to them with even greater admiration.

They reported for duty. Things got quieter in the house. The children once again had long discussions in the evenings in bed about dying and death. Now death was something different than earlier, no longer an unexplained accident as it had been when in Friedrichsbrunn a small child had fallen into a shaft and drowned.

No, dying was now something quite solemn and sublime, something in service of a grand cause, and the children accordingly no longer simply referred to "death." No, now they spoke about the "eternity" into which every person would someday enter. And though the idea admittedly unnerved them somewhat, at the same time it carried with it a modest, wistful promise of happiness.

Then in April 1918 a letter arrived. Walter had been wounded. His legs were full of shell splinters, and he was lying in a field hospital after an operation. Dietrich's mother had reticently asked, "Shouldn't we go visit him, Karl?"

Dietrich's father quickly scanned the letter again. "He expressly does not want us to."

"Of course he wants us to. You know that."

Karl Bonhoeffer shook his head—and for the rest of his life, he never forgave himself for doing so. "No. We will respect Walter's wishes." Dietrich, however, pictured himself lying in just such a field hospital, with heavy bandages around his head and body, a beatific, Madonna-like nurse at his bedside, gazing at him tenderly, a red cross on her white hat, to whom he would dictate his last words, words that would then enter into the immortal treasury of quotations alongside Goethe's "More light!" or Nelson's "England expects that every man will do his duty."

Walter, too, had dictated a letter, had spoken about the probability of a second operation. The letter had sounded cheerful, almost playful.

Dietrich's parents had smiled at each other. "Our brave boy!" And then the day came. It was early afternoon, when everyone and everything was quiet in the house on Wangenheim Street. The doorbell suddenly rang, shrill, clanging, abrupt.

The telegram messenger.

Dietrich had wanted to run to the door himself, but his father was quicker. The boy heard him exchange a few words with the messenger, then saw him go into his study. From the hallway, through the half-open door, he could see his father sit down, slit open the envelope, read, stare blankly, and then, suddenly, with a dry sob, let his head sink down on the desk, where it remained for several seconds, unmoving, silent.

Dietrich had never seen his father this way. He shrank back when Karl Bonhoeffer, with short, wooden footsteps, walked right by him as if blind and went upstairs to his mother's room, where she was taking a midday nap.

Dietrich just stood there, fixed, rigid, his arms hanging at his sides. Finally he dared to go into his father's study, which otherwise the children could do only with his permission. He picked up the telegram, which had fallen on the floor, and read it, his eyes blurring. "I must inform you that your son . . ."

Walter was dead.

A cry came from the second floor of the house, not really human, more like a mortally wounded animal. It was Dietrich's mother, who cried out and then sank into a convulsive, unceasing fit of weeping. How Dietrich would have liked to go upstairs to her, caress her, kiss her, hold her tenderly, indeed, whisper to her that soon he himself would report for duty, would go to the front and avenge his brother's death. But something held him back, and with slumped shoulders he instead merely slunk back into his room.

Perhaps death was not so beautiful and sublime after all.

His mother was not at dinner that night. His father merely remarked that he had taken their mama over to relatives for a time so that her heart might find peace again. And then he added, "But now let us pray for our deceased Walter!" Dietrich bowed his head, as did all the others, and yet was also astonished to hear something like this from, of all people, his father, who normally never really prayed at all and instead was inclined to cut a wry smile at the mere mention of "God" and religion.

The war was over. But there was no real peace yet. Men with red armbands marched through the streets of Berlin, singing the "Internationale" and talking about human rights, and calling themselves "Spartacists" after the slave leader Spartacus. One could hear the dull clatter of their machine guns all the way out to the Grunewald section, and Dietrich's mother had told their cook, Anna, "Make sure we always have a good pot of coffee on hand and plenty of pastry so we'll have something to offer them." But the Spartacists never made it as far as Grunewald.

Here everything remained quiet and green and, really, wholly unchanged.

There was no more emperor. Members of the Bonhoeffer household bore this fact with equanimity, not least because they had never really had that high an opinion of the second Wilhelm. When rumor had it that he would be whiling away his considerable free time in Dutch exile chopping wood, Dietrich's father quipped, "Well, at least that's something he may have some understanding of."

Other names were mentioned with considerably more respect, and one with increasing frequency, namely, the new foreign minister, Walter Rathenau. Rathenau was an industrialist who had taken care of supplying the home front during the war. "He's one of us, cut from the same cloth, and also quite bright. One can expect great things from men like that," Karl Bonhoeffer had said. He then read a newspaper article to Dietrich's mother about the Treaty of Rapallo. The German Reich and the young Soviet Union would be exchanging diplomats, mutually waving all war reparations and offering mutual economic support. "Now, that's the way things should be done!"

"But Karl, an alliance with those horrible Bolsheviks who murdered the tsar and his entire family?"

Karl Bonhoeffer remained composed. "The Russians call the tsar 'Daddy,' and that wonderful professor Freud in Vienna believes that everyone must kill his father at one time or another if one is truly to be free."

Horrified, his wife raised her hand toward him, *"Charles, mon cher! Ne pas devant les enfants!"* Such things were simply not to be uttered in front of the children.

Rathenau actually did not live far from the Bonhoeffers, in one of the most beautiful villas in that section of town. The house had an excruciatingly narrow front door through which politicians, intellectuals, and artists would squeeze, and then, at a considerably later hour, occasionally also young fellows with well-muscled bodies and short blond hair over their rather low brows.

There was considerable speculation and rumor concerning Rathenau's inclination for these somewhat dim, strapping lads with their broad shoulders and tight derrieres. The general public, however, knew Rathenau only as the ever-irreproachable gentleman with the goatee and melancholy gaze whose chauffeur would drive him from Grunewald to his ministry every morning. Just as he did on this particular day, June 22, 1922.

The car drove up. Rathenau leaned back in the seat and glanced briefly over at the car on the opposite side of the street. But then he froze.

Several men were sitting there, leaning over as if lurking or lying in wait. Rathenau thought he recognized one of them. Wasn't he one of those who had recently squeezed through Rathenau's front door? Kern, that was his name. And now he was holding a revolver pointed directly at Rathenau.

Then the shots rang out.

I'll Create This Church Anew

The students had jumped out of their seats and run over to the window. The schoolwork on their desks was utterly forgotten. That sound, that dry, barking sound, that must have been shots! And really close! "No, no, those weren't shots. I was in the war, I know what shots sound like. They sound different." But even the teacher had gotten quite pale. "Just keep working at your desks!"

Then during recess, the seniors at the Grunewald Higher Secondary School learned that, only a few streets away, Germany's foreign minister, Walther Rathenau, had just been murdered. "Those swine!" That was Bonhoeffer's reaction, one of the seniors, his face beet-red with anger. "These right-wing Bolsheviks just shoot down the best we have. Someone ought to just shoot them down as well, like mad dogs!" The other students gaped in astonishment. This student, with all his sixteen years and bright blue eyes, was the youngest in the class, someone the others did not really take all that seriously. But then again, he could occasionally demonstrate passionate and remarkable clarity far, far beyond his years and stature.

"Someday our Dietrich will become a great defender of the people." The others laughed.

Although hearty toasts were proposed to Rathenau's murder—and to his murderers—in more than one back room in the city, the general grief for the dead statesman was considerable and genuine, and two hundred thousand Berlin citizens gathered for demonstrations three days later in the Lustgarten, the grand park near the castle. Speeches were delivered amid a sea of banners. The murdered man was never as popular during his lifetime as now.

Bonhoeffer, too, was among these thousands, alongside him Gerhard Leibholz, four years older and actually more his brothers' friend than his own, though he certainly shared Dietrich's admiration for the deceased Rathenau. "Why on earth must such a man die?" Bonhoeffer shook his head while the speaker up on the castle balcony spoke about Rathenau's will to peace and his intelligent politics of reconciling earlier enemies.

It began to drizzle, gently. Umbrellas appeared, opening up among the crowd; collars were turned up. Bonhoeffer, too, hunched his shoulders, shivering. "Why only him?"

"Perhaps only now will people recognize who he was and what he wanted," Leibholz answered softly, "and perhaps also where our real enemies are to be found."

Bonhoeffer brushed his wet hair back from his face and continued looking toward the speaker. "You're saying a person has to sacrifice himself before people finally understand the cause for which he stood?"

"Possibly, yes."

"Like Moses, who never even set foot in the Holy Land, where he wanted to lead his people. . . ?"

"What? He never actually made it there himself?"

"You can read about it yourself in the Bible."

Leibholz laughed. "You're much more familiar with it than I. And apparently with the history of the Jews as well."

The demonstration was over. The crowd dispersed. The two young men walked away together, silently. After a while, Leibholz, quietly, hesitatingly, finally asked, "Do you maybe think . . ."

"Do I maybe think what, Gerhard?"

"That they shot Rathenau because he was a Jew?"

Bonhoeffer did not answer. Like everyone else, he was familiar with the slogans people had painted on walls. Beat him to death, that Rathenau! That goddamned Jew pig!

"Things could get really dangerous for us Jews again," Leibholz said.

"What do you mean, 'us Jews'?" Bonhoeffer did not understand.

"Well, I'm one myself, in case you've forgotten."

"But baptized. A Protestant now."

"Maybe that won't make any difference soon."

There was no school today. Then day-to-day life picked up again, although it was never particularly difficult for Dietrich Bonhoeffer. He may indeed have been the youngest in the class, but he was also the best, in fact so good in most subjects that his teachers even found their way clear to put up with his atrocious handwriting.

"If only all these things you write could also be deciphered," his teacher had once sighed when returning Dietrich's essay on "Germany's Situation before the World War." "But your presentation, how the naval rivalry between England and Germany was the real reason leading to the war—no one has yet come up with that. Very good, very intelligent."

The teacher had leaned over to speak with Dietrich, so close in fact that none of the other students could hear what he said. "You're quite gifted, Dietrich, almost too gifted. All possibilities are open to you—even though," here he let out a gentle sigh, "that sort of thing can also be a great burden."

This statement followed Bonhoeffer home. *All possibilities*, he thought, sitting at the piano in the house there on Wangenheim Street. But which is the right one, the true one for me? His fingers glided over the keys.

Perhaps a pianist. Indeed, he had once even played for a real one. Or a physician, like his father, in a white coat, a look of kindly seriousness in his countenance. Or a professor, standing at a lectern high above his students—their teacher, their mentor.

"I want to be a theologian."

That was at dinner. The family members were just eating their soup, and Dietrich himself had no idea what prompted him to announce such a thing at precisely that moment. Even though the idea itself had long taken hold in his mind, he had never spoken about it so directly with others. It would have been like revealing a shameful hidden secret in his soul, like showing himself naked to the others.

And now the anticipated response. His brothers broke out in laugher. "You want to go to work for the church? For this lame, petit-bourgeois edifice?"

His father had not yet said anything. He merely calmly put his soup spoon down and gazed at his son for a moment with his dark, searching eyes, as was his custom. This time, however, his son perceived something different in those eyes, something like worry, concern, and a touch of anxiety.

"So, a theologian like your grandpapa and your uncle; well, yes," Karl Bonhoeffer finally said. "But the church is different today than it was during their time. No longer the high man on the totem pole; it's . . ."

"But didn't you yourself once consider becoming a theologian?" Dietrich's mother had just entered the conversation.

"Well, yes, for a short time." Karl Bonhoeffer laughed out loud. "But the prospect of having to stand in a pulpit every Sunday and be the only one to speak—no, no, that would simply have been too boring for me."

He had picked up his spoon again, animatedly. "Yes, indeed: boring. That is what the church has become, unfortunately. At least for a lad as gifted as you." And his son, to his own astonishment, now heard himself respond, "Then I'll just have to make it exciting again, Father!"

"You, Dietrich?"

"Yes, me. I'll create this church anew."

Hastily, as if having just inadvertently blurted out a blasphemy, Dietrich went back to eating his soup.

THEOLOGY MAKES A PERSON LONELY

The early 1920s really were not a particularly good time to be studying theology.

The time was past when prominent theologians such as Bonhoeffer's own later mentor, Adolf von Harnack, wrote speeches for their emperor, putting such delectable words into their mouths as, "I no longer know parties; I know only Germans." In August 1919 the church-state alliance had been sundered once and for all, and an enormous, deep emptiness threatened the country now that the classic "alliance between throne and altar" no longer existed.

But what, then, was the church today? That is, beyond the gentle, twilight interiors of its houses of God? Merely the keeper of Sunday piety? The backdrop to weddings, baptisms, and funerals? That is, now that its function as "keeper of the state" had been taken from it?

The clerics themselves were baffled. Many reproached the new leaders as "red pseudopoliticians." Others wondered where it would all lead. And who—above all—would study theology now in any case? And why?

Bonhoeffer himself, if he were honest, did not know the answer to that question either. He stood at the window of his room, smoking—a habit he had picked up at school—and gazing out at the icy blue Neckar River.

This was not Berlin, not the huge, shimmering, boiling cauldron convulsed by inflation and post-inflation with all its street fights between the left-wingers, the right-wingers, and who knows who else. This was Tübingen, where his father had attended the university earlier. Where all the Bonhoeffer children traditionally began their university years. And where Grandmother Bonhoeffer still lived. Frau Julie Bonhoeffer, eighty-two years old. It was a bitterly cold January day in 1924.

The grandson stepped outside and began his walk over to his grandmother's on Neckarhalde Street, ice skates over his shoulder. After his visit he wanted to do a bit of ice skating on the frozen river. He walked along whistling softly, "Jesus, lead the way. . . ." A "red" hymn, he thought to himself. Such was his classification: "red" hymns like this one stood for life and faith; "black" hymns like "Now May All Give Thanks to God" stood for doctrine and the church.

But what doctrine? For what was God to be thanked? For watching over everyone like the faithful keeper of a flock? That is, for being a utilitarian God? As if made by human beings—and if so, then what, exactly, were his servants supposed to be? Higher officials of the highest power? A power that held sway over its creation as if it were a large business?

Bonhoeffer didn't know.

He arrived at Neckarhalde 38. Standing before the door and the inviting stucco facade of the house with its colored glass windows, Bonhoeffer looked around once more. Tübingen, with all its Biedermeier tranquility, had always seemed to him like an almost self-enclosed world, like a world that was somehow already part of the past. And occasionally even Grandmama herself—he smiled tenderly—seemed like a remnant of the past.

An old but handsome woman, her magnificent steel-gray hair meticulously combed back, her face still alive with the clear, self-assured energy of a woman who had always known what was best both for herself and for others. The grandson kissed her hand and cheek.

"Your suit is wrinkled again; it needs ironing. And your tie is crooked," she chided.

"Well, you know how I am about clothes." Since moving out of his parents' house, domestic tidiness and neatness were not exactly Dietrich's strengths.

"Help me, child." Bonhoeffer supported her beneath her arms. She groaned. "These bones of mine. They just won't cooperate anymore. Pretty soon I won't be able to do for myself. Then I think I'll probably accept your father's offer to move in with all of you in Berlin." Cautiously, arm in arm, they walked over to the tea table. Bonhoeffer wondered what he ought to talk about.

Perhaps about the "Hedgehog," the student fraternity to which even his father had once belonged. A fraternity without the traditional dueling loft and student duels, and instead of the gaudy, colorful caps, members wore a demonstratively prickly cap with a hedgehog on top.

"Karl-Friedrich and Klaus are not planning on joining the 'Hedgehogs' here in Tübingen," he told her. "They're opposed to students supporting the imperial army against uprisings, either leftist or rightist."

"And you? Do you have a different opinion than your brothers'?"

Bonhoeffer shrugged. "Well, I don't think it's so bad. And I was there when they called us up for military exercises so we could learn how to handle weapons. I just thought it was a nice change of pace."

"And? Was it fun? Were your comrades nice fellows?" She pushed a bowl of his favorite cookies over to him.

"Yes, yes, quite nice. A bit reactionary, maybe. But otherwise. . . ."

Earlier in his life, to be honest, he had never really established any genuine contact with others. Such was also the case here in Tübingen, where, once again, he was "the youngest," just as he was in school earlier. Popular and always in the middle of things. No one danced as gracefully, no one sang as well as he. And right up there with the best of them in sports. Masterful in tennis. The little star that, with cool radiance, seemed to revolve around itself.

He did indeed have a circle of friends. But no best friend. No lady friend.

"I'm still too young for that," he occasionally remarked, thinking at the same time that Ursula, however, was not too young. She was already engaged to her Rüdiger, Rüdiger Schleicher, the jurist. And Christine would probably marry the Dohnanyis' Hans. His astute brotherly attentiveness sensed it. As it also did—not without a slight sting of jealousy—Sabine's inclination for Gerhard Leibholz. His consolation was that his elder brothers did not seem to be in quite such a hurry with the marriage thing. And he himself . . .

He could see his own reflection in the silver teapot. A somewhat chubby young man with a slightly haughty smile peered back at him from the reflection. Dietrich could not really say whether, should he meet that fellow on the street somewhere, he could warm up enough to him to want to become friends.

"You're rather lonely, child, aren't you?" His grandmother, whose gaze, like his father's, was dark and searching, fathoming everything, looked over at him. As if in response, he shoved another cookie into his mouth. Ginger cookies. He smacked his lips, savoring the flavor.

Well, yes, he probably was lonely. And why should he not be? How could he explain to others what he was really seeking in theology, his major at the university? Security? Certainty about who he was? Who would understand?

"Theology makes a person lonely, Grandmama."

Although they spoke about other things that afternoon as well, this particular idea accompanied him as he walked down toward the Neckar River. It stayed with him while he put on his ice skates and then pushed him along as he glided across the ice. And perhaps that is why he was less attentive than usual.

In any case, it suddenly seemed as if the ground were opening up beneath him, with nothing there to support him anymore. He slipped, skidded, and his legs suddenly seemed to be jerked forward out from under him. He fell backward, the back of his head slammed against the ice, and then he saw only blackness with bright, shooting flashes of light. The last thing he heard were the cries of the people on the riverbank who had apparently seen him fall.

"Yes, yes, I'm doing much better now. What an imbecile, slipping and falling like that on the ice." The brilliant winter sun shone in the hospital room. His parents, who had arrived from Berlin for his birthday, were sitting on the edge of the bed. Their son was eating some of his birthday cake with what was obviously a robust appetite.

Perhaps too robust, and his laugh was perhaps too merry. His father wondered what was going on.

"That was not a matter of his body; that was a matter of his soul. That's why he fell," he later remarked to his wife in the hall outside Dietrich's room. "He's overtaxing himself, clearly."

"Are you saying," Dietrich's mother cast an anxious look at her husband, "that our Dietrich is working too much?"

An orderly rolled a hospital bed by them. They waited till he passed.

"Well, it's probably not the work itself. All that's easy enough for him, too easy in the final analysis, just as it's always been. What he's really searching for there is himself, and that's what he cannot find. So—he literally lost the ground beneath his feet."

Karl Bonhoeffer took his wife's arm. "Come, Paula. Let's consider what is the best thing to do for our youngest child." And after a short pause, "Maybe have him go abroad. To Italy. Rome. Where he can experience a different world for a change."

Tegel, night of 5/6 April, 1943

The cell is cold and dark; it stinks, and the guard has just snarled, "In with you, you hooligan," before pushing Bonhoeffer into the room. Then the door closes behind him.

Dietrich Bonhoeffer is alone.

A couple of tentative steps over to the plank bed against the wall. He would like to sit down, pull the covers around him against the cold. But they smell too foul. Bonhoeffer retches. Then goes over to the opposite wall and crouches down on the floor.

Outside, deep night.

"It is also one of the duties of a Christian citizen to endure, with dignity and the certitude of his own innocence, the experience of investigative detention." But who had said that? Harnack? Barth? He himself?

It was Schlatter. Adolf Schlatter, the Swiss biblical scholar, at the time still teaching in Tübingen. It was he who had said it. With the certitude of his own innocence. . . .

The notion increasingly gnaws at Bonhoeffer.

Is he really that innocent? And will he be able to prove it?

"They have nothing concrete against us." Again, Dohnanyi's sharp voice.

"Really nothing, Hans?" he had asked in response at the time. The other man had attempted a calming smile. "All the documentation that could in any way be construed as compromising, all our plans, the names of all the accomplices. . . ."

"Am I on that list as well?"

"Of course you are. Aren't you an accomplice, and indeed even more? But don't be afraid. It's all locked away in a 100 percent secure safe. No one will ever find it there."

"But why is there any documentation at all? Why hasn't all that material already been long destroyed?"

His brother-in-law had shrugged. "That would be best, perhaps. But some of us. . . ." He had appeared to want to name names, but then swallowed them. "Some of us just think we need proof for later concerning why we made the plans we did, and proof that we're not just traitors." Dohnanyi's smile had turned wry. "I guess that's just how we Germans are. Proper even in the middle of our own downfall. Nothing happens without documentation. Not even a catastrophe."

What a brother-in-law!

In the semidarkness of his cell, Bonhoeffer sees Hans's face before him, narrow, pointed, slightly haughty, as if he knew all the riddles of this world along with all their solutions, and suddenly he is seized by a feeling of rage, violently, unjustly.

Why on earth did his brother-in-law ever draw him into everything? Indeed, why did he, Bonhoeffer, allow himself to be drawn in?

Vanity? Pompousness? Was he really all that indignant about this regime and its misdeeds, or was he in reality more concerned with his military deferral, with not having to go to the front, with not having to go where death was present on such a grand scale— or with not disappearing into some concentration camp?

In the final analysis, was it all just a matter of cowardice? Of avoiding the unpleasant?

No! No! A thousand times no!

Bonhoeffer scrunches up more tightly, pulling his knees up even closer to his body with his arms. His teeth are chattering, but not because of the cold. It's fear. What awaits him? Interrogations? Increasingly malevolent, increasingly insistent? Night after night after night in this tiny bit of hell here?

They have nothing concrete against us. His mind repeats this phrase with the monotony of a Tibetan prayer wheel. He believes it because he wants to believe it. It is with these thoughts that he passes the night, until finally the first gray of dawn creeps into the darkness outside the window bars. Bonhoeffer has fallen into a modest slumber.

A sobbing noise, at first quite soft, then increasingly loud, lamenting, startles him. Someone is weeping on the other side of the wall. Someone is wailing out of fear before the emerging day, weeping out into the half-darkness of this early morning. Will he, too, whine like that? Like a child crying for its mama?

Never!

But what will protect him against what's coming? He envisions the politely smirking face of the military prosecutor in front of him—or was it a senior military prosecutor? His name is Roeder, and somewhere, Bonhoeffer is quite certain, he has heard that name before. . . .

The sobbing in the adjacent cell ebbs, becomes softer, falls silent.

"Herr Pastor." That is how Roeder had addressed him. So, at least that much of his identity is intact. His title. His doctorate. "Just say 'Barth.' One can take titles from me, but I will be 'Barth' until I draw my very last breath"; that's what Karl Barth had once told him.

So, Bonhoeffer. Quite simple. Without "Pastor" or "Doctor" in front of his name. And what else was left to him in this stinking, damp dungeon?

His education. His knowledge. His three languages. But here only one is spoken, and that quite suffices. Education and knowledge count for nothing. Nor does the Bonhoeffer family tree hanging there in the hall in his parents' house. Nor the ancestors' pictures on the walls, nor the silk coverings on those walls, nor the gilded book spines in the library, nor the silver in the buffet.

Vanity of vanities! He once had preached on that topic when he lived in London. But what had he said in that sermon?

Shouts outside the cell. Slamming doors. Morning seems to have come. Soon the guard will be standing in front of him. "Come on, you criminal." With what will he counter such an address? With his fluent Latin, as he once did with "Reich Bishop" Müller? Or by telling the guard he's a Christian, not a criminal, and indeed, a Christian from the Confessing Church? He sees the guard grinning.

But that's exactly what I am. A Christian. My faith remains. The shouting is getting closer.

Bonhoeffer presses the back of his head against the wall, envisions, behind closed eyes, black-clad figures, with torches, hooded. They will put him on the rack, make him denounce his faith. Then what will remain of him?

A bloody body. That's what Bonhoeffer will then be. With only memories in his head. No one can take those away from him, not even here in this dungeon cell. He can still flee into that paradise, far, far away from everything here.

Perhaps to Barcelona. Into the fine dust clouds above the Ramblas section of the city. Into the shouts and heat of the bullfights. Only New York was hotter. And Cuba. But how on earth had he ever ended up in Cuba?

It had been while he was in New York, in 1930. "Fräulein Horn? You? Here? . . ." Maria Horn, the governess from his childhood, was suddenly standing before him. How had she ever gotten to Cuba? Ah, yes, as a German teacher. "And are you still as enthusiastic about the emperor, Fräulein Horn?" Dietrich had recalled how, to his father's great amusement and his mother's equally great chagrin, Fräulein Horn always jumped up and ran over to the window whenever one heard the ta-ta-too-ta of the horn on the imperial limousine. . . .

The shouting is now quite near. The key turns in the door. Bonhoeffer anticipates the sound of clanking steps, then distorted faces, can already hear the voice barking orders. But the door is only cracked open slightly, something flies in. Then everything is quiet again. The shouting moves on further.

Bonhoeffer feels his way forward, feels the object between his fingers. Half soft, crumbly. A piece of bread. Bonhoeffer smells mold, retches again, but still takes a bite. Not so much out of hunger. But just to have something to do. And then conjures up, coerces up his memories again.

The bitter-sharp aroma of a freshly brewed cup of espresso. With fruit as well, perhaps orange juice. The sun is shining. He's in Rome.

What Makes the
Church a Church?

1924–1929

*"I think I'm beginning to understand
the concept of 'church.'"*
—Italian diary, 1924

Laocoön, Too, Was a Priest

Many of prisoner Bonhoeffer's dreams during this period were bathed in Rome's warm sunshine, which enveloped him like a soft, comfortable cloak.

In reality, however, its rays were harsh and searing back then, around Easter 1924, when he and his brother Klaus had set out for Italy. But Bonhoeffer had hardly noticed it as the two brothers wandered through the streets, stopping at every church, every palazzo, or simply sitting before a trattoria, preferably at the Trevi Fountain.

There they had eaten domestic cheese, drunk clear, white wine, and simply people-watched, surrounded by the raucous activity of the Roman streets.

Bonhoeffer stretched a bit, sighed, and felt quite comfortable.

"So, what are you dreaming about, Dietrich?" That was his brother. Klaus was even more impatient and more curious than Bonhoeffer himself. "Shouldn't we get going again?"

"Aw, can't we just linger a bit longer with our dreams here? Just a bit?"

"Well, then let's at least drink another cup of coffee, an espresso, as they call it here."

Espresso for two. Bonhoeffer took a sip.

He honestly thought he already knew Italy before they even arrived. He had studied his Baedeker travel guide more thoroughly than any schoolbook. "We almost don't even need to go there. I already know all about everything," he had remarked to Klaus in the train while crossing the Brenner Pass into Italy.

But then *this* Italy! Completely different than any postcard or even the travel guide. Much more colorful, much louder, sometimes even unbearable, especially in Rome, where people shouted in the streets as if constantly crying out for help. Bawling children, women pushing flower carts through the milling crowd in the impossibly narrow streets. Everyone seemed to be getting in everyone else's way. And yet there was room for all.

And the smells! The colors! The people with their dark, darting eyes and black hair! Bonhoeffer, blond as he was, cast an envious glance at Klaus's dark hair. He did not stand out quite as obviously as Dietrich himself. And the sky above it all! So blue, so clear! And utterly without the soft haze that envelopes everything in the north.

Bonhoeffer sighed yet again.

"What are you thinking about?"

"Saint Peter's."

It had disappointed him at first. Smaller than he had expected, and not nearly as grandiose as the greenish Colosseum, amid whose ruins the entire magnificence of antiquity still seemed to hover and the pastoral god Pan still shrilly piped out his tunes with pagan cheerfulness.

Then Palm Sunday had come, with the celebratory mass in Saint Peter's. The two brothers stood boxed in among the throngs of the faithful. Up at the altar, a cardinal read the mass, surrounded by priests and seminarians. Bonhoeffer stared in genuine astonishment.

He saw white, black, and yellow faces, saw white, black, and yellow hands folded in prayer, united in the same prayer and in the same faith. The magnificent robes seemed to enhance this sense of universality with an element of the otherworldly, the mélange of different colors taking on its own, almost glowing radiance, the haze of incense creating a sweet, heavy fragrance around everything. Bonhoeffer felt enveloped by a magic spell.

No, indeed, this was anything but the frugal, severe black-and-white of Protestantism. This was fullness, color, life. This was music. Bonhoeffer hummed a few bars while sitting with his brother at the Trevi Fountain.

"I'll bet you're still thinking about the young nuns of Trinità dei Monti, aren't you?"

They had visited the convent that afternoon. Forty young girls, still almost children, really, with yellow and violet sashes over their chests, had sung—sung with such young voices and with such freshness and such immediacy. Bonhoeffer recalled hours he himself had spent sitting at the piano, times when, after immersing himself in the printed music, he then, suddenly, heard only music, all around him and in him. That was how he had felt while listening to these girls sing.

Pious, yes indeed. His feeling, then as now, was pure piety. And ultimately—his thoughts, accompanied by the rushing of the Trevi Fountain, pondered this notion—ultimately faith is like music. Not a matter of the understanding, not like the spoken, written word. No. Feeling. Sensuousness. Yes, that, too.

That is religion. And that, too, must be reflected in the image of the church.

"I think I'm beginning to understand," he heard himself suddenly say, to his own amazement. "I am gradually understanding what the church is."

His brother looked at him in surprise. "Namely?"

"Something powerful that makes demands on the entire person, on his heart, on his body. . . ."

"And less on his brain, eh?" Klaus's inclinations were sooner agnostic, like those of their father. Klaus was a born natural scientist who as a child preferred to be bent over a microscope and as an adult could not resist getting in such affectionate little digs at his brother Dietrich. But Dietrich did not take the bait. "The brain, too, of course, yes. But not as exclusively as our Protestant theology does."

"What do you have against our good old Protestantism?"

"Perhaps it's just old, and not so good at all. Somewhere along the way it became a 'national church' and in the process got detoured into becoming a state agency. At the same time, it's become a gathering place for people who call themselves Christians but do not really take faith seriously."

It's dead, he thought. Its own insistence on equating itself with the state has killed it. The church, however, if it is truly to win over both the heart and the mind, must be *alive*.

Like the church here in Rome.

Klaus motioned to the waiter, pointed to his empty espresso cup, and raised two fingers in the air. Unlike his brother, Klaus was wholly disinclined to speak any Italian, making do instead with a bit of pantomime, all the while admiring his younger brother, who, utterly without inhibition, regularly unloaded his hodgepodge of Latin and German on the Italians and as a rule—behold!—was even understood.

"Admit it," Klaus laughed, "you are probably hoping to conjure up a pope as well!"

No, precisely *not* a pope. They had already seem him from afar at an audience, a rather sullen figure void of either splendor or grace who seemed interested in nothing *less* than in the believers around him. "We already have enough characters at home like Pius XI."

The second espresso arrived. Bonhoeffer did without sugar. The sight of the overly slender Italians had once again made quite clear to him that he could stand to lose a few pounds.

"I just don't know," his brother began, watching several children tossing coins into the air while shouting, "Santos!" and then enthusiastically clapping when the copper piece landed on the right side. "Catholicism may have its advantages. But even just this thing with confession, the mere thought of confiding one's most intimate thoughts to a complete stranger. . . ."

Klaus shivered at the thought.

"I don't find it all that bad." Bonhoeffer remained composed. "I visited the Maria Maggiore on the day of confession, and every confessional was occupied. And the people's faces were so serene, almost as if redeemed. The confession must have done them some good. Perhaps," he paused a moment because the children's cries had become particularly loud, "perhaps confession offers the best possibility for speaking directly with God."

"Oh, Dietrich, Dietrich." His brother shook his head, laughing. "I can already see you returning to our beloved Protestant fatherland as a devout Catholic." For several seconds things were very quiet between the two brothers.

"As for myself," Klaus began again, "antiquity is what has most fascinated me here in Rome. The Belvedere Apollo alone. And then the Laocoön group...."

"Unbelievable, yes. I was almost stupefied."

"Well, that's certainly understandable. The sculptures of the human body they were able to produce, and so long even before Christ...."

It was to Laocoön's face that Bonhoeffer had paid particular attention. In the sculpture group, as Laocoön fights off the stranglehold of the deadly snake, his face's features are distorted in the most extreme torment, as if he wanted to draw all the suffering of humanity onto himself—like Christ later, on the cross.

Yes, perhaps Laocoön was the prototype of all portrayals of Christ in this sense, and the two martyrs representatives of a promise of new glory—whose reflection could be seen in the colors and magnificence of Saint Peter's itself. "Wasn't Laocoön also a priest?" he suddenly asked.

Klaus looked at him in astonishment.

"No, I will certainly never become a Catholic." Bonhoeffer set his cup down so forcefully that his brother started. "But I do still want to see more, learn more, understand more, other things, new things, the East, Africa ..."

"Our travel funds will allow for a trip to Sicily, and maybe even for a hop over to Africa." Klaus signaled to the waiter for the check. "And when our wallets are finally empty, we'll return to our gloomy, foggy Germany."

He flicked a fly away. "There's also considerable beauty to be had between the Rhine and the Spree Rivers, you know."

JUST READ WHAT BARTH HAS WRITTEN!

And though the brothers genuinely did travel on to Africa, they returned in a considerably more sober frame of mind, and Bonhoeffer's travel diary reported after their return to Italy: "With what enthusiasm did we then revel in a landscape that evoked such a sense of home for us."

Bonhoeffer had the same experience when in the summer of 1925, decked out in a checked shirt, shorts, and a backpack, he gazed over at the gentle incline of the vineyards across the Main River. "It's beautiful here, isn't it?"

He was not alone. His companion on this hike along the Main River was one of his cousins, Hans-Christoph von Hase, a year younger and a student in Göttingen.

"Yes, quite beautiful." Hans-Christoph panted, trudging along with beads of sweat rolling down his flushed face. The summer was hot, the sun brutal. "But to get back to the topic we were discussing yesterday. . . ."

Bonhoeffer knew what was coming and whose name would now be mentioned. That of Karl Barth, a pastor and son of a pastor from Basel, currently a professor of theology in Göttingen whose words, like thunder, were causing considerable quaking in the theological world. Some called him a heretic, others a spoiler of religion, still others a new Luther, or indeed even a church father.

"He grabs us by the collar and pushes our noses down into the only thing that matters: God's word, just as it appears in the Bible," his cousin had said the night before, full of enthusiasm, while they ate fresh fish from the Main and drank clear, savory wine together in a small inn. "I absolutely cannot get enough of him."

"But you're studying physics, not theology," Bonhoeffer had countered, astonished.

"Well, as of now." His cousin looked around, as if some eavesdropper might get wind of his most secret plans. "I intend to switch to theology. And you, Dietrich, should consider whether you, too, ought not study in Göttingen. With Barth."

Bonhoeffer took a long—a very long—sip of wine and busied himself with the fish, which, prepared this particular way, one ate whole, including the head, bones, and everything else. His cousin's suggestion was not all that outlandish.

Since the summer semester 1924, he had been enrolled in the department of theology at Berlin University, surrounded by the splendor of illustrious professors. One, however, outshone them all: Adolf von Harnack, who among other things was one of the authors of the Weimar constitution. Although he was over seventy years old and actually already retired, he still taught seminars at his home for a select group of students, and Bonhoeffer belonged to that select group. Nor did he have far to go.

Harnack's villa was in the immediate vicinity of Bonhoeffer's parents' house, and for all practical purposes Bonhoeffer himself merely moved from one Gobelin easy chair to another. There, at Harnack's, he now experienced how this man with the hard Baltic "r" in his pronunciation went about theology, viewing it as the most select of *all* the scholarly disciplines, a discipline according to which knowledge of God represented the ultimate goal toward which everything else—from culture to morality to historical knowledge—ultimately should lead.

Bonhoeffer was not always entirely comfortable with this notion of God as the highest goal of culture and education, and occasionally he even contradicted the old gentleman. In his own turn, Harnack knew enough to appreciate such bold precocity, since it added extra flavor to his own statements, and for the rest Bonhoeffer was in any event his declared pet who occasionally accompanied him through the city as far as the train station when Harnack took a trip, or even—the highest honor of all!—was allowed to carry his satchel.

The name of Karl Barth had already been mentioned on several of these jaunts, albeit in an unusually heated tone of voice.

"That fellow was my student once," Harnack said vehemently, his Baltic accent clipping over the various syllables even more forcefully than usual. "And what's he doing now? Instead of flying the honorable flag of scholarship, he blathers on about how the scholarly discipline of theology, which in his *great* beneficence he even grants a certain right to exist—" Harnack gently laughed, and Bonhoeffer dutifully and politely concurred, "how the discipline of theology is not really so *wrong*—but has taken a wrong *turn* and now must find its way back to God's revelation. But where, I ask, are we to *find* that revelation? Well? Bonhoeffer?"

Bonhoeffer was not quite sure what the old gentleman wanted to hear, and so remained quiet. Harnack was not really expecting an answer in any case, preferring instead to offer it up himself. "Solely in the Bible. There alone does God reveal himself. Not in science, not in scholarly disciplines. This . . . this . . ."

Harnack paused for a moment, searching for the right word, then, having finally found it, almost spit it out onto the Berlin street. "This *revelatory positivist.*"

Bonhoeffer did not entirely understand his professor's agitation. But he was reminded of precisely that agitation when that autumn a fellow student grasped him by the arm and, with bright-eyed enthusiasm and using the familiar form of address, asked, "Have you read what this Barth is writing?" Not even among fellow students was Bonhoeffer particularly fond of such excessive familiarity and the overly hasty use of the familiar forms of address. So he merely looked at the student with a polite, querying expression. "But you really *must* read it, Bonhoeffer."

Bonhoeffer took his time.

Winter came. Bonhoeffer coughed and snorted and wheezed; his head was feverish. The flu had gotten hold of him. On his bedside table lay not only various volumes of Ibsen but also issues of *Between the Times,* the periodical with Barth's essays and lectures. Between thermometer readings and hot lemon juice, Bonhoeffer began reading Barth, albeit still with rather modest expectations.

But his drowsy condition was soon at high alert, and it was with increasingly feverish anticipation that he read what he found there.

The church, he read, in its abject surrender to the ruling powers, has failed; by making compromise after compromise, not only was it unable to prevent the war, but also—this was Barth's particular concern, and was also why some people called him "Red Barth"—was unable to find any real answer to the social question.

There must be conversion, a turn, and a new church must emerge, a church whose God, rather than hovering about in some faraway, hazy "beyond"—from which he can then be summoned as a kind of cure-all for human concerns—instead reigns as the lord of our entire life, the *whole* of life.

Bonhoeffer leaned back on the pillow and wiped the sweat off his brow, which in this case was not caused by his fever. Just as his experiences in Rome had opened up his senses, so also had Barth's words now opened up his understanding, and he suddenly saw God as clearly as he had during his childhood in those Bible illustrations by Schnorr von Carolsfeld.

No, no, it was not that he thought of God as an old gentleman with a long beard. But he did indeed think of him as a phenomenon accessible to the senses, a phenomenon that spoke to human beings through the Bible. And that was no doubt what Harnack, the man of culture and education, had wanted to denounce with his cranky, vehement reference to *revelatory positivism*. "Barth is taking us back to the Middle Ages, back to where things are darkest of all," he had cried out, his Baltic accent cascading and rumbling forth like the advancing flood of Noah.

Bonhoeffer reached over for the milk and honey his mother had set out for him and drank it in small sips.

No, he thought, these ideas do *not* lead us back to the Middle Ages. They open up a completely new door for faith, for all faith. What Barth's writings had *not* told him—at least not yet—was exactly where that door itself would lead.

There was still too much to come to terms with, too much to work through, and Bonhoeffer repeatedly wanted to object to what this man from Basel was saying. Bonhoeffer was, however, certain that the church would indeed have to be renewed, have to become something different than before if it were to be a church again. He turned over in bed to face the wall, pulling the covers up over his ears so he could sleep off this horrible flu. But it was not working.

He tossed and turned, feverishly, with all these new ideas flitting to and fro in his head in no particular order, and whenever he sank into a brief period of sleep—from which he invariably awoke with a start—he saw the powerful edifice of Saint Peter's Basilica before him, the stone-and-concrete expression of a power next to which Protestantism seemed like merely a modest sect. "Catholicism arouses love and bliss, Protestantism arouses—well, boredom," he once mumbled, shocked at his own heresy.

Certainly, he immediately thought, the Catholic Church itself, in all its omnipotent grandeur, was not yet the true faith, but more a bulwark on the road to that faith. It was the Bible alone, however, that could point that road in the right direction.

This was not a word *about* God, but God's word *itself*. And next to it, Harnack's theology seemed to sink to the status of a mere utilitarian object within the world of culture and education, a world to which it belonged just as did Dürer's drawing *The Praying Hands* hanging on the wall, or the Bechstein grand piano in the parlor, or the first edition of the collected works of Goethe on the bookshelves.

Precisely this world, however, was also Bonhoeffer's world. This was the world into which he had been born and in which he had grown up. His entire existence was rooted in this world. He could not simply extract himself from it, and certainly not so facilely.

From this point on, Bonhoeffer would embark on a search, would take a path leading equally to Barth and yet not far past Harnack. And at first Bonhoeffer had no intention of simply dispensing with the traditional notion deriving from Martin Luther, namely, that faith and the world were two different entities, and that the world should not misuse faith just as faith should not use worldly means.

At the same time, however, he already realized that a faith completely divorced from the world could never satisfy him.

So it came, then, that the Bonhoeffer of these years found himself searching for a connection between two theological worlds. At first he was unsuccessful, lacking contact with those who through fellowship might have brought more clarity to these questions. For now, he was to remain alone with the questions: Who am I? Where do I belong?

And thus did he sit there, pondering, surrounded by clouds of smoke from nervously smoked cigarettes. A doubter, a seeker who perceived his surrounding world as if through a veil and then stood by with a modest, melancholy smile as, once again, that world came alive, in all its grand bourgeois splendor, there in the house on Wangenheim Street.

Festive illumination in all the rooms, the entire family assembled together, even the most distant, faraway relatives had come; a lone uncle had declined the invitation, saying he would not attend the wedding of a Jew. Little girls all in white, flowers in their hands, entered and began singing Carl Maria von Weber's "We Wind Round Thee the Bridal Wreath." The young man in the dark morning coat tenderly squeezed his bride's arm at his side.

It was April 26, 1926, and Dietrich's twin sister, Sabine, was marrying Gerhard Leibholz, who, after getting his Ph.D. at nineteen and his LL.D. at twenty-two, was well on his way to a brilliant legal career.

The Bonhoeffer house was radiant on this day with dancing, singing, and a huge buffet. Susanne, the baby of the family but wearing rather audacious lipstick today, recited verses that their grandmother had once composed for the party before their own mother's wedding. "Nicely done, sister," her brother praised her across the table, offering her a glass of fruit punch at the same time. But she had responded with, "I'd rather have a gin fizz." Then "Could I bum a ciggy from you?"

A ciggy?

"You smoke?"

Instead of answering, she nodded toward the dancers. "Kind of a 'death-dance' for the bourgeoisie, don't you think?" Bonhoeffer shook his head at his heretical little sister.

No doubt about it, some rather wondrous things had found their way into the Bonhoeffer home since the end of the war. There was Karl-Friedrich, the eldest son, opining in favor of socialism and going on about how it was actually not all that bad, while the parents' own conversation sank to the level of a whisper when they spoke about the mother's youngest brother's illicit liaison with a young woman who was a painter *and* a Communist. And now Dietrich's sister put her arms around his neck. "Let's dance, my darling brother! You dance so well! And soon you can come to one of *our* parties and see how things are done *else*where."

Indeed.

There—"*else*where"—everyone was immediately on a first-name basis, sat on the floor, chain smoked, and spoke about the most intimate things as if it were the most natural thing in the world. Bonhoeffer learned that the person sitting to his left was actually a homosexual who, truth be told, would nonetheless like to sleep with his own mother because of what Dr. Freud had written. Then a girl across from him loudly extolled the sexual customs of the Papuans. Finally a breathy, smoky voice whispered into his ear, "And who might you be, darling?"

Two dark eyes, encircled by rings as black as those of the cinema diva Pola Negri as she knelt at the casket of Rudolf Valentino before the cameras, immersed themselves into his own.

"I'm a theology student."

"A pope? Here? I must be losing my mind!" the voice, no longer so smoky or raspy at all, shrieked.

"No, no, not quite yet a pope. Still just a student. In fact I'm working on my doctoral dissertation."

"And what might its topic be, my blond darling?"

"The community of saints." Now everyone's eyes had turned toward Bonhoeffer. "Well, then you certainly are in the right place here with us," someone yelled, and the others roared with laughter.

No, he was not in the right place here, but neither was he entirely in the right place anymore in his parents' house either. In fact, he was not really in the right place anywhere just now, something he himself sensed in a dull, half-conscious fashion. In any event, he was happiest when he went to the parish hall of the church in Grunewald to assist the pastor there with the children's worship services.

Anyone who saw him there among the children and heard him tell the story of the Bible like one big, grand adventure—an adventure at least as exciting as Karl May's westerns or James Fenimore Cooper's

Leatherstocking Tales—might think that at this very moment this young man himself had become a child again. And that is exactly how Bonhoeffer felt: liberated and free.

On December 17, 1927, Dietrich Bonhoeffer, twenty-one years old, received his doctoral degree in theology, the only one among twelve candidates who did so summa cum laude. He also immediately passed his first examinations for church service and presented the required sample sermon.

"But why, son?" his father wanted to know. "You have all the goods for a splendid academic career. Surely you don't just want to become a simple pastor somewhere?"

Bonhoeffer avoided his father's scrutinizing gaze, thinking instead of Karl Barth's assertion that in the future, what would be needed were pulpits, not lecterns.

The telephone rang. A familiar voice was on the line, Max Diestel, Bonhoeffer's superintendent in the church administration. "You're looking for a position as an assistant pastor, aren't you, Bonhoeffer? Well, I might have one. Brother Olbricht has just written to me saying he urgently needs an assistant pastor."

He hesitated for a moment. "Of course, it's in Barcelona."

You Can Find Shelter with Us

"Holy mackerel, Dietrich! Now that's what I call a *palace!*"

Klaus Bonhoeffer plopped roughly down on the unsteady bed and looked around. His gaze drifted from the almost totally clouded window with its tattered curtain over to the worm-eaten chest of drawers on which his brother had placed photographs of all the family members, including his new brothers-in-law with their wives, Rüdiger Schleicher with Ursula, Hans von Dohnanyi with Christine, and Gerhard Leibholz with Sabine.

"Soon I'll be in that group, too, with my Emmi, and Karl-Friedrich with his Grete," Klaus said after examining the gallery. He had just become engaged to Professor Delbrück's daughter, and Karl-Friedrich to one of Hans von Dohnanyi's sisters.

For now, however, he merely lay on Dietrich's bed and laughed heartily at his brother's shabby accommodations.

For his own part, Dietrich sat on the only chair in the room and made a long face. "You think this is good, you should see the washroom accommodations. By comparison, the third-class lavatory on the train is a marble Roman bath. But," he sighed, "it's cheap, and I'm doing a good deed at the same time, since the two older ladies who are renting this magnificence to me can use every peseta."

He got up. "Come on, Klaus, let me show you something different now: beautiful Barcelona, and then this afternoon a *corrida*."

"A bullfight? Must we?"

"It's more fun than you think. But first let me show you Barcelona from above."

The cableway carried the two brothers squeakily to the top of Tibidabo, the mountain overlooking the city.

"During the spring this was like a dream, with all the almond blossoms," Dietrich said. "The whole world was cloaked in white enchantment." Then he quoted a Latin phrase: "*Omnia tibi dabo si cadens adoraveris me*, those were Satan's words to Jesus in the wilderness when he showed Jesus all the kingdoms of the world, 'All these I will give you if you will fall down and worship me.' *Tibi dabo*. The Catalans named this mountain after this phrase."

Although one could not see quite *all* the kingdoms of the world from the café on top of the mountain, one could indeed see all of Barcelona and far out into the Mediterranean Sea, which on this particular day lay before them in radiant, sparkling blue. "This tastes horrible," Klaus grumbled, poking with his fork at the pink sugar coating on the pastry in front of him, which a sullen waiter had served.

Bonhoeffer's was garishly green and tasted even worse. He pushed it aside and instead took a sip of the ink-black coffee. "Stick to the coffee. It's really good here. And stick to the museums and palaces. The old part of the city here is the filthiest thing you can imagine, even filthier than what we saw in Naples. And gloomy. Like the hearts of most of the people here."

He looked toward the churches. "You remember how the Catholic Church so impressed me in Rome? Here, I must unfortunately say, I merely find the old Protestant prejudice confirmed, namely, that the purpose of the Catholic faith is to make people stupid."

"But surely not all of them?"

"You'll never really get to meet any of the few who are not. The minute they hear you're from the church, they flee. For them, the clergy is the enemy of all enlightenment and reason. And, of course, they're not entirely wrong. But let's go on to the *corrida*! *That* is the Spaniards' real celebratory mass."

Their seats in the arena were located in the uppermost grandstand. Klaus observed his brother out of the corner of his eye and was astonished at how enthusiastically he got caught up in the excitement of the crowd, crying, "Olé!" and groaning mightily after the matador almost missed the deathblow. Klaus himself became rather green around the gills and would certainly have preferred to look away entirely. But Bonhoeffer never noticed his brother's unease.

"That's a slice of real life, isn't it? What gargantuan passion!" he said later as they were pushed along toward the exit by the throng of the crowd.

"But the poor animal. . . ." Klaus had still not completely regained his composure.

"Which do you think he would prefer? To be smashed on the head with a hammer in some slaughterhouse or to die here in the sunshine through a dagger thrust?"

Klaus just shrugged. His brother remained unperturbed. "You have to focus on the mythical pattern behind it, the struggle of light against the powers of darkness. We pastors are also a kind of matador. . . ."

"Well, then why don't you let our parents know precisely that?" Klaus laughed and pushed his brother toward a poster wall just outside the arena. The poster depicted a bull with lowered horns and a torero with a drawn sword, but the latter's face was cut out, and customers could place their own heads into the hole from behind. "Go ahead, Dietrich, do it! Have a photograph made! You as a matador! Then send it home."

"Our boy seems to be feeling quite at home," Bonhoeffer's father chuckled at the breakfast table in Grunewald as he handed the postcard to his wife. "He signs it: 'Greetings from the matador.'" Bonhoeffer's mother also smiled. "Well, the main thing is that he's doing well down there."

As a matter of fact, however, during this period Bonhoeffer himself was not all that sure he really was doing so well.

The German congregation was small, at just three hundred members. Hardly forty showed up regularly for Sunday services in the church: upright businessmen and their families, petits bourgeois for whom church membership was in reality not much more than membership in the card club or the chorus. And their pastor, Fritz Olbricht, a somewhat phlegmatic fellow with an inclination for red wine and good cigars, did little to change any of this.

Bonhoeffer tried to introduce a few modest innovations, implementing a children's worship service, putting on a nativity play, and once again displaying that particular, unaffected sense of authority when dealing with children which he often lacked around adults. A good example was the day one of the children came to the worship service completely exhausted from crying. His dog, Caro, had died.

"So, why are you crying? Caro is now in heaven. And you'll see him there again someday." Bonhoeffer was not being hypocritical. He believed it himself.

"Do dogs go to heaven, too?" The little boy was still sniffling but looked inquisitively at Bonhoeffer.

"Of course they do. Even Dr. Luther himself said, I simply cannot imagine that my Fido will not get into the kingdom of heaven." The child stopped crying.

His most interesting work involved his daily responsibilities in the German Auxiliary Mission.

The German Auxiliary Mission was where all the Germans who needed some sort of help or assistance showed up. There Bonhoeffer counseled the nightclub dancer who was about to be "reassigned" to a brothel; a member of the Foreign Legion who was tired of feeling his sergeant's boot on his neck; and the circus acrobat who, though unafraid of working in the lion cage, did indeed fear the whip of the head groom in the small itinerant circus.

Human fates, human faces. Sometimes grimacing, distorted faces. And they told of things that Bonhoeffer had never thought possible. He listened, wide-eyed, attentive, and thought of his own family standing on the train platform at his departure for Barcelona. "You'll always have a place here with us. You can always find shelter here with us," his mother had called after him even as the train was pulling away.

His family, waving to him from the platform that day, had disappeared in the locomotive's gray steam.

Shelter! Could there be such a thing in a world in which stories took place like the ones Bonhoeffer heard here? No, people here were not sheltered. Nor was he himself. Nor did he want to be. He did not always want to have to play the role of the prince from a good family.

Pastor Olbricht was waiting for him in the parsonage. He pushed a box of cigars toward Bonhoeffer. "I had some visitors, Bonhoeffer. The congregation presbyters. They would very much like to keep you here."

"Me? Here? In Barcelona?"

"Not a bad offer at all. Think about it."

Bonhoeffer did not have to think about it. He had indeed enjoyed the work, and he liked Olbricht well enough even though he did not think all that much of him as a pastor and preferred to hear him talk about wine rather than about Jesus.

But one year with him was quite sufficient. It was time to say goodbye, time to move on to the future, a future over which hung a gray mist similar to that hovering over the Mediterranean Sea just now as Bonhoeffer once again traveled up to the top of Tibidabo.

Indeed, with a little imagination one could visualize palaces, towers, walls emerging from behind that grayish silver veil—the kingdoms of this world—and the tempter once again whispered—just as earlier in the wilderness: "Over all this you can rule if you but want to. . . ."

The voice became more urgent, hissing, "And not just here in Barcelona! Think about the rest of the world as well, about Rome!

Convert to the religion of the others, think of all you could become there, at the very least a cardinal, perhaps even pope. . . ."

A slight laugh, rumbling, crude: "But Germany is not so bad either. Reform that church, become a new Luther, appoint yourself highest bishop. . . ." And then the voice became a seductive, silken whisper. "All you have to do is get on the right terms with me, Dietrich Bonhoeffer. . . ."

Bonhoeffer started abruptly and looked around.

He was alone.

TEGEL, APRIL 1943

One can get used to anything. To the cell, measuring two by three meters. To the covers on the plank bed, which no longer smell quite so foul. To the peephole in the door, to being lonely and yet not really alone. To this entire, giant edifice in south Berlin, the "Military Detention Center." To the food, which no longer automatically makes one vomit.

During these initial twelve days, Bonhoeffer has even gotten used to the pail over in the corner of the cell.

"That's the worst, most humiliating part about being in the slammer. Having to live in one's own privy." But who had once told him that? With whom had he ever even spoken about prison?

It had been a writer, one with a Jewish name, Ernst von Salomon. He had been involved in the Rathenau murder and had been sentenced to five years in prison. Recently, however, especially in Jewish circles, he had been celebrated as a kind of intellectual boulevard darling ("Just think, a real assassin!"), and Bonhoeffer still remembers the odd feeling he had when shaking precisely this man's hand while simultaneously recalling the shots fired at Rathenau.

But when had they met? And where? Perhaps a hundred years ago. In a completely different reality. And what is reality now?

Reality outside is represented by the view from the cell window. If one stands on tiptoe, one can just make out that other world, or at least a slice of it, maybe a portion of sky, sometimes gray, sometimes blue. It's far in the distance, hidden from view, that everything else begins, Berlin, Grunewald, his parents' house. And his parents themselves are somewhere out there, and his siblings, his friends, and somewhere his fiancée as well. . . .

That's right. He was engaged. To Maria von Wedemeyer, nineteen years old. But when was it again that she had accepted his marriage proposal? This past January? January the previous year? Or . . .

In any event, in another world.

Reality, here, that would be this cell. The stool. The wall shelf. The food bowl. The guards. Their steps. Their gazes. Their silence.

Sometimes he wishes they would yell at him again, revile him with abusive names, like at the beginning. But merely creaking door hinges in the morning, creaking door hinges at night, silent, rejecting faces, and nothingness in between. Nothing but waiting. Endlessly. Pointlessly. For something indistinct.

His eldest brother, Karl-Friedrich, had once told him about his experiences at the front. "It's not war itself that's so bad in war. What's bad is the eternal waiting." Now Bonhoeffer knows what he meant.

Everyone waits here. All eight hundred inmates in the Tegel Military Detention Center. For their trials. For their verdicts. And to learn whether they will receive a death sentence. This latter thought seems to afflict them especially at night.

It is then that Bonhoeffer hears them crying and whimpering, and some of them seem to be fettered. Bonhoeffer can hear the chains rattling.

Toward morning, things get quiet again. The guards' steps are the first noise of the new day. On the third day, one of them, grinning, had shoved a Bible into the cell. The only thing Bonhoeffer is permitted to read.

And he does read it. Learns by heart whatever he does not already know by heart. And waits. He, too, waits. Almost with yearning, eagerly, then with increasing urgency until, finally, that too—whatever it is he's waiting for—becomes almost a matter of indifference. Except that something is now different. He hears a voice again. Eyes are again watching him, focusing on him, not merely looking through him, as the basilican stares of the guards seem to do.

At some point they must finally interrogate him. At some point must tell him what it is he is guilty of. And then he will put on the carefully rehearsed face of the naive, somewhat simple, and politically unsophisticated pastor whose Sunday services attract especially old women, who think he chats just so *nicely* about death and eternity and such.

He wishes he had a mirror so he could learn to control that mask better. Instead, he sees a different mask in front of him, that of Senior High Court Military Prosecutor Roeder, polite, obliging, and hears a voice, a not entirely unpleasant one . . .

Suddenly he remembers where he had come across the name "Roeder."

It had been a little over a year ago. His brother-in-law Hans had mentioned him. In connection with the Communist "Red Orchestra" group in the Reich Ministry of Aviation. A certain Harro Schulze-Boysen had belonged to it, a friend of Ernst von Salomon, and Arvid von Harnack, the nephew of Bonhoeffer's own first, great teacher, and his wife Mildred. All of them had been executed after being tortured. And their interrogations, Hans von Dohnanyi had said, were conducted by a certain Manfred Roeder.

So, a henchman. A torturer. Not like those in the Middle Ages. Today's torturers do not wear black hoods, nor do they need racks and thumbscrews. They have other methods. Worse methods. More thorough methods.

Would Bonhoeffer be able to resist? Be able to remain steadfast? Or would he divulge everything he knew, all the names, all the secrets? Would he emerge from this imprisonment having betrayed not only the cause, but his co-conspirators as well?

He would rather be dead. Would rather choose death freely. Suicide. The most unpardonable of mortal sins. Really?

Once, in fact at the very first funeral sermon he ever delivered, he had stood at the casket of a person who had committed suicide. That had been in Barcelona; a man who had gone bankrupt and hanged himself. Pastor Olbricht, ever well-meaning, had nonetheless not denied the man a Christian burial, though he had turned the sermon over to his younger assistant pastor.

"For heaven's sake, what on earth should I say?"

"Say anything. Just say that this person was not strong enough in faith to bear the sufferings of this world and for precisely that reason deserves our sympathy, not our contempt."

And that, more or less, was what Bonhoeffer had indeed preached, albeit not without a bit of discomfiture. Never, not even later, did he like speaking at funerals, and it had always cost him enormous effort to overcome his disinclination. As did the letters he had to write to the mothers of fellow seminarians who had been killed in action. And he himself never quite understood whether the reason was a general, more universal anxiety in the face of finitude or his own, completely personal fear of death.

"I do not fear death. What I fear is lying cold, unmoving, and helpless in a black box." One of his colleagues had once divulged this to him.

Bonhoeffer now nods to himself. Now he understands that colleague. And at the same time he wonders whether he has not already been long lying just as cold, just as unmoving, and just as helpless in just such a box, namely, in this cell here in the Military Detention Center. Whether—a wave of fright washes over him at the thought—he has not already long been dead.

If he were now to bring a quick, harsh end to this existence— one could not really call it a "life" anymore—freeing himself from the fear of somehow doing harm to those who were still alive, then only a body would really die, and no longer a spirit.

But how? How do you kill yourself? What do you make a noose out of? And from what do you then hang it? Or should you instead slit your wrists? With what? And how do you make sure you cut exactly, precisely on the artery? He once read that you are supposed to slit it lengthwise, not crosswise. . . .

In any case, killing oneself is not that easy. It would be a rather circumstantial affair. Bonhoeffer laughs. Practical things had never been his strong suit. His sister Christine had already told him as much when she had taken care of housekeeping during their brief time together in Tübingen. And now his practical skills are not even up to the task of ending his own life.

The bell. Clanging. Shrill. The real master of this world here. Omnipotent. It now summons him to the exercise yard.

The same yard. The same exercise. Bonhoeffer trudges along his accustomed path around the yard. He thinks of death.

Death can be gentle or brutal, a quiet departure, a final cry. He wonders, how had his fellow seminarians died out there on the front? Or the other soldiers, in the other war? Or his brother? His cousins? Or the millions of unknown soldiers? How did they die?

Bonhoeffer sees an image before him. Soldiers in a trench. Boyish faces. One of them turns around, sees a flower up on the edge of the trench. The image begins to flicker. A film. It seems to be coming to an end.

Bonhoeffer is in a movie theater. In New York.

The New World—
A New World

1930/1931

"In the Negro churches, it is clear that
whenever the gospel itself really is mentioned,
their participation peaks."
—report on his year of study, 1931

WHEN THE SAINTS GO MARCHIN' IN

The soldier reached for the flower, intending to pick it. Then the shot rang out. The soldier slumped down, dead, and that evening, the report from the battlefield would read, "All quiet on the western front." Up on the screen, however, were the words "The End." The film was over.

"Come on!" The young man in the parquet nudged him. But Bonhoeffer needed a bit more time to get back to reality.

They pushed up to the concession stand in the foyer. Bonhoeffer's companion, very slender, very dark, bought a package of chocolate-covered peanuts and offered some to Bonhoeffer. Although he normally really liked sweets and always got hungry in the theater, this time he had lost his appetite.

They stepped outside into the bustling activity of Broadway with all its garish advertising and glaring colored lights and headed toward the nearest bus station down the street.

"That was a good film, wasn't it?" Bonhoeffer's companion remarked. His name was Jean Lasserre. He was a Frenchman and, like Bonhoeffer, a fellowship recipient at Union Theological Seminary in New York. "Yes, very good," Bonhoeffer nodded. Then, softly, "I'm ashamed standing here before you, Jean. I have to ask your pardon."

"For what?" Lasserre popped another peanut into his mouth and looked at Bonhoeffer a bit perplexed.

"For the way those people in the theater howled and laughed and applauded when the French were shot."

"There were probably a few Germans in the audience." Lasserre remained completely composed.

Bonhoeffer responded, "And you're a Frenchman. I'm ashamed."

"As a Christian, a person is neither German nor French. But you already know my opinion on this. Nationalism and Christianity are mutually exclusive. And Christ's commission is more important to me than that of my *grande nation*.

"Nonetheless. I'm still ashamed."

"Ah, what a model German you are. . . ."

Lasserre laughed, put his arm around Bonhoeffer's shoulders, and walked on farther with him.

A model German. Well, yes, that is indeed what Dietrich Bonhoeffer was here in New York. And that is exactly what he wanted to be. In Germany he had already read all the American books and newspaper articles reviling Germans as half-civilized barbarians who were constantly at the throats of their peaceful neighbors. And now he was determined to disprove precisely that reputation. Always polite. Courteous. Modest. Well brought up. With his slightly blushing, roundish, boyish face.

And thus, too, did he mount the podium for the lectures that—with remarkable frequency—he was invited to deliver during these months. He spoke about the disgraceful Treaty of Versailles. About how all the war guilt had been foisted solely on the Germans. And he spoke well, garnering considerable applause. But also some wry smiles: So, Germans can also be like this—educated, well-read, born romantics, and a wee bit inexperienced in the ways of the world.

But when Bonhoeffer's own thoughts drifted back to Germany during this period, it seemed to be somewhere far, far away, far beyond the ocean, in a completely different reality.

The unemployment numbers were climbing daily there, and a political party that previously had elicited no more than an amused smile from people was now becoming more and more the topic of conversation. The National Socialists. Their Dr. Goebbels—what in heaven's name did he have a doctorate in?—had just become their district leader for Berlin. And in October 1929 one of the last hopes for the Weimar democracy had died in the person of Reich Chancellor and Foreign Minister Gustav Stresemann.

Here in New York, however, Bonhoeffer thought less about Stresemann than about Adolf von Harnack, who had also recently died and whose eulogy Bonhoeffer himself—not without a twinge of bad conscience—had delivered. Everything else, however, even his parents' house on Wangenheim Street, was enveloped in a fine, gauzy mist. And even when Bonhoeffer, conscientious as ever, wrote letters to his father, mother, grandmother, siblings, and friends—his mail connection had never been sundered, not even in Barcelona—he nonetheless first had to clear away this mist and consciously reinsert himself into his earlier life, his earlier world over there in Europe.

For this was America. The New World. And America was different. A genuinely new world. Including here at Union Theological Seminary.

Here, in the cafeteria, Bonhoeffer sat across from Asian students who were homesick for their rice and chopsticks. In the library, he found he had forgotten his pencil and ended up borrowing one from a Negro. And yet another student told him how his own ancestor was an almost full-blooded American Indian. Everything here was quite international. A real mix of nations and races. And always so noisy in the halls, laughter, everyone constantly saying, "Hello!" Saying it to everyone each time they met, and so heartily, so spontaneously, as if seeing that person for the very first time. That was the custom.

At the beginning, Bonhoeffer took that custom more seriously than it was really meant. Every time someone said, "Hello!" he stopped in mid-stride, smiled cordially at the person, prepared to introduce himself, and extended his hand in greeting with a "How are you doing?" But that other person had already long hastened on his way. And Bonhoeffer already heard the next "Hello!" and stood there rather helpless with his hand extended in greeting.

Only one person had actually stopped and shook his hand. "Hi, I'm Paul," he had said, and it was only later that Bonhoeffer learned that the full name of this young man about the same age as Bonhoeffer himself, was Paul Louis Lehmann. Bonhoeffer also had to learn that everyone addressed everyone else here by his first name.

"So, you're already a real professor?" the new friend had inquired.

And Bonhoeffer was indeed. He had qualified to lecture, the youngest assistant lecturer at the university in Berlin. He had also already passed his second theological examination. The only thing left now was ordination. But problems had developed.

"Twenty-four is rather young to be getting your own pastorate. You have to be at least twenty-five for that," his fatherly mentor, Max Diestel, had explained. Diestel had looked at him questioningly, then continued, "And you are intending to pursue an academic career in any case, aren't you, with all the splendid opportunities you have now?"

Splendid opportunities. Yes, such opportunities were indeed available. That's what everyone was saying. And he suddenly thought of his brother-in-law Gerhard Leibholz, who had just become a professor in Greifswald.

He had visited Gerhard and his wife, Dietrich's sister Sabine, there in their attractive house, with one child and another already on the way. And thus would things continue to go for them. After Greifswald a larger city, and then an even larger city, and at some point Berlin itself. And at every stage Gerhard would have an attractive house, an attractive position, the proper wife, a growing gaggle of children, everything very smart and attractive, predetermined, unalterable. . . .

Would that be his own path as well? His own fate? Was this professor, husband, and father really Dietrich Bonhoeffer?

He had shaken his head, slowly, hesitatingly. "No, I'm still just much more inclined to enter the pastorate, to be there on the front lines, where life is, and with life also faith. At least since Barcelona, faith for me is increasingly more . . . more . . ."

He had tried to find the right word.

"More humanistic?" Diestel had suggested with a gentle smile.

"Yes, more humanistic. Yes, that's what it's become." Bonhoeffer had nodded. But he did not go on to say that since his return from Barcelona the atmosphere at the university had seemed increasingly stuffy, and all the academic goings-on increasingly artificial and removed from reality.

Diestel had reflected for a moment. "Perhaps a good transition would be a fellowship abroad, in England or America. Let me encourage you to apply; I'll support your application. After all," his smile had turned a tiny bit mischievous, "why does one cultivate one's connections with the World Federation of Churches?" Diestel knew that Bonhoeffer had hitherto not been particularly interested in the still-nascent ecumenical movement, whose most important German representatives included Diestel himself.

As it turned out, Bonhoeffer ended up in New York, at Union Theological Seminary, almost a century old, the most respected, progressive theological seminary in America.

And he was quick to throw himself into the whirlpool of this breathless, sleepless city, a city that made Berlin in comparison seem like a staid provincial town. In fact, he got so caught up in this maelstrom that his parents had already received a letter insisting that "if you really try to experience New York completely, it almost does you in." He also found himself in the midst of student life that was completely different from that in Europe, much looser, much more natural, much more democratic.

To be sure, this particular type of university study did seem to lack seriousness and discipline. Dietrich Bonhoeffer, who had grown up a product of strict Prussian academic discipline, could only shake his head.

Everything was done in teams, and often enough everything was also discussed to death in endless, endless discussions. "What about the scholarly work of the individual?" And Bonhoeffer visited churches that offered tea dances, concerts, lectures, sports, and sometimes even a worship service. He heard pastors preach about every conceivable topic, and occasionally about Jesus Christ. With all the arrogance of the typical European, he asserted: "America has no theology!"

"You really think so?" His friend Paul Lehmann looked a bit crestfallen. And Bonhoeffer began to talk—about a congregation that was a community of Jesus, about God's word as revealed in that community, and he quoted from his own qualifying dissertation, *Act and Being*: "God *is* present, not in eternal nonobjectivity, but palpably, tangibly in the church." That was one of the key passages in that work.

These conversations were continued outside the seminary as well, in bars or in coffee shops. At one such time, Lehmann got up suddenly in the middle of a heated discussion, said, "Sorry," and headed for the restroom. Once he was gone, however, a young man at a neighboring table turned around to Bonhoeffer and said in German, "You know, sir, there is quite a bit of Barth in what you are saying there."

The unaccustomed sound of German and the equally unaccustomed use of the more formal "sir" startled Bonhoeffer as much as did the name "Barth," which, while not entirely unknown in America, was more likely to elicit a condescending smile than serious conversation. Here he was sooner viewed as a bit over the top, like so many over there in *old Europe*. Quite without thinking, Bonhoeffer invited the young man over to his table.

"My name is Erwin Sutz." The somewhat shuffling lilt of the man's accent betrayed that he was Swiss.

"You're familiar with Karl Barth?" Bonhoeffer asked.

The young man smiled. "Quite familiar, actually. I was his student." Lehmann returned to the table and looked at the new guest with a bit of surprise. The young man continued, "You probably do not know Barth personally, do you?" Bonhoeffer shook his head. "Too bad. He would like you. An educated young man from a good home. Unfortunately, most 'Barthians' are often rather remarkable oddballs. Everyone wants to be even more 'Barthian' than Barth himself." Bonhoeffer himself had already seen that.

During this period, Sutz became yet another of Bonhoeffer's good friends. For some reason, Bonhoeffer seemed to make such contacts more quickly in America than in Germany. In fact, he was even beginning to feel at home here. On Sundays, however, when the seminary campus was caught in its sleepy weekend repose, one could occasionally see him inconspicuously leaving the building next to the Riverside Church and hastening over to Harlem, New York's black district in the immediate vicinity of the college.

He walked down increasingly narrow, increasingly dirty streets, where eventually not a single white face was to be seen and where curious stares followed behind him. He walked on further before finally stopping in front of a shabby building. He listened at the wooden door—whose paint had long since worn off—and heard singing, clapping, stamping. As gingerly as possible, he pushed the latch down and entered the low-ceilinged room full of singing, clapping, boisterously stamping people.

But solely Negroes. With brightly colored, cheerful clothing. Swaying from the hips, bobbing back and forth, and singing about how old Pharaoh should finally let the children of Israel move on to the Promised Land, shouting and cheering, "O praise my Lord!" and "Sing hallelujah!"

The pastor stood up at the front, black like everyone else, singing along with them, clapping in time, swaying to and fro, holding the Bible, the word of God, in his right hand. It all seemed more like a festive celebration than a worship service.

Bonhoeffer had taken a seat in the back row. Hardly anyone even noticed him; nothing could distract these people during all the singing and clapping. Their voices grew ever louder, their singing ever more urgent. At first Bonhoeffer had involuntarily folded his arms, as if defending himself against something.

But then his own feet started to move, his own lips started to mouth the words, first silently, then more powerfully. The rhythm grew stronger, almost into a march: "Oh, when the saints. . . ." And finally he, too, started singing and clapping his hands along with all the others, "Oh, when the saints go marchin' in. . . ."

Bonhoeffer sang well, his trained tenor lilting above the others, who turned toward him and smiled, without mockery, without reproach.

The white man over there in his gray flannel suit was just like them now, his skin could have been just as dark, his tie just as colorful as those of the other men, it made no difference. "Oh, when the saints...."

"So, this is where you're hiding!"

Bonhoeffer looked up and saw a dark face with strikingly delicate, chiseled features, an almost classically formed nose, and a high, classic forehead. His fellow seminarian Albert Frank Fisher. *So, Negroes can be handsome as well*, Bonhoeffer had thought after their first meeting, *despite the black skin.*

No, precisely because *of their black skin*, he now thought. A beautiful, handsome skin whose supple, dark hue shone in the opalescent lighting. Where was it written that only white was handsome?

But not just the dark complexion, it was also the velvet black gazes and supple movements that made these people, women and men alike, handsome. *Their beauty must come from some inner source*, Bonhoeffer thought while clapping and singing and swaying his hips—Fisher also sang and clapped along—and gazing over the crowd. *Their enthusiasm, their devotion, their piety also make them beautiful; the warmth in their hearts.* That warmth seemed to emanate like a silver radiance from all these black faces. He smiled at Fisher like a brother. Fisher smiled back.

It was Fisher who had first taken Bonhoeffer along to a worship service among Harlem's poor, and Bonhoeffer had been very taciturn when they left the shabby building together.

Fisher had put his arm in Bonhoeffer's, as if to support him. "Dietrich, you didn't like it?"

At the time, Bonhoeffer himself didn't know. He, ever cool and ever keen on remaining composed and in control, had been peculiarly moved by the ecstasy of the others. In fact, to be honest, he had also been a bit put off, as if he, the only sober person, had just stumbled into a bunch of drunks.

At the time, he resolved never to attend such a worship service again. After all, a white man was an intruder in any case. He didn't belong there. And yet this Sunday experience had stayed with him.

And the very next weekend he became peculiarly restless, as if he were missing something that could never be retrieved again.

He had finally gotten up and walked over to Harlem again, back to the worship service. He was otherwise rarely to be seen at the daily chapels at the seminary and, quite frankly, even earlier had never been a particularly avid churchgoer. His parents had never insisted on it in any case, and he himself had often found the Protestant ritual too rigid and cold. But what he experienced here, in Harlem, was something entirely different. Fisher, who had felt compelled to come to this little church on this particular Sunday more on a whim, could not help smiling a bit today at his friend's enthusiasm.

But Bonhoeffer was not to be deterred.

"This is real faith, real piety, real community. Grace, promise, sin, and forgiveness are all still taken quite literally here," he later remarked as the two returned to the seminary.

Fisher observed him not without a touch of melancholy while Bonhoeffer continued. "The community of saints. That was the title I chose for my doctoral dissertation. My demand was that *every* congregation be such a community, that *every* congregation be the living, concrete continuation of Christ. And yet, honestly, I myself," he laughed, a bit embarrassed, "saw it more as a utopia, a beautiful dream that could not really be fulfilled in reality. But now, finally, here, I can see that it is quite possible."

"Then let us pray that it remains such as well," Fisher sighed.

"Why would it not?"

"Our young people are getting impatient. The God to whom their parents so ardently pray, whom their parents so ardently entreat, and in whom they so ardently believe, has not brought them what they hoped. No social freedom, no equal rights for all races. Despite all the singing and clapping, he's remained the God of the whites, while they themselves remain slaves, not slaves in chains, but slaves caged up in the separation of the races."

"Things are that bad for all of you?"

"Worse." And Fisher had taken his friend along on a driving tour to Washington, D.C.

"Shouldn't we travel there by train? Wouldn't that be cheaper?"

"Well, yes. If we want to sit in two compartments, you in the white one, I in the black one."

On the way to Washington—Fisher drove; Bonhoeffer, amid considerable agony, was still trying to get his driver's license—Fisher had laughed out loud. "Apparently the whites are more annoyed at this separation than we Negroes. Their compartments are always overcrowded, those of the Negroes always virtually empty. Moreover," his words took on a slightly derisive tone, "our compartments are also allegedly much cleaner. Even though we 'niggers' are supposed to be so filthy."

His laugh sounded angry.

They visited all the sights in Washington, the museums, the White House, but Bonhoeffer was most impressed by the Lincoln Memorial. "He must have been a very special man. I'll have to learn more about him sometime." They were sitting in an attractive restaurant that offered French cuisine. Bonhoeffer had invited his friend to dinner, and had already ordered onion soup, giant oysters, and cheese afterward. "You'll see: the French make the best cheese in the world."

Then he spoke about Lincoln. "Yet another person whom they had to murder before his ideas could come to fruition." He had thought about Rathenau's murder. The waiter, a Negro, brought their soup. But only one bowl. He set it down in front of Bonhoeffer.

"You seem to have forgotten my friend's soup."

The waiter rolled his eyes in feigned horror and hastily retreated. Bonhoeffer reached for his spoon. "May I go ahead and begin?" The second bowl of soup still did not come.

The waiter brought the oysters. Again only one serving.

"What's going on? When are you finally going to serve my friend?"

"Never. Negroes can't be served here. And it's only because he's with you and you yourself, sir, are obviously a foreigner that he is even allowed to sit here in the first place."

"We're leaving, Frank."

And they left; Bonhoeffer speechless with rage. Fisher seemed to take it with considerably more composure. "Well, Dietrich, now you know how it is here." Bonhoeffer laughed loudly. "And over there in Germany, my brother-in-law Gerhard Leibholz—who's a Jew—gets so huffy and indignant when he hears a couple of anti-Semitic remarks at the university and when some idiots in brown shirts yell, 'Judah, to hell with you!'"

"But I recently read in the paper that all that is getting even worse in Germany."

"Nonetheless. Compared to the racial problem, our so-called Jewish question is a joke." He shook his head. "And to think: one of your own kind treats you that way."

"An 'Uncle Tom.' Surely you're familiar with the book by Harriet Beecher Stowe. During her time, it still took courage to show a Negro as being a nice person who was always polite and respectful and always obedient when serving whites, and everyone wanted to be an Uncle Tom. But today, believe me, there's nothing our young people despise more than these Uncle Toms."

These were the kinds of experiences and impressions that increasingly and with increasing harshness brought Bonhoeffer's attention to the social situation in America.

He was already giving religious instruction every Sunday to young Negroes in a Baptist church in Harlem, though he was doubtless learning far more from his pupils than they ever could from him. And he wanted to know even more, wanted to immerse himself even more in what was for him a completely new, completely different world.

He visited his pupils' parents at home in their apartments. He made the rounds of all the record stores in Harlem and was soon quite proud of his modest collection of spirituals, a collection he played— and not always with the blessing of his fellow seminarians—almost incessantly on his little record player. He read—and was profoundly moved by—"black" literature. And with increasing frequency he attended the lectures of Harry F. Wand, the professor responsible for courses on Christian ethics.

Professor Wand's gaze, like that of a predatory bird, glided over the heads of the students sitting before him, and his squawking voice pierced their ears, derisive, disdainful, while his nose seemed to peck at them like a sharp beak. "Well, fine, now let's leave all those sweet, dear little angels up there in the clouds where they belong and direct our attention instead to the poor devils here on earth." And then he spoke about economic structures, about the reasons behind the financial crash, about child labor, and about the nonsense of prohibition.

Bonhoeffer didn't like the man. But he did learn from his lectures. And he learned about the woman who was denied citizenship because she never in her life intended to pick up a weapon. And about the efforts of Father Flannagan on behalf of delinquent boys in his Boys Town. And he began to comprehend what it had meant for hundreds of thousands of small investors to have lost absolutely everything down to the very last penny on Black Friday in 1929.

Yes, he was learning more and more about the interplay of forces within capitalism, things people certainly never learned amid the beautiful villas of Berlin's Grunewald district. He came to the conclusion that "the large banks are the real power here in America." And he thought to himself, *My apolitical behavior now seems impossibly frivolous to me.*

Sutz could only listen to such statements in astonishment. Fisher smiled. And Lehmann merely shook his head. There was one person, however, who nodded forcefully in agreement. That was his friend Jean Lasserre.

Having grown up in France's poorest region, Lasserre resolved quite early to use Christ's word in opposing all the misery in this world and to seek the proper home of his faith not among the rich but among the poor of this world. But first he invited his friend Bonhoeffer to go to a movie, *All Quiet on the Western Front*, based on the novel by Erich Maria Remarque.

Bonhoeffer had already read the book back in Germany, where shortly before his departure it had become a huge—and surprising—bestseller.

Now, however, he was doubly smitten by the fate of Paul, the private so senselessly shot down on that quiet summer day. "That could easily have been one of my brothers, or even me," he remarked after they had arrived back at the seminary and sat down to chat a bit in his room, as usual with the door wide open. That, too, was something that took some getting used to for Bonhoeffer, namely, that the doors were always open and that anyone could just come into your room at any time. Closing your door—and certainly closing it and locking it—would have been perceived as crudely impolite.

"Any of us could be this Paul," Lasserre had responded. "Rich or poor, German or French. Dead is dead; everyone shoots down everyone else. And none of it will stop until we, all of us, finally take Christ and his Sermon on the Mount seriously when it says, 'Blessed are the peacemakers'. . . ."

"But isn't that meant to be taken figuratively, as a promise of blessedness applying to the beyond?" Bonhoeffer objected hesitatingly. Lasserre threw his dark head back and laughed heartily. "Oh, you Germans! Always so wonderfully abstract and removed. Why can't you just take things as they are, as tangible, concrete? Especially— *especially*—God's word."

Lasserre kept talking. "No, the Sermon on the Mount is *not* some symbol. It tells us exactly how we ought to be, here on earth—here and now, not somewhere else—if as Christians we ever hope to become disciples ourselves and take seriously the *imitatio Christi*. Or did Christ only *symbolically* allow himself to be nailed to the cross? Without any real, earthly suffering or real, concrete pain?" And once more: "We're his disciples, Dietrich, that is, if we really are Christians. And we must also act accordingly."

Discipleship. Henceforth that word would never leave Bonhoeffer. And the Sermon on the Mount, seen in this light, became a new key to faith, a key that opened up that faith as never before.

It was with Lasserre that Bonhoeffer traveled to Mexico. At the beginning of the trip, Erwin Sutz had also gone along. In a decrepit, borrowed jalopy, they had rumbled through the Ozarks, prompting an indulgent smile from Sutz: "For a comparison you both really need to have a look at our Swiss Alps." Bonhoeffer, too, who had expected an imposing mountain range like the Rocky Mountains, could not hide his disappointment.

The car creaked and rattled and groaned. "And we're supposed to drive all the way to Mexico in this thing?" Sutz laughed. "No, friends. I'm afraid I won't make it." So he left them when they arrived in St. Louis, and the other two journeyed on. And, indeed, they did make it all the way to the Mexican capital.

In Mexico Bonhoeffer stood beneath giant, deep green cacti on burning red ground. He saw the temples of the Aztecs and their altars, where the hearts were cut out of living victims as an offering to the gods. What impressed upon him even more, though, was the poverty all around Mexico City. "Thinking that we, with our modest faith, can lead these people to the Promised Land where milk and honey awaits them—what presumption," he remarked later after they had returned to New York.

But the lure of faraway places had gotten into Bonhoeffer's blood. The travel bug began to gnaw at him. "Now I want to go to the East, to India. I've always wanted to go there," he told his friends.

"And what do you plan to do there?"

"I plan to look. To learn. To understand even more. There are so many things I know absolutely nothing about."

"Why don't you just stay here with us in America instead?" That was Paul Lehmann. "We need men like you. Pioneers who can renew faith, breathe new life into it, rejuvenate it. Otherwise faith is just going to turn into another utilitarian object, like a new car or a new toaster." Nonetheless, Bonhoeffer still made increasingly frequent inquiries at the harbor to see how expensive a passage to India would be for a person of modest means.

And then the day really did come—in the summer of 1931—when a ship with Bonhoeffer on board departed from a pier in New York. But it was not headed to India. It was headed to Germany. A letter rustled in Bonhoeffer's pocket. The position of student chaplain was to be created at the technical college in Berlin, and in that letter, Superintendent Otto Dibelius had written that Bonhoeffer could have the position if he so desired.

So, back to Germany it was! And once again, just as a year earlier upon his arrival in the New York harbor, Bonhoeffer stood at the railing, looking back at the Manhattan skyline. *Metropolis*, he thought.

Just like the skyscrapers in Fritz Lang's film. A piece of the future, captured in stone. He cast one final glance at the Statue of Liberty as it gradually disappeared beneath the horizon. "You, too, Madam," he chuckled, "I probably will not see again for some time."

Thus did Bonhoeffer return to Germany, where he was met by a country in which the number of unemployed was quickly approaching six million, where the chancellor, Brüning, was grasping at emergency decrees trying to save what, really, could hardly be saved now, and where that party, the National Socialists, had just achieved their first breakthrough successes in the last election.

In Berlin, too, *All Quiet on the Western Front* was being shown at the Mozart Hall Cinema. At the premiere, Arnold Bronnen, a writer and a vehement opponent of Erich Maria Remarque, had turned white mice loose in the room, and somewhere in Berlin, that Dr. Goebbels was delivering one of his speeches—against Remarque, against his book, against the film, against, as he never tired of bellowing to his listeners, this whole, rotten, degenerate, Judaized Weimar system.

He concluded his speech with the cries: "Germany! Wake up!" and *"Sieg Heil!"*

MILITARY COURT, APRIL/MAY 1943

The two men stand across from each other, face to face, and at first Bonhoeffer hardly even recognizes his brother-in-law. Not because he looks wretched or miserable, but because he looks so good.

Perhaps no longer quite so pointed, or so slender, and without glasses his gaze seems somewhat darker, softer. Bonhoeffer looks surreptitiously for any signs of mistreatment but finds nothing. Hans von Dohnanyi looks quite fresh, clean shaven, and is dressed in a clean white shirt.

"How are you?" they both say in the same breath while shaking hands, and neither can help laughing at the mundane, conventional character of that question.

"So, they incarcerated you as well?" Bonhoeffer adds, sounding not much more original than when posing the initial question. In the background, behind his desk as if behind a protective barrier, Senior High Court Military Prosecutor Manfred Roeder clears his throat.

"Yes, me too," Dohnanyi says, "and Christine immediately afterward as well, and in Munich our Josef Müller, his wife, and Anni, his secretary. But why them?" His voice gets louder, almost shrill, then his gaze turns to Roeder, "And why Christine?"

"Your wife, like you yourself, is under suspicion of high treason, at the very least through privity."

"My Christine, a traitor? The storybook wife and mother? She doesn't even know what that is." Dohnanyi laughs out loud.

Bonhoeffer pictures the self-confident face of his sister, a university-trained biologist who could hold her own with any man in even the most sharp-tongued discussion. He also pictures her sitting across from this Roeder, the good German wife with a loyal gaze, her hands folded quite demurely in her lap, the quintessence of quiet feminine devotion from her head all the way down to her oh-so-primly positioned feet.

We Bonhoeffers, Bonhoeffer thinks silently to himself, *are not such bad actors at all.*

"And you gentlemen do not otherwise have anything to say to each other? Or to me?" Roeder's voice is no longer soft and polite, but cutting, malicious, threatening.

"Only what I have already told you several times." Dohnanyi is speaking. "Namely, that it is an insulting insinuation to assert that I helped my brother-in-law secure a position in the intelligence services merely so that he might avoid direct military service."

His voice gets loud again, sounding exactly like the voice his brother-in-law knows so well, slightly nasal, sharp, with a hint of arrogance. "And your other insinuation, namely, that I secured military deferrals for people for money in order to finance my house purchase in Sakrow, will have consequences. Not for me. For you, Herr Prosecutor."

Bonhoeffer admires his brother-in-law. One might even think that he, not Roeder, is the accuser here. Roeder no doubt senses that nothing is to be gained by juxtaposing the two brothers-in-law like this, no gushing confessions, no grand moment of truth.

He dismisses Dohnanyi with a hand gesture, then stares angrily at the door as it closes behind him. "He thinks he's superior to me, the jerk. Won't he be surprised. . . . ," he mutters before turning to Bonhoeffer again. "Well, now to you, Herr Bonhoeffer. . . ."

He has long since dispensed with "Herr Pastor." No more "Dr. Bonhoeffer" either. "Among us academics," Roeder had smiled so obligingly during the very first interrogation, as if meeting Bonhoeffer at a horse race at Berlin's Hoppegarten racetrack, "such is not really customary," with which, of course, he quite deftly drew attention to his own academic degree.

It was on April 12 that Roeder and Bonhoeffer had first sat across from each other here in the interrogation room of the Reich War Court. Easter had been celebrated afterward in all its gorgeous beauty, and Bonhoeffer, in his cell, had listened, longingly, to the distant pealing of Sunday church bells, imagining himself sitting with his parents and siblings over in the garden of their Grunewald villa, having Easter breakfast, brightly colored eggs on the table. His father would have squinted into the sunshine, lit a cigarette, and said, "Every year it seems as if the world is being born anew."

Here in the gray gloom of the interrogation room, however, with Hitler's malevolent eyes glaring down from the portrait on the wall, the world is certainly *not* being born anew. Here the world is a soulless apparatus, eternally the same, eternally, obstinately revolving around itself, and the man over there behind his desk, though hardly older than Bonhoeffer himself, seems like the ancient, fossilized guard of an order that no longer asks about justice or even custom, existing instead solely, exclusively, for its own sake—dead, malicious, evil, merciless.

Bonhoeffer now sits on the edge of his chair before this man like a schoolboy whose final examination is at risk, sheepishly knitting his sweaty hands, stammering, repeatedly asking that the questioning not proceed so quickly, since otherwise he simply cannot keep up. For the rest, Bonhoeffer does acknowledge with an embarrassed smile that, well, yes, it is certainly possible that someone like him, someone rather removed from reality and naive, might have made this or that mistake in the strange, alien world of the intelligence services. But what might he be accused of now?

Subversion of the military. Aha! That he has avoided military service by alleging that he—Pastor Bonhoeffer—was needed by, of all things, the intelligence services.

"But they did need me. That is what my brother-in-law told me."

"At the behest of Canaris and Oster?"

"Exactly. Admiral Canaris asked specifically for me. It was practically an order. There is no way I could have refused it."

"And the fact that you were thus not called up for normal military service—even though your age group was due—that presumably broke your heart."

"Indeed."

Bonhoeffer says this so loudly that Roeder almost starts. But even more than Roeder, Bonhoeffer himself is now astonished as he continues, and not without some passion: "Was I not in the United States in 1939, just before the war broke out? Could I not have stayed there quite comfortably except for the fact that I did indeed want to have a part in the destiny of the fatherland? But no, I returned immediately and almost forced myself into the position of a military field chaplain. It was not my fault that I was not accepted." And Bonhoeffer now visualizes himself sitting there in the room as precisely such a person experiencing completely sincere, heartfelt indignation and chagrin at not being allowed to serve the fatherland, on the verge of weeping genuine tears of disappointment from behind his glasses.

You are, he thinks to himself, *not such a bad actor at all.*

But then he says loudly, "I belong to the Confessing Church and I am quite familiar with our reputation. Do you think it doesn't hurt us for my colleagues and I to be labeled as unwilling participants who would prefer to just hand their country over, defenseless, to the Bolshevist onslaught? No," he laughs out loud, proudly, derisively, "absolutely not; we are determined, indeed driven to prove exactly the opposite to the world." Nor is Bonhoeffer lying in this instance.

He thinks back to the day during the 1930s when he had read a newspaper article to his seminary students about the reintroduction of compulsory military service. And about how all those young fellows had cheered, one of them then declaring, "Well, now the others can see whether we really are cowardly draft dodgers!" Although Bonhoeffer had quickly put the newspaper aside and turned the conversation to other things, that enthusiasm echoed in him long afterward.

Bonhoeffer has now put aside all pathos and is projecting pure dignity, pure objectivity. "Here Prosecutor, 90 percent of all the pastors in the Confessing Church have been conscripted, and 16 percent of those have already been killed in action. I would not shy away from taking exactly the same path except that I am able to serve my country in better ways than with a weapon."

"And what might those better ways be, Herr Bonhoeffer?"

"Do you know what the ecumenical movement is?"

Roeder finds this question so arrogant and haughty that he would prefer to jump up and shout Bonhoeffer down as he already has Dohnanyi on several occasions. But that had not been of much help with the wily lawyer, and Roeder senses that here, too, it would not yield much. So he forces himself to listen to Bonhoeffer's explanation with a certain measure of composure.

"The ecumenical movement, or the World Federation of Churches," Bonhoeffer commences with the tone of voice and amiable patience of a teacher who is explaining something to pupils who, although certainly willing enough to learn, are also slightly slow-witted, "is a worldwide alliance of all the larger churches, except for the church in Rome, with connections to the highest strata of society in their various countries. I think I may flatter myself that I am acquainted with virtually all the most important gentlemen in the organization, and indeed even rather good friends with some, such as the bishop of Chichester. Can you understand now why Admiral Canaris particularly wanted me as an agent?"

"To sound out the ecumenical movement?"

"So to speak. To learn what their opinions and attitudes are toward Germany, particularly toward Germany after the final victory." Bonhoeffer nods as graciously as if, finally, even the slowest pupil in the class had understood the lesson. "Nor was it at all easy for me to accept this commission, since it did, after all, mean misusing my friends' trust at least to a certain extent."

His voice begins to quake slightly, as if suppressing a sob. "In a manner of speaking, I have sacrificed my own ecumenical connections for the sake of the fatherland. I do not know whether I will ever be forgiven for that and whether I will not stand there one day as a traitor. But before Germany itself, that is a matter of indifference to me. Germany will understand what I have done for my country."

After speaking these words, he feels a bit queasy in his stomach and fears he may throw up. These last sentences have come out of his mouth with such concentrated urgency that he himself almost believes what he is saying. He now essentially sees himself just as the man sitting across from him is supposed to, namely, as an upright patriot who is prepared to surrender everything he has hitherto held sacred for the sake of Reich and *Führer*.

How he would have liked to wash his hands at just this moment, so sweaty and dirty did they suddenly seem to him. But he continues to look at his interrogator with the utmost sincerity.

And the latter does indeed seem impressed, jotting down a few notes and then looking up at Bonhoeffer again. "And it doubtless has nothing to do with your family ties with Herr Dohnanyi that for the role of agent he chose precisely *you*, a man whom, a short time before, the state police had forbidden to speak publicly and even to publish?"

"I asked him about that myself. He merely remarked that the intelligence services must work together with everyone, with Jews, Communists, with . . ."

"With someone like you, Herr Bonhoeffer?" Dohnanyi has already given him the same answer. Roeder raises his voice. "With a pastor accused of making statements hostile to the state?"

"Show me even a single sentence in my sermons that can be construed as hostile to the state!" Bonhoeffer is almost shouting, and it is only an assuaging gesture from his counterpart that prompts him to slide back into the role of indignant innocence. "I do not expect you to be familiar with my book on discipleship, though it is certainly not entirely unknown." Bonhoeffer does not have to feign this modest pride at the success of his book. "There you can read what I have to say about the obligation of every Christian with regard to the authorities, as drawn from my own interpretation of Paul's letter to the Romans. Never, I think, has this point been made as clearly and unambiguously."

He leans back in the chair and once again envisions the person he has just portrayed. No "Reich bishop" could have presented himself as more loyal to the state or more submissive to the authorities. And again he feels slightly nauseated.

In the meantime, Roeder seems to have only half listened. Quite unexpectedly he pulls out a letter and, with knitted brow, carefully peruses it. Then he looks up again. "You are not the only one who has not served in the military. You have also tried to save others from serving, for example, your colleague Wilhelm Niesel. You no doubt know him."

Bonhoeffer can only nod confusedly.

Roeder picks up the letter again. "I read here in a letter you wrote to your brother-in-law that Herr Niesel was facing the threat of being called up."

He drops the letter on the desk. "The threat is indeed there, Herr Bonhoeffer."

"But . . . but . . ."

"Well?"

The surprise suggests exactly the right gesture for Bonhoeffer. He almost squints in confusion, his hands fluttering helplessly in the air for a moment. Then, as if in total shock, he puts his hands on his cheeks, and his eyes and mouth get wider and wider. "That sounds horrible. Absolutely horrible. But you must understand . . ."

"What, exactly, must I understand, Herr Bonhoeffer?"

"It is not that Brother Niesel is facing the threat of being called up, no, it is us, his church, that is facing the threat of losing Brother Niesel if he is sent to the front. After all, we really do need every good man here, on the home front, for church work. . . ."

Roeder seems satisfied. The guard comes in to take the prisoner back to his cell. Roeder watches them walk away.

"Do you know the joke about the pushcarts?" he suddenly asks. Bonhoeffer, almost outside the room, turns around in surprise. The last thing he has expected is that this man, at this place, after such a conversation, would want to tell him a joke.

"There is smuggling going on at the border. Nonstop. But no one really knows what's being smuggled. People are pushing pushcarts back and forth, and every single cart is thoroughly examined. Empty. All of them. Finally, the head customs officer entreats the head smuggler to reveal to him, with a guarantee of immunity, what it is he's smuggling. Do you know what the smuggler answers?"

Roeder leans forward, without even the trace of a smile. "Pushcarts, Herr Customs Officer, pushcarts."

Bonhoeffer does not know whether he is supposed to laugh or not, and Roeder, too, does not seem to find the joke funny, and instead leans his upper body even farther, like a predatory animal about to leap. He then hisses, "I will find your pushcart, Herr Bonhoeffer! And then may your Jewish God—about whom you preach so nicely—may your Jewish God help all draft dodgers."

With that, Bonhoeffer is in reality already dismissed. But to his own astonishment he now walks back to the desk so forcefully that even Roeder momentarily shrinks back. "Do you know what you are saying there?"

Roeder almost lifts his hands up as if to ward off an assault.

"You are insulting a man whose fiancée comes from a family that has already paid an enormous toll in lives in this war. And a man who lost his own brother in the last war. . . ."

"You're engaged?" Roeder almost stammers the words out.

"With Fräulein Maria von Wedemeyer. Who even as we speak is weeping at the death of her father *and* her brother. And such a woman is supposed to be engaged to someone like me? To someone who is a coward and is trying to duck service at the front?"

Poor Maria, Bonhoeffer thinks later as he sits in the prisoner transport truck. *Holding her up as a moral alibi for this whole thing. Why on earth did she have to end up with precisely a fellow like me?* And his smile turns gentle, tender, just as it always does when he visualizes Maria's narrow, clear, girlish face.

"What's with the stupid grin?" a voice barks from the side.

Knobloch. The crudest of all his guards, though other guards have in the meantime become much more courteous, at times even almost friendly with him. A "prole," he thinks. And then he immediately remembers that, as a matter of fact, such "proles" occasionally even prefer to call themselves that, seeing it as a kind of honorific title.

"Workers of the world, unite, that's the way to lose your chains!" Isn't that how the song went that Bonhoeffer heard so often in the working-class district of Berlin, Prenzlauer Berg, during those days long ago when he himself had found a home there?

Quite without thinking, he purses his lips and begins whistling a melody. "Forward, without forgetting where our strength can be seen now to be, . . ."

The man next to him glances over, says nothing, merely nods slightly. He seems to know the song.

~

Leader and Seducer

1931–1933

*"Only the leader who himself stands in the service
of the penultimate and ultimate authority can elicit loyalty."*
—from a radio speech, 1933

GOD LOVES THE CURSES OF THE WICKED

Bonhoeffer had changed trains in Frankfurt after visiting his brother
Karl-Friedrich and his wife. He was on his way to Bonn, where, finally,
he would make Karl Barth's acquaintance. His *personal* acquaintance.
Finally. Erwin Sutz had promised.

It was July 1931. Hot. Almost sultry. Bonhoeffer pulled the window
down in the train compartment. So, tomorrow he would actually
meet Karl Barth.

Bonhoeffer had already seen photos of Barth. And Sutz had also
described him several times. Smallish in stature, compact, not a
particularly imposing figure. And yet on first seeing the much admired,
much disputed man, Bonhoeffer would be startled, and even later, in
Tegel, whenever he thought of Barth, he always recalled this very first
impression.

Even though Barth was only in his mid forties at the time, every
time he entered the main lecture hall—the *auditorium maximum*—on
Seminary Street in Bonn, it seemed as if an old man were shuffling in.
Bonhoeffer could not know at the time that Barth had had to endure
a terrible case of diphtheria of the ear. That same day he had written
to Sutz, "Barth looks terrible. Does he always look this bad?"

Sutz had accepted a position as an apprentice vicar near Zurich after returning home to Switzerland from America. Bonhoeffer was back in Berlin, and the city seemed to have grown peculiarly strange, even alien to him. Everything seemed that way to him, even his parents' house, which had never seemed so quiet and empty.

All his brothers and sisters were now married, even cheeky Susanne, who to the quiet amusement of not a few family members had become the staunchly upright wife of Pastor Dress. The first children were arriving, and his siblings all had their own circles, their own small worlds, their own lives. *But why not me?* Bonhoeffer occasionally wondered to himself. *Does a twenty-five-year-old still belong in his parents' house?* And that was not the only self-critical question he raised regarding his life.

He received his doctorate. Then his secondary dissertation qualifying him to lecture. Then assistant lecturer. Soon a student chaplain. "So young and already so far along," people whispered behind him when in radiant blond self-confidence he walked through the halls, a favorite child of fate, a perpetual golden boy. "We'll be seeing him again as a bishop, at the very least."

But this self-assurance was only feigned. Behind it lurked an element of tormenting self-doubt. Who am I? How can I presume to teach others what I myself do not really know?

Bonhoeffer looked around him. Harnack, despite all criticism, had been a standard. But now he was dead. And the other professors were teaching a theology that was no longer really his own. So his thoughts drifted over to the Rhineland, to Bonn, where something new was stirring. Karl Barth was teaching there.

In the spring of 1930, the man from Basel had become a professor of systematic theology in the city where Beethoven had been born. The sleepy town had been roused from its slumber and then overnight had become the center of modern German theology. Accordingly, Bonhoeffer, too, set out on a journey.

"Wouldn't you rather spend a few weeks resting up in Friedrichs-brunn before starting the difficult work as a student chaplain?" his father had asked, full of concern. He had precisely registered the changes that had taken place in his son's disposition and nature, and his inner restiveness.

No! Anything but rest! Anything but standing still just now! The train trundled along through the Rhineland low country, Bonhoeffer gazing out of the compartment window. Everything was so green and peaceful, and yet behind it all lay Germany—tormented, battered, and vulnerable to every sort of seduction. After his experiences in New York, Bonhoeffer could not understand how he could have ignored all the misery earlier.

Poverty. Unemployment. Hunger. Yes, genuine hunger now among Germany's almost six million unemployed. The lines outside the soup kitchens were getting longer and longer, the faces of those waiting increasingly grim. Those who were accepted into the so-called SA, the Brownshirts of this Hitler—and who was this fellow again?—were fortunate.

Those Brownshirts were offering something like "self-help"— apartment rent, some clothes, a piece of bread each day. And Bonhoeffer had once walked down a street behind a small boy who was barefoot despite the cold weather.

"Hey, young fellow, shouldn't you be wearing a pair of warm shoes?"

"I don't got any. I'm growing too fast. My parents can't afford to buy me new pairs that fast."

Bonhoeffer stretched out his legs in the train compartment and looked down at his feet. Impeccable shoes. He was almost ashamed. The train pulled into the Bonn train station.

Only seven o'clock. The master loved lecturing early. Bonhoeffer had taken a seat in the back row of the *auditorium maximum*, uncertain, uneasy. A hitherto unfamiliar shyness came over him. He was no longer an assistant lecturer, but a student again, just like everyone else here in the overflowing hall.

No, not exactly like the others.

Those others had the look of haughty priests, members of a caste that was closed off to nonbelievers, a caste sworn to allegiance to he who would soon utter words of ultimate truth from the podium. And Bonhoeffer was the bastard among purebloods. An intruder, the only black man among whites, just as in the Harlem churches he had been the only white man among blacks.

No doubt they will soon ask me to remove my shoes and socks to check whether the soles of my feet are white, he mused to himself, finding the notion not at all funny.

Then, finally, the door opened. Barth entered the room, shuffling, shambling along. Every step he took toward the podium seemed to require inordinate effort. Finally, at the podium, he gestured. First a small devotional moment during which each person might collect his or her thoughts. Then a chorale. Bonhoeffer sang along and started feeling a bit more secure. These verses, sung together as a group, somehow brought all these different people together, turning them into a community. Had that not also been the case in Harlem?

There, it was "Oh, when the saints go marchin' in!" Here, "Sacred God, we praise thy name!" Then the singing stopped.

Barth had begun to speak, and Bonhoeffer was genuinely surprised. It all sounded much more spontaneous and direct than he had expected. What had particularly disturbed Bonhoeffer about Barth's written works was the rigidity, the dogmatic element in his understanding of faith, faith that is revealed *only* through God's word.

But now this man up at the podium seemed to have his own doubts about everything. He, too, seemed to be a seeker, full of questions. Bonhoeffer suddenly understood the man standing there and felt closer to him than he ever had to someone like Harnack.

"So, how do you like this Karl Barth of ours?" That was Hans Fischer, a personal friend whom Erwin Sutz had asked to help Bonhoeffer navigate all the university hustle and bustle in Bonn.

Bonhoeffer did not answer until after a short pause, and then only with some hesitation. "There seem to be two Barths. You have to see him away from his books as well."

Fischer smiled. "You'll soon have more opportunity for precisely that. He has invited you over to his house this afternoon along with some other students."

These others—yet another surprise—were Benedictine monks from the nearby abbey Maria Laach. Barth liked to stop by the abbey now and then, and the monks for their own part occasionally sat in on his lectures. They were a cheerful bunch, quite open to the world, and Bonhoeffer immediately felt comfortable among them. *A genuine community of Christians,* he thought. *Why can't a community like this emerge everywhere—regardless of denomination?*

The shyness that had come over him like a fever now subsided, and when someone laughingly quipped, "Come on, we can't just sing, 'Hallelujah!' day in and day out all the time!"—the topic of discussion was how to persuade non-Christians—Bonhoeffer heard himself say to his own astonishment, "Not least because the curses of the wicked are often more welcome to God than the hallelujahs of the faithful!" But then he immediately regretted saying it.

The room fell completely silent. A solitary fly buzzed about in the July afternoon heat. Barth brushed at it with his hand. Then he, like all the others, looked over at Bonhoeffer. "What do you mean?"

"Well, I, um," he tried not to stammer, "I mean, whoever curses God is actually praising him. What that person is really cursing is not God himself, but all the stones and thorns and obstacles blocking the path to God. The wicked—the godless—are usually seeking God. In any event," he hastily added, "I didn't come up with the expression myself."

"But rather?" Barth held his fingertips together and looked even more searchingly at Bonhoeffer.

"It comes from Martin Luther."

"From Luther himself? Excellent. I didn't know that." Barth's eyes sparkled like a young boy who still loves surprises. Bonhoeffer suddenly liked Barth.

That time in Bonn turned out to be a very good time indeed.

Bonhoeffer had the opportunity on several other occasions as well to visit the two-story apartment on Siebengebirg Street where Barth and his family lived. Sometimes Bonhoeffer went with others, other times alone. And on those visits—when he went alone—he occasionally caught himself engaging in a rather voluble openness that he otherwise generally preferred to keep concealed behind a mask of cool, smiling superiority.

He spoke about America, and about Barcelona, and about all the social misery he had seen there, and which—even more—he had also smelled, felt, tasted, and breathed into the depths of his own soul there. "We Christians cannot simply turn away from these things." Nor did he conceal his earlier criticism of Barth, the excessive and one-sided focus on the Bible, a focus that seemed to have not the slightest inkling of the real misery in this world. "I sometimes wondered whether Karl Barth had ever spent any time abroad," he concluded, startled at his own audacity in saying such a thing.

"Well, certainly not as long or as intensively as you have." Barth smiled and put his fingertips together again. "And you may well be right. Perhaps I withdrew too often to my Swiss summer retreat, my *Bergli*. I do realize that must now change. Why otherwise would I have joined the Social Democratic Party this past May?"

Now Bonhoeffer was genuinely baffled. Barth was amused by his astonishment. "Yes, yes, I'm a registered Social Democrat now. Not that I see salvation coming from socialism, but I do think we need something concrete to counter what seems to be coming at us now."

He did not specify what that might be, but did add, "Too bad you were not in Berlin during the spring when I delivered my lecture about our church's current distress. The great hall of the university was overflowing. Fourteen hundred people were crowding into. . . ."

Barth never failed to mention such details.

Then he laughed. "Let's just say that not everyone was enthusiastic about what I had to say. Namely, that our church's distress consists precisely in its perpetual inclination to accommodate itself, in this case to nationalism, which is once again becoming fashionable. 'Christianity must be German. Or it will not *be* at all.' Who was it that came out with this rubbish recently?"

Bonhoeffer did not know either.

"Of course, it's all nonsense, this 'hyphen' between Christianity and nationalism and national character and what not that is becoming so fashionable. What we need is a Protestant, not a German-Protestant church. But, yes, saying something like that publicly does take a certain amount of courage. And I was promptly reviled as a foreigner hostile to Germans." Barth sighed; this recrimination hurt. "But there is no better way for a Swiss living here to articulate his love for this country. But come, Bonhoeffer," he stood up with a bit of effort, "let's have a glass of sherry before my wife calls us in for dinner."

On their way to the dining room, Bonhoeffer remarked, "Perhaps the World Federation of Churches is the counterforce you would like to see, or at least part of it." Since returning from America, he had overcome his initial slight disinclination toward the ecumenical movement and now even added with a bit of pride, "In September I'll be attending the annual conference in Cambridge. Max Diestel— perhaps you know him. . . ."

"A good man, even though I do not entirely share his enthusiasm for the ecumenical movement."

"He suggested me as a member of the German youth delegation."

No real friendship developed between Bonhoeffer and Barth during these three summer weeks in Bonn. Nor was it only the age difference.

Bonhoeffer's personality emanated a flickering, slightly rebellious nervousness during these early years, something that made the more peasantlike, robust Barth slightly nervous. He once remarked to his wife at dinner, "Bonhoeffer really does scare me a bit. In fact, he seems almost eerie."

Nelly Barth looked up in astonishment. "You mean this nice, blond, lucid young man? He of all people?"

"Blond and lucid? I don't know. He is indeed bright. Almost too bright. Probably brighter than me." He coughed out a laugh, since in reality he did think this was *highly* unlikely. "Someone who guides others and yet is looking for guidance himself. That can be a dangerous mix."

"You don't like him?" Nelly Barth was quite astonished because she had always thought her husband had a particular fondness for precisely this Dietrich Bonhoeffer.

"No, no, I like him well enough. He just doesn't always make it *easy* to like him. The imperious element in his disposition, his inclination for the unqualified and the absolute, all that can quickly become a problem for others. I fear," Barth hesitated, then looked over toward the window, "that he is very lonely. And will always be so."

He rolled up his cloth napkin. "He just doesn't know it yet."

"FORWARD, NOT FORGETTING . . ."

The stamping footsteps had gotten closer, the singing voices oppressively loud, really more like roaring. Bonhoeffer had stopped briefly to listen. What were they singing? The Communist *Internationale* or Horst Wessel's nationalist *The Flag on High*? Bonhoeffer was not interested in having an encounter with either group, so he quickly ducked into a doorway.

The marchers turned the corner toward him. "So comrades, come rally, and let us face the last fight . . ."

That meant they were Communists. Red armbands. They marched by. Bonhoeffer breathed a sigh of relief and walked back into the street. Let's hope they don't come across the others—the Nazis—he thought. Then there would be bloodshed. Again. For that was how things went in the Wedding district of Berlin during the early 1930s, where Hitler Youth had already been shot to death and, on the other side, Communists trampled to death by Brownshirts.

Bonhoeffer put his collar up. It was drizzling.

The marchers in the distance had now changed songs. "Forward, without forgetting where our strength can be seen now to be. . . ." A beautiful song, Bonhoeffer had to concede as he involuntarily hummed along. "Forward, not forgetting our solidarity! . . ."

Solidarity. Peace. A reconciliation of the nations. Actually, he thought, those are the same things that were debated this September in Cambridge at the annual conference of the World Federation of Churches, and there, too, right-wingers had whistled in derision at them, insisting that there would be no understanding among the nations as long as the Germans continued to be oppressed by their neighbors, "and anyone who thinks any differently is a crazy fool."

"So comrades, come rally. . . ."

Bonhoeffer whistled the melody as he continued on through Wedding, with its tenement blocks and stinking courtyards and grim canyons between buildings, where the hurdy-gurdy piped its sad song up toward the building facades, and where the corner bars, even at this early morning hour, were already full of sad figures who could still afford beer and sometimes even a schnapps.

Several weeks had already passed since Bonhoeffer had first made his way through this section of Berlin. Pastor Müller, from the Zion Congregation in Wedding, had accompanied him, huffing and puffing and muttering something about "You'll see, they're a bunch of urchin animals." Bonhoeffer had smiled at the remark and thought about the Sunday schools in Harlem. He had responded with just a simple nod of his head when asked to take over confirmation instruction from his clearly overtaxed colleague in Prenzlauer Berg.

"Can't you already hear the mob of them?"

They had entered a musty gray building. The stairwell smelled of chalk dust and floor polish and echoed with the shouts of fifty young boys whose voices were just at the breaking stage. As the two men climbed the stairs, they were pummeled by squawking laughter and an assortment of garbage. Up on the top stairs, the boys emptied the garbage can down on them. "You just wait, you urchins. . . ."

Müller stormed up the four flights of stairs, his face beet red, breathless. Bonhoeffer followed. "Get on into the classroom, all of you, now! . . ." Müller herded the boys into the room, slapping at the one or the other, while the others continued to laugh and shout. Bonhoeffer leaned against the wall, his hands in his pockets.

"This is Herr Pastor Bonhoeffer. He'll be instructing you from now on."

"*What's* the guy's name with the bicycle on his nose?"

"Bon–hoeffer."

"*Bon bon bon bon bonnnnn,*" the group cackled. Then one of them, the most audacious, with red hair and freckles, asked, "So didja bring us any *bonbons*, seein' 's how that's your name?"

Bonhoeffer, his eyes half closed, smiled.

"Well, no, not yet. And what might *your* name be, '*seein' 's how*' we're already on a first-name basis?"

"Teddy. Like Thälmann, the workers' leader."

The boy was obviously quite proud of this coincidence.

"Teddy. Nice. I used to know a Teddy, over there in New York. But he wasn't a workers' leader. He was black."

"A real nigger?"

The others had gotten noticeably quieter. Bonhoeffer, still standing against the wall, merely nodded briefly as Müller, with a dismissive wag of his hand, quickly stole away. Bonhoeffer's voice remained soft, really almost just a whisper. The boys had to strain to hear him.

"Nice boy, that Teddy. Just too bad they put him in jail."

"He was put in the slammer?"

This was something that did indeed get these boys' attention. Their fathers, uncles, brothers, neighbors had often enough spent time in jail, and they—the boys themselves—knew they eventually probably would as well.

"Not just jail. The electric chair as well. That's what they call it there. That's how criminals are executed."

"So what'd he do, this Teddy?"

Bonhoeffer had no idea what this Teddy might have been up to. To be honest, he had never even *known* a Teddy. But that just gave him all the more to relate. For the next several hours, he talked at length about "Teddy," and about "Bill" and "Tom" and about "Chinese Charlie," and about one particular other fellow he had met in New York. "Just imagine, guys, this fellow had *genuine* Indian blood flowing in his veins, just like Karl May's character Winnetou."

The boys had indeed listened. Picking their noses, belching, squatting there in their ragged jackets and endlessly patched pullovers. And wanting to hear more from "Herr Paster," as they now called him. And this Herr Pastor continued to tell his stories; and told them well. Including about the two brothers, one of whom was supposed to inherit a vegetable store from his father—but one time he was ravenously hungry.

So his younger brother served him a bowl of pea soup with bacon. "That's something you guys like as well." And because the older brother was *so* hungry, "like an animal," the younger had managed to talk him out of the vegetable store in exchange for the soup.

"What a swine!"

"Naw, I don't think so. I think he was purty darn clever. The brother could also have eaten a fatback sandwich. Right, Herr Paster?"

"And that really happened? In New York?"

"Nope, not in New York. In the Bible. The fellows' names there are Jacob and Esau. And *next* time I'll tell you about somebody else—about Joseph—whose brothers sold him off to Pharaoh."

It was not like all these boys now turned into little angels under Bonhoeffer's guidance. They were the same, impudent, cheeky kids from Wedding, unwashed, uncombed, with skinned-up knees and the first "fags" hanging from the corners of their mouths.

Bonhoeffer, however, increasingly found himself almost eagerly looking forward to the next class with the boys. And he played chess with them, taught them a couple of phrases in English, even visited their parents at home now and then, where he was served a hard-roll sandwich that, quite frankly, he ate not without a bad conscience, since they often hardly had anything to eat themselves. *Can one really talk to such people about some distant heavenly kingdom?* he thought. *Wouldn't a paradise full of ham and sausages be a more welcome sight to them?*

Christmas was approaching. Bonhoeffer sat in his parents' parlor in the house on Wangenheim Street, wrapping packages with festive, colorful paper and gold ribbons and bows.

"And what might you be doing there, Dietrich?" It was his grandmother, who was now living with his parents. She pushed a cup of tea over to him followed by a bowl of his beloved ginger cookies.

Bonhoeffer took a bite out of one of the cookies. "Christmas presents for my confirmands. Otherwise they won't get anything. Their parents just don't have the money for presents." He wrapped the next package in blue paper with silver stars. "I've already written to all my brothers and sisters. They won't be getting any presents from me this Christmas. I need every penny for the confirmands."

"You're a good boy."

Was he really? He didn't know.

He only knew that this confirmation instruction had become much more important to him than his work as a student chaplain, not least because the students at the technical college were inclined to view their spiritual shepherd more, let us say, from the "bright" side. More often than not, he merely sat there alone during his weekly office hours. But these boys in Wedding, *they* were his real congregation. And he felt at home among them.

"By the way, Grandmama, I'm moving out right after the New Year. Into a furnished apartment in Wedding."

"You're going to leave us?"

"At least for the three months leading up to the boys' confirmation." He thought about what Teddy had once said to him. "You tell us all these really nice stories about paradise and all, Herr Paster. But then you head on back to your own house, with all the pretty trees, and you have it good there, a kinda paradise, while we're all stuck back here in Prenzlauer Berg. Tell you the truth, I think I like Ernst Thälmann better. He's promising that we'll all be living in prettified houses someday, just like you. . . ."

"Forward, not forgetting our solidarity. . . ."

"What are you humming there, my boy?"

"Well, not a Christmas carol, Grandmama." Bonhoeffer laughed. "We can't just let Thälmann take over."

"The Communist?"

Julie Bonhoeffer had become an avid newspaper reader here in Berlin. "There is this Dr. Goebbels now. He says that his leader, Hitler, and his party are the only protection we have against Communism."

"Oh, my, Hitler. The fool with the sjambok whip. He won't be able to do anything to counter someone like Thälmann. No, it is we who must get going, each at his own station. I'm already thinking about applying for a pastoral position in the eastern part of Berlin, in one of the workers' congregations."

He put the wrapped package over with the others. "Can you loan me some money, Grandmama?"

"I'd be glad to. But for what?"

"I need a bolt of blue fabric. For my boys' confirmation suits."

WELL SAID, HERR PASTOR!

All fifty boys stood before the altar of the Zion Church in Wedding in crisp new blue suits, myrtle-sprig bouquets in their lapels. Bonhoeffer, in a robe and clerical collar, could not help feeling a bit melancholy looking out over the neat, slickly combed heads.

He had already firmly resolved to stay in contact with these boys. But the hard truth was that these boys were no longer "his congregation." He commenced with the confirmation sermon.

He spoke about Jacob this time as well, but now about the one who wrestled with the angel to gain blessedness. And again Bonhoeffer's gaze, with quiet sadness, drifted across these bright, open, youthful faces. He wondered what blessedness life might have in store for them.

It was March 13, 1932.

It was on this same Sunday that the new Reich president was elected. Although both Hitler and Thälmann had campaigned for the office, the overwhelming victor was Paul von Hindenburg, "our ersatz emperor," as Bonhoeffer's father ironically muttered, adding with a sigh, "I certainly hope he's brighter than the original."

In any event, the danger of a radical turn to either the left or the right seemed thwarted.

The fad of nationalism, however, did not just exist in Karl Barth's imagination, and it had become more than a mere fad. It was rampant now and was also creeping into the church. A new party had already emerged, the "German Christians," whose program read as if dictated by Dr. Goebbels himself: the principle of the leader—the *Führer*—a Reich Church, the exclusion of all Jews, and the destruction of diabolical Marxism.

Precisely this party had achieved considerable initial successes in the regular elections in the Prussian church in November 1932. And Bonhoeffer—who had hitherto found these "German Christians" along with their founder, Joachim Hossenfelder, more comical than anything else—was not the only person for whom these successes utterly shattered the otherwise customary tranquility of the church.

It was with almost grim determination, as if in response to this advancing nationalism in Germany, that Bonhoeffer threw himself into his ecumenical work. He was now one of three youth secretaries, organizing conferences from England to Czechoslovakia and speaking with increasing ardor about how any Christian who raises his weapon against another Christian is also raising that weapon against Christ himself. Bonhoeffer's friend Lasserre would have been happy.

Although he was living back on Wangenheim Street now, his ties with Wedding had remained close.

Bonhoeffer visited his confirmands often, took excursions with them in the countryside, once even spent an entire week with them at his parents' country house, quite to the horror of the caretaker. But only a single windowpane had been broken. And at some point amid these excursions Bonhoeffer came up with the idea for a "Youth Hall," a place where young people could meet and talk, but also laugh, party, and simply be happy.

"Youngsters need a home, a place where at least for a couple of hours they can feel safe and secure, just as we Bonhoeffer children always did here in our parents' home," Bonhoeffer remarked. "The political parties are now providing that for their young members, the Nazis no less than the Communists. We need to create something like that as well."

That was at the evening meal to which Paula Bonhoeffer—her husband was away on a lecture trip—had invited not only Dietrich but also his sister Susanne and several of their friends, including Susanne's former schoolmate Anneliese Schnurmann, a budding psychologist from a wealthy Jewish family. She was fascinated by the idea.

"I could see helping to finance something like that," she said, "with maybe five hundred marks a month. Then," she laughed gently, sadly, "then perhaps Jewish money will be doing some good." Anti-Semitism was also increasingly rampant.

His mother interjected, "But it's not just money that Dietrich needs. He also needs help. Or are you intending to do it all yourself again, what with being a lecturer now with so many students, and with being a student chaplain and who knows what else in this World Federation of Churches?" Her son waved her off. "My students will just have to step up. It can only do them good to experience a bit of the world *outside* the lecture hall. . . ."

" . . . and besides, you already have them eating out of your hand in any case." That came from a young man at the other end of the table. "Your son, Madam," he turned to Paula Bonhoeffer, "is a born leader . . . and seducer. It won't be long before his students become his 'congregation' and start referring to him as their Jesus."

He wiped his mouth with his napkin and folded it daintily. "The 'Bonhoeffer circle.' That's what they're already calling themselves—a considerable number of are, I might add, women. No other lecturer is attracting as many students as is your son."

"What nonsense, my old adversary!" Bonhoeffer laughed, annoyed and yet also flattered.

Bonhoeffer had gotten to know Franz Hildebrandt, also a student of theology, even before the trip to America. Because they actually tended to be theologically at odds with each other, they affectionately and jokingly addressed each other as "old adversary."

And yet Bonhoeffer was attracted to this slender young man, three years his junior, to his sharp understanding and quick wit, and whenever Hildebrandt let go with one of his *as de Reve* stories in his absolutely inimitable semi-Yiddish, Bonhoeffer usually could not resist snorting with laughter even before the punch line, once even laughingly remarking, "One could almost believe, Herr Hildebrandt, that you really are a Jew. . . ." Bonhoeffer was still disinclined to get on a first-name basis with people. That would change only after his year in America.

"I *am* a Jew, Herr Bonhoeffer. On my mother's side."

"And you intend to become a pastor?"

"Who if not Jews?" Hildebrandt flashed a slightly mocking smile. "After all, we are constantly having to remind Christians where the roots of their faith are."

In the Bonhoeffer household, Franz Hildebrandt was soon as welcome as all the children's other friends, and Paula Bonhoeffer was particularly fond of this dark young man whose musical sensibility she admired even more than his two doctorates. And even now, she asked, "Ah, Franz, could you not do us the pleasure of playing something together with Dietrich?"

Bonhoeffer, however, quickly stood up from the table. "Another time, Mama. We're going to the theater." And to Hildebrandt, "We need to get going, Franz! We're already late as it is. We're going to miss the 'Prologue in Heaven.'" A performance of Goethe's *Faust* in the theater at the Gendarme Market was currently attracting considerable attention, especially because of the rousing performance of the role of Mephisto by a young actor named Gustaf Gründgens, who previously was better known for playing villains in B thrillers.

"This Mephisto is a kind of leader and seducer all in the same package," Franz Hildebrandt remarked after the performance as the two friends were having a glass of red wine in a wine bar. "We must be on our guard against this smooth smile and seductive gaze lest we, too, end up descending into hell at his beckoning. Then every soul will be lost."

"Being a leader—a *Führer*—is not really all that bad a thing, not in principle." Bonhoeffer sipped the wine and nodded to the waiting server to go ahead and fill the glass. "Human beings long for leadership; that's something I saw time and again in Wedding. What's bad is when the leader no longer leads us to God, declaring *himself* to be God instead. And by the way," he raised his glass, "I just received an offer from Berlin Radio. They're broadcasting an afternoon series of talks on topics of interest especially to young people. How about 'The Leader and the Individual in the Young Generation'—that would be something, wouldn't it?"

Hildebrandt nodded his agreement. They toasted.

Time passed. The Charlottenburg Youth Club came into existence, where young Christians, Communists, and Jews could spend time together in harmony, and it seemed to be turning into a genuinely successful undertaking. In November the National Socialist Party—the NSDAP—suffered a serious election setback, losing two million votes. General Schleicher became the new Reich chancellor. Bonhoeffer participated in a conference on ecumenical youth work and lectured at the university on the theological topic of "creation and fall."

Thus did the year 1932 pass, for many people the worst in German history considering the unimaginable misery of the unemployed masses. But then 1933 came, and with it that particular day in January— January 30—when Adolf Hitler did indeed become Reich chancellor.

The Brownshirts celebrated his victory with torchlight processions, the German Christians rejoiced, and in the provinces pastors recast the hymn "Praise the Lord" into "Praise the *Führer*" and opined that Herr Hitler was governing them quite well indeed. Even more moderate observers looked favorably on these recent developments.

The Marxist threat seemed to have been thwarted. No one like Teddy Thälmann was now in a position, like Lenin in Russia, to preach as a *Führer* to the masses that "religion is the opiate of the people"—and in any case, which party program except that of the Catholic Center was explicitly professing its allegiance to Christianity, which the National Socialists' program alleged to be something quite "positive"?

Although no one quite knew what to make of such a notion, most people were satisfied enough simply to hear the words "positive" and "Christianity" in the same context.

Two days after this "seizure of power," which some were already calling a "national revolution," Bonhoeffer was on his way to the Vox House at the radio station on Potsdam Street, his manuscript under his arm.

He walked into the almost palpably quiet studio. An amiably grinning sound engineer behind a glass panel would be his only audience here. Otherwise he saw only a table, a chair, and a microphone. No pulpit, no congregation. Bonhoeffer cleared his throat and noticed that his palms were sweating slightly.

A final cigarette, then "Can we begin?" and "All right, Herr Pastor!" A red light came on. Bonhoeffer began, at first in a somewhat strained fashion, then gradually freer, looser.

He spoke about authority. About authority that first really becomes authority only when we ourselves acknowledge it as such. And he spoke about young people, who want to choose their own leader and who are not interested in some imposed authority such as a father or the state. The sound engineer nodded to him behind the glass panel.

Bonhoeffer was feeling more secure now. He spoke further about the individual, who remains alone and cast adrift without an earthly leader, until finally, some day, he stands before the only real leader, namely, God. Bonhoeffer's conclusion was then that every leader is thus subordinated to other, higher authorities. Any leader who denies this simple fact is elevating himself to the status of the highest deity, and this ultimately leads to idolatry.

Bonhoeffer was now speaking as freely as if he were in the pulpit. "For leaders or offices that set themselves up as gods are in fact mocking both God and the individual, who becomes lonely before him, and are bound to collapse. Only the *Führer* who himself stands in the service of the penultimate and ultimate authority can elicit loyalty."

Bonhoeffer closed his eyes, allowing these final words to resonate in his ears, and enjoyed the intoxicating notion of having just spoken to thousands of people instead of, as was usually the case, only a few dozen.

The red light went out. In fact, it had already gone out some time ago, but Bonhoeffer, following the sound engineer's admonition to "just keep talking even if the light goes out, Herr Pastor," had not given it any more thought.

The program was over. "Well said, Herr Pastor!" That was the sound engineer. Bonhoeffer smiled at him gratefully. "Really too bad," the man continued, "that we had to break off in the middle of it."

"What? Break off?"

"Didn't you notice? Right when you got to the part, 'Only before God does a person become what he really is . . . ,' the light blinked. We had gone on too long. Too bad, really, and just when you were getting into a rhythm. On the other hand. . . ." He stopped. Bonhoeffer, speechless with anger, gathered up his manuscript.

"On the other hand," the man continued, lowering his voice as if betraying a profound mystery, "we already have a *Führer*. And we don't want to run him down now, do we?"

Bonhoeffer looked at him. Only now did he notice a *Bolschen*, the party emblem, on his coat lapel. Previously many members had only worn them on the *underside* of the lapel.

MILITARY COURT, JUNE 24, 1943

"And now we probably need to have another look at one particular issue. At this one." Roeder leans over the files. "At this Q7."

"Q7?" Bonhoeffer is all attentiveness, all politeness, with a touch of astonishment.

Roeder holds the file label up closer to his eyes. "Well, it could be an *O*. Yes, it's an *O*. Ah, here at the bottom we have it: 'operation.' So: 'Operation 7.'" He lays the file back down. Bonhoeffer merely raises an eyebrow, waiting, anticipating.

"It has been demonstrated that your brother-in-law—nor does he deny it—assisted seven, let us call them 'non-Aryans' in immigrating to Switzerland."

"Not seven. Fourteen."

"So, you know the exact numbers?"

No one can appear more innocent at this moment than does Bonhoeffer. "My brother-in-law told me about it. More peripherally, really. Something about trying to smuggle a network of agents into Switzerland."

"And they just happened to be Jews?"

"Who would arouse less suspicion in Switzerland than Jewish émigrés? And the intelligence service . . ."

" . . . and the intelligence service must work together with everyone, with Jews, Communists, and so on. Yes, I now know that. Your brother-in-law has emphasized it to me often enough." Roeder has to force himself not to fly into a fit of yelling. He picks up a ruler and taps on his fingertips.

"And so you, Herr Bonhoeffer, suggested the Jewess Friedenthal as a suitable candidate. . . ."

Charlotte Friedenthal. Her parents were still practicing Jews, while she herself was a baptized and active Christian, and her own religious practice was characterized by the traditional German—one might say, *Prussian*—inclination toward thoroughness. During the Great War she had worked as a nurse in a military hospital. During the 1930s as a secretary in the Confessing Church. And then she had sat before Bonhoeffer and said, "I have to get out of Germany. Preferably to Switzerland...." She was wearing a Star of David on her coat. To Bonhoeffer it had seemed like a wound, just yellow instead of red.

Bonhoeffer envisions her face. Clear, beautiful. *She'll resemble Grandmama someday*, he thinks. *And my Maria, yes, she will perhaps look like her.*

"Why the smile, Herr Bonhoeffer? Have I perhaps said something amusing?" Roeder is still tapping the ruler on his fingertips.

Bonhoeffer is startled. His thoughts have drifted. He forces himself to concentrate. "No, not 'suggested.'" He tries to gain a bit of time by stammering. "Fräulein Friedenthal simply asked me once whether I thought taking on a task with the intelligence services could be reconciled with a Christian conscience."

"What sort of task?"

A bird pecks against the windowpane. Roeder briefly glances over, then looks back at Bonhoeffer. Silence. The tapping of the ruler is the only noise in the room.

"I asked: what sort of task?" Roeder repeats after a lengthy pause.

"She didn't really offer any details about that either, nor did I really want to know. I merely remarked that my brother-in-law was a believing Christian himself and would surely not ask her to do anything unchristian."

"And when was this?"

The critical issue, since in an earlier conversation Bonhoeffer had carelessly mentioned spring 1942 as the beginning of the O7 undertaking. But since the deportation of Jews had begun in the autumn of 1941, Jews were no longer allowed to travel outside the country the following spring in any case. And it is on this point that Roeder is now building his case.

The entire maneuver—thus Roeder's argument—had nothing to do with the intelligence services at all. The sole purpose was to remove Jews from state jurisdiction with the help of the intelligence services and, not least, also through funding from the latter.

"No, it must have been earlier, much earlier. I can never remember dates, I constantly get them confused," Bonhoeffer stammers, this time, to his own horror, not needing to pretend: "But why earlier? And when?"

He thinks of a way out. "It was in the fall of 1940. Yes, the fall of 1940." When there was as yet no talk of any deportation of Jews.

"And just like that, all of a sudden, you know exactly when?"

"Yes, exactly when, Herr Prosecutor. Because in 1941 I was sick, in fact extremely sick. Pneumonia. In both lungs. . . ."

"Extremely unfortunate for you, Herr Bonhoeffer, but what, may I ask, does it have to do with the matter at hand?"

"My brother-in-law visited me at the time. And during his visit he told me . . . I remember exactly . . . he said . . ."

"What exactly?"

The hospital room. Early sunshine. Flowers and books on the bedside table, and a few pieces of fruit. Hans von Dohnanyi had entered the room, smiling. "Well, the thing with Fräulein Friedenthal is in order. We finally have the exit permit. It's taken an entire year." Indeed, "Now I remember quite precisely: 'one year' is what he said at the time, in the autumn of '41. . . ."

Bonhoeffer relates the incident as if it really had happened just that way.

"So, if I figure back, then the plan for Operation 7 was already in place in the autumn of 1940?"

Bonhoeffer nods, and feels infinitely relieved. *They have nothing, absolutely nothing concrete against us.* The triumphant thought from the early hours of his incarceration returns.

They would have no choice. They would have to release him as one accusation after the other collapsed. No more talk about his allegedly conspiratorial trips abroad, about trying to help others avoid military service, and no evidence regarding Operation 7, which was conducted quite legally.

I'll soon be free. Bonhoeffer was elated. No more cell, no bucket in the corner. No more snarling Knobloch. Just his parents, his siblings, his friends. And Maria. She above all.

The first thing I'll do is plan the wedding, Bonhoeffer thinks. And he can already see himself in a morning coat alongside Maria, she completely in white. Children scamper before them, strewing flowers. *How fiercely have I avoided precisely this vision,* he thinks, *or even feared it. And now there is nothing I am looking forward to more.*

Roeder has cleared his throat and put down the ruler. Bonhoeffer looks over at him, seemingly in expectation, and yet inwardly triumphal. *You, too, Herr Prosecutor, can no longer prevent it from happening.* The state's avenging angel now cuts a rather pitiful figure. Bonhoeffer almost feels sorry for him.

Roeder also feels sorry for himself.

A year earlier, with his conviction of the Red Orchestra group in the Ministry of Aviation, he had achieved his greatest success. And recognition. Even official decoration. Göring, who as head of the Air Force was considerably embarrassed, had taken the bull by the horns and ostentatiously honored Roeder, inviting him to his country estate north of Berlin, "Karin Hall." There Roeder had stood at the brightly blazing fireplace alongside Marshall Göring himself, Göring's wife, Emmy, on the other side. A kiss on the hand for the sublime lady. The Marshal had even toasted Roeder.

He wants all that again. But grander. With even more honors. And from the very top this time.

Perhaps the Berghof itself. The *Führer*'s country house on Obersalzberg. A blond lady, Eva Braun, about whom there was so much whispering. And Dr. Goebbels in the background, displaying his broadest grin for the cameras. And Roeder will relate how with the cunning and instinct of a hunting dog he had scuppered an even more dangerous ring of traitors, in the intelligence service itself. Indeed, a ring led by the unfathomable Admiral Canaris, the self-assertive Colonel Oster, and this slippery eel, the arrogant Hans von Dohnanyi.

At first Roeder did not have any proof. Then, however, certain irregularities in the foreign exchange accounting of the intelligence service had come to light. The "Cash Fund Deposit Affair," as it was called, had been initially investigated by the Gestapo, then, at Himmler's explicit directive, was transferred to the jurisdiction of the military courts. That is how Roeder had gotten involved. An ideal starting point for him.

So, the immediate arrest of Dohnanyi had been the first order of business, then of his wife shortly thereafter—whom in the meantime they had had to release. But her arrest had nonetheless been a sobering shock for the family, and in that sense certainly was useful enough. As was the arrest of Dohnanyi's brother-in-law Bonhoeffer.

Roeder does not really think Bonhoeffer is guilty. Bonhoeffer comes across as too simplistic and naive for that. But for precisely that reason, he may well divulge something—unwittingly—about his brother-in-law.

But this man of God is either too naive after all to know anything really useful—or he is much more sophisticated than Roeder had imagined. In any event, the interrogations of the past eight weeks have produced nothing of note. Essentially a washout. The photo opportunity before the Berghof fireplace recedes. Roeder sighs deeply.

"I will have to bring charges against you, Herr Pastor." For the first time since the arrest, Roeder uses the address "Herr Pastor" again with Bonhoeffer. "One thing that remains certain for me is that you avoided military service through pretext. You . . ."

"I did not . . ."

"That," Roeder looks up, appearing almost resigned, "is something the judges will decide at your trial."

"And when will that be?" Bonhoeffer almost leaps up at the question. *Surely soon!* he thinks. *Hopefully soon! A trial can only end in an acquittal, and then I am truly free. Once and for all.*

Roeder merely shrugs his shoulders and stands up. Bonhoeffer almost thinks Roeder is about to shake his hand and has already offered his own. But Roeder makes a vague gesture. "Take it easy, Herr Pastor! It doubtless won't be too long. And for today I have one more surprise."

Bonhoeffer withdraws his hand.

"A visitor for you."

"My parents?" It was exactly four weeks ago that his parents had been allowed to speak with him for the first time.

Roeder shakes his head, smiling, almost charmingly. "I really wanted to get to know your fiancée."

The door opens. Bonhoeffer turns around. Maria walks in.

The Church Must
Remain the Church!

1933

"Where Jew and German stand
under the word of God,
there is the church."
—"The Church before the Jewish Question," April 1933

PARLIAMENT IS BURNING!—ALREADY?

On January 27, 1933, at about 11 P.M., the news came over the radio that the Reich parliament building was in flames. In the Bonhoeffer house, where the family was sitting together downstairs, brother-in-law Rüdiger Schleicher smacked the table with the flat of his hand. "I told you so, right after he was named Reich chancellor. This Hitler, he's dead set on war."

"This is not war. What's happening is that the parliament building is burning; that's all," Karl Bonhoeffer had tried to calm him.

But his son-in-law would not be deterred. "That *is* like a war, an unmistakable challenge to begin striking out at every imaginable adversary, every imaginable opponent. I wouldn't be at all surprised if Hitler himself had not set fire to parliament."

That, however, really did seem a bit far-fetched to everyone.

At this very hour, Herr Hitler walked out of the still smoldering parliament building in a trench coat and a black slouch hat. He turned around once more, his blue eyes smoldering with the cold passion of pure, lustful delight.

He loved such scenes. Their glowing, fiery red drama reminded him of the finale in his favorite opera, the *Twilight of the Gods* by his revered Richard Wagner. And Goebbels, limping alongside Hitler through the smoldering, smoking corridors, had heard him whisper hoarsely, "What a gift from heaven!"

So, now he simply stood there, gazing transfixed at the gutted building from beneath the black brim of his hat, Wotan in a trenchcoat, drawing the ring of fire around his magnificent child Brünnhilde, and if he had had a sword, he doubtless would have rammed it into the ground as once did Germania's father of the gods and declared, "Whosoever fears the tip of my spear shall never pass through the fire!"

A car pulled up. An extremely slender, elegant gentleman in a tuxedo and bow tie got out. Franz von Papen, the vice chancellor.

Hitler turned to him, seized his hand as if unwilling ever to turn it loose again, and his voice became even coarser, even more guttural. "If it be the case—and I am utterly convinced of it, Herr Vice Chancellor—that this is the work of the *Communists*, then we must exterminate this rabble with an absolutely iron fist!" Papen maintained his perpetually smooth, straight smile. "Oh, yes, and I have heard to my considerable joy that neither the Gobelin tapestries nor the library were damaged."

"Not a bad idea," thought a reporter who had overheard the conversation, "not so stupid at all. Downplay the entire incident to the level of an insurance claim." Papen had already turned and hurried back to his waiting car. "I have to go make a report to Herr Reich President."

"Also not a bad idea," the reporter thought, jotting down notes. "Hitler is immediately reminded that there are other, higher authorities than he. Very clever."

It was, however, considerably more than merely an insurance claim, and that highest authority, the ancient Paul von Hindenburg, was only too willing to place himself at Hitler's service. That very night, he signed an emergency decree "for the protection of citizens and state" which, quite frankly, read as if it had been prepared long beforehand.

And the first "Have-you-heard-the-one-about" jokes were circulating. "'My *Führer*! Parliament is burning!' Hitler glances at his watch. 'What? Already?'"

But anyone telling a joke like this did so only in a whisper, and only after making sure no one uninvited was listening. Life in Germany had gotten dangerous.

Private letters and private phone conversations were a thing of the past. Anyone, anytime, anywhere could be arrested without cause, without official orders, and often enough such people simply disappeared, without a trace, in one of the quickly emerging "wild" concentration camps. During this first night alone, four thousand Communists were apprehended, including the one who had been caught inside the parliament building the night of the fire, a Dutchman who could hardly speak even broken German, Marinus van der Lubbe. He was found to be carrying a device for starting fires, albeit one that could hardly start a fire in a garden shed, much less a large building.

Nonetheless, van der Lubbe, who in his youth had been a member of a Communist organization, was viewed as the arsonist and ended up being the ideal excuse for the National Socialist regime to begin systematically persecuting and hunting down all its opponents, whether Communists or Social Democrats or simply critics, regardless of their stripe.

"Lubbe has performed such *eminent* service to the party that they will have to award him their Golden Party Emblem," Franz Hildebrandt, never at a loss for jokes, had remarked. Everyone except Karl Bonhoeffer laughed.

"Van der Lubbe has started a hunger strike, and I am scheduled to examine him and determine to what extent he is still of sound mind." Although Karl Bonhoeffer let out a heavy sigh reflecting the anticipated burden, one could nonetheless discern the modest pride he felt at being singled out for this honorific task. At the same time, however, his scientific curiosity had also genuinely been aroused. "Of course, having the opportunity to see this fellow up close is also not entirely uninteresting."

The poor fellow had squatted apathetically in his cell, staring dully ahead at nothing in particular, with a runny nose that he occasionally wiped with the back of his hand. Professor Bonhoeffer had sat down next to him, in an almost fatherly fashion, and had spoken to him, cautiously, gently.

Finally van der Lubbe had also begun to speak, falteringly, sometimes in German, sometimes in Dutch. One could hardly make out his words, and even then, those words didn't really make any sense. But he did genuinely seem to have been the arsonist, though his motives were not entirely clear.

Karl Bonhoeffer's colleague Jürg Zutt had been allowed to accompany him. "What's your assessment, Herr Professor?" he had asked.

"Not a malingerer. Doubtless a psychopath. And an aberrant idealist who was intent on accomplishing something great. Very easy to turn a fellow like that into one's tool." He had stopped in the corridor. "Give me a cigarette, Zutt. I can't stand this prison smell." Karl Bonhoeffer lit the cigarette and inhaled in hungry breaths.

"Are you saying, Herr Professor, that there are others behind him? But who? Really the Communists? Or the Nazis?"

Karl Bonhoeffer quickly rubbed the cigarette out with his foot. "No political speculation allowed, Herr Colleague. We're physicians, nothing more. We have nothing to do with politics."

But politics has plenty to do with us, with your scientific discipline as well as with my church, Dietrich Bonhoeffer thought later when his father made such statements. And soon he saw the swastika banners hanging over altars and heard not a few of his pastoral colleagues preaching that "the swastika is our hope!" Of all symbols, why did it have to be one dredged up from the primeval Aryan-Mongolian period?

"Who will you be voting for?" Dietrich asked Franz Hildebrandt on March 5, the day of parliamentary elections, the last halfway free and secret election for a long time. But no one suspected as much at the time.

Franz Hildebrandt took a leisurely sidestep and kicked a stone against the wall of the next building. "The Christian People's Service seems the most reasonable party to me."

"Most reasonable, perhaps, but also powerless." Bonhoeffer stared straight ahead. "I'll probably vote for the Center."

"The *Catholics*?" Hildebrandt was so surprised that his youthful grin vanished.

"The Center is backed by Rome and the pope—by a strong church. It hasn't splintered into silly factional struggles like ours. Ultimately it's the only group that might halfway be able to maneuver or direct Hitler in the future. And it's the only thing that genuinely has had an enduring existence for almost two thousand years now. It will also weather a thousand Hitler years." He envisioned the dome of Saint Peter's in Rome and recalled the words of one of the Benedictine monks in Barth's apartment in Bonn, who maintained that when the pope reads the final mass, judgment day will have come. The Protestants Barth and Bonhoeffer had offered no objection.

In the meantime, Hitler, winning just 47 percent of the votes, had not won a particularly impressive victory in the election. But with the 8 percent of the German Nationals, it was enough to remain in power, and on March 21 the official state ceremony did indeed take place in Potsdam.

For the occasion, Superintendent Otto Dibelius preached in the Nikolai Church there, admonishing those in power to return to their otherwise well-behaved, cordial demeanor after all the election battles. At the same time, Hitler and his minions conducted a quiet devotional service at the Graves of the Old Warriors. But then he and Hindenburg met at the gravesite of Frederick the Great for a copiously photographed handshake. All the church bells were rung, their pealing broadcast by radio into the farthest corners of Germany.

"Well, perhaps we really have gotten through the worst," Karl Bonhoeffer remarked in the house on Wangenheim Street, turning the radio off. His son Dietrich had his doubts.

He had in the meantime been permitted to deliver his talk in full, albeit not over the radio but at the College of Political Science. One of the teachers there, Theodor Heuss, who was also a member of parliament, had invited him. Moreover the manuscript itself had been published in one of the newspapers, the *Kreuz Zeitung*, to which his grandmother subscribed. She could not read her grandson's talk often enough.

"You said all this so wonderfully, and so accurately," she praised, "For what is a human being without leadership and guidance? And yet what is a leader who elevates himself like a god above other human beings? An idol." They were sitting together at tea again. She looked at Dietrich apologetically. "I'm so sorry I don't have any more ginger cookies. But I'll get some tomorrow at the Department Store of the West, which always has the best ones. I have to go into the city anyway."

The chauffeur drove the ninety-one-year-old into the city. Along the Kurfürstendamm Avenue, she leaned forward in horror. "What's all this supposed to mean? All those fellows in the brown shirts in front of the stores? And what's that they're shouting?" She rolled the window down. Now one could understand the voices. "*Germans, defend yourselves! Don't shop at Jewish stores!*" Julie Bonhoeffer sank back into her seat. "Have they gone crazy? Or is it some sort of joke, here on April 1?"

The car drove on.

"I don't believe it's meant as an April Fools' joke, ma'am," the chauffeur responded. "It said in the newspaper that today was to be a general boycott of Jewish stores." They drove on toward the Department Store of the West. There, too, a line of brown-shirted protestors carrying placards: "*Don't shop at Jewish stores!*" The chauffeur cleared his throat. "It's probably better if we just turn around, ma'am."

"We'll do nothing of the sort! *I* still decide where I go shopping." Julie Bonhoeffer did not wait for the chauffeur, as was usually the case, to open her door. With small but energetic steps, she made a beeline for the Brownshirts.

"Well, now, and where do we think we're going, little mama?"

The elderly woman assessed the rather ordinary face beneath the brown cap. "*We? Little mama?*" She smiled, and the man blushed. "I have no idea where *you* want to go, sir, and, frankly, I don't really care. And for the rest, young man, I'm afraid I cannot really recall ever having given *birth* to *you!*"

She entered the department store.

FORTUNATELY ONLY A PASTOR. AND A JEW.

"For heaven's sake, Klaus, why are you so restless? Why are you constantly listening at the door? Do you think the maid is eavesdropping on us?"

Paul Lehmann laughed and clasped his hands behind his head while Klaus Bonhoeffer, with an embarrassed shrug of his shoulders, returned to the table where his brother Dietrich was sitting with his New York friend and the latter's young wife, Marion. "Unfortunately, that's necessary in Germany these days. You'll find faithful servants like Minna von Barnhelm's Francisca only in plays by Lessing." They had been sitting together here in the house on Wangenheim Street and conjecturing how long Hitler would be able to hang on. Doubtless not very long.

Lehmann, who in 1933 was on a European trip with his wife, looked at the beautiful antique furniture and at the walls, which seemed virtually covered with paintings. He stirred his tea. "When you used to talked about Germany, Dietrich, I imagined it all just like here at your house. Peaceful, quiet. And all the people just like you: cultured, educated. But it seems there is another Germany as well."

"And other Germans, very different Germans." Bonhoeffer nodded.

There were indeed. And precisely these others were quite visible during these April days in 1933.

Bonhoeffer drove out to Sanssouci with his guests, visited all the museums, even accompanied them to the State Opera for a universally extolled performance of *Electra*. But none of Strauss's operatic sounds were as shrill or piercing as those coming from the First Reich Conference of the German Christians, who were demanding that one put a stop to impure blood in German pulpits and to Christian marriages between Aryans and non-Aryans.

But not all the speakers were merely populist loudmouths, nor did everything sound entirely unreasonable. Bonhoeffer himself agreed, for example, with the demand for a single Reich Church instead of the previous twenty-eight independent regional churches. "A rather imprudent demand on the part of the German Christians, wanting something like that," he remarked to Franz Hildebrandt, "since in a strong Reich Church they would soon enough be pushed into a sectarian corner." Hildebrandt was not so sure.

But the idea of a Reich Church with a Reich bishop at its head was now on the table. It generated interest elsewhere as well, and now three gentlemen set out, carrying with them an honorable commission from the German Evangelical Executive Committee to work out a constitution for this future church. Their destination was the Loccum Monastery, where one of the three, Hannover's regional bishop August Marahrens, was also the abbot and was always *delighted* to be photographed with his bishop's crosier and miter.

"It seems we are not the first to arrive," remarked Hermann Kapler, president of the Church Federation Council. Marahrens and the Elberfeld pastor Hermann Hesse also were a bit startled to see an imposing black car parked in front of the monastery. They were indeed not the first ones there.

The man who had arrived before them was a bit chubby, with pinkish skin and rather simple features, none of which suggested the presence of a particularly high intellect. He had surfaced on the periphery of the Reich conference, a military chaplain named Ludwig Müller from Königsberg who merrily entertained the others with the frequent reminder that he saw himself as a kind of old warrior who had early on sensed Hitler's divine calling, "earlier than any of you, gentlemen." But the merriment quickly vanished.

For behind this seemingly harmless and, frankly, somewhat ridiculous man there soon emerged—in a fashion that was anything but ridiculous—the shadow of Adolf Hitler, a shadow that also now cast itself over Loccum Monastery.

For his part—that much was obvious enough—Müller was comporting himself quite civilly. Although he did indeed speak quite often about the *Führer* principle, he never mentioned the "Aryan Clause" which had so horrified Bonhoeffer during early April.

He had been at the Dohnanyi's when his brother-in-law Hans, who was now working at the Berlin Supreme Court and would soon be working in the Reich Ministry of Justice, had taken him aside and said, "Tomorrow's the day."

"What day, Hans?"

"The Law for the Reconstitution of the Civil Service will be passed with an 'Aryan Clause' prohibiting all people of Jewish descent from being civil servants. I'm just hoping it won't be extended to the church as well." At the time, Bonhoeffer still thought that highly unlikely, since the church was, after all, not a state agency, nor were pastors civil servants.

Nonetheless, he sat down and wrote his essay "The Church and the Jewish Question" as a kind of clarification of the issue. Not the least of the issues for Bonhoeffer was that, because "the baptized Jew is a member of our church," the Jewish question was posed differently for the church than for the state.

In May his twin sister, Sabine, came for a visit from Göttingen. Dietrich was utterly taken aback by how radically his sister had changed, with dark circles under her eyes and deep wrinkles around her mouth. Her personality seemed to have lost every trace of its earlier cheerful optimism.

"What on earth is bothering you, Sabine?"

"You wouldn't believe what's happening at the university now. Gerhard is constantly being harassed, Brownshirts march up and down outside the lecture hall and try to prevent students from even entering because, after all, they couldn't *possibly* learn anything from a Jew. And in school the teacher is telling the other children not to wave their hands a certain way, since only *Jews* do that—Jews like that little Leibholz kid. We feel like lepers. . . ."

She sobbed. Her brother did not know what he should say. "But don't you have any friends?" he stammered.

"Well, we did. Until recently. Now they quickly cross over to the other side of the street when they see us coming."

"All of them?"

"No, not all of them. Walter Bauer, the theologian, recently paid us a really ostentatious, open visit, saying he was ashamed to be a German. And the elderly Ortmann, the professor of civil law. . . ."

A gentle smile crept over her face. "You have to realize, he's half deaf. And as soon as he sees Gerhard, he walks directly over to him trumpeting as loudly as he can about what he thinks of the Nazis, and half the city can hear him."

Her smile quickly disappeared again. "Gerhard is suffering unspeakably from all this. He recently remarked that he had been thinking about emigrating." *Yes*, Bonhoeffer thought, *the emigrations have started*. Anneliese Schnurmann, the patroness of the Youth Club, had been one of the first. And the Youth Club itself was also long a thing of the past. A gang of Brownshirt bullies had seen to that.

"Poor Gerhard," Sabine sighed, "and you, too, Dietrich—I hate to have to tell you—you, too, have made it very hard on him." Bonhoeffer knew only too well what his sister was referring to.

His brother-in-law's father had died in April, and Leibholz had asked him, as a pastor, to accompany the deceased on his final journey. "But your father was a Jew, Gerhard. He belonged to the Jewish congregation."

"Nominally. He just lacked the courage to take the final step. And he always thought so much of you, Dietrich. 'A pastor like him,' he always said," Leibholz had managed a weak smile, "'a pastor like him will manage to convert me once and for all.'"

Bonhoeffer had shrunk back almost in horror. Compliments always embarrassed him. He had told his brother-in-law he would speak with the superintendent. But the latter would hear nothing of a Christian burial for an unbaptized Jew. "In this day and age? My dear, dear friend, that would be nothing short of sheer provocation. Please, please, just forget it."

Bonhoeffer did not forget. Not then, not later. And no excuse helped in his own eyes. The others forgave him, yes, but he never forgave himself. For in this first, modest test, he had failed. Nothing could change that. And the memories of that failure pursued him, maliciously, painfully, all the way into his Tegel cell, all the way into the interrogation room with Roeder.

"Your sympathy with Jews doubtless comes from your brother-in-law and your best friend being Jews," Roeder had once barked at him. But that was only partly true. His shame with regard to this one, modest disgrace involving the funeral counted at least as much.

"That was stupid and cowardly of me. I myself can't even understand my timidity now," he told his sister. And he repeated what was to remain his view on the matter till the very end, namely, that "a church where Christians and Jews are not permitted equality before God's word is no longer a church."

The German Christians, with Ludwig Müller at their head, saw things quite differently indeed. Acceptance of the Aryan Clauses was part of their platform.

But the regional churches once more stayed a step ahead of them when in May they appointed Friedrich von Bodelschwingh, head of the Bethel Community, as the new Reich bishop—a bishop without a church, as it were, since no Reich Church really existed yet in any case. The German Christians raised a stink, and the struggle began, a struggle waged with every conceivable means. Bodelschwingh, who understood neither power nor tactics, quickly resigned and withdrew. But the struggle continued, now with increasing intensity and harshness. Finally, at Hindenburg's own behest, Hitler himself intervened.

Church elections were set for the summer of 1933. And Hitler himself, currently in Bayreuth paying homage once again to his idol Wagner, stepped up to the microphone as the supreme campaigner for the German Christians.

"Well, we certainly can't keep up with that." Franz Hildebrandt sighed, a wry grin on his face. He and Bonhoeffer had just listened to the speech on the radio. But Bonhoeffer stayed composed. "We didn't do so badly ourselves." He had penetrated all the way into the headquarters of the newly formed Gestapo when the German Christians had the opposition's flyers confiscated.

"No, not badly," Hildebrandt remarked, "but what can we accomplish against all the others?"

"A great deal, Franz. This wretched Aryan Clause alone makes the German Christians look ridiculous."

"I confess I can't really laugh about it, Dietrich. That clause will be accepted sooner than we think. Have you already forgotten what some of our own leaders, not just the German Christians, said after the Jewish boycott on April 1? Even though they agreed that some of the excesses were less than flattering, they could understand the Nazis, considering how the Jews had everywhere oppressed the poorer Germans, in the press, in art, probably also in the church."

He paused and tried to crack a smile. "Have I ever oppressed you?"

"Constantly, old adversary!"

But this attempt to flee into a bit of humor fell flat. His friend remained grim. "I can even understand our elder colleagues to a certain extent. The ties between 'throne and altar' for which they have longed for so many years seem to have been reestablished. Hitler pats them on the cheek and tells them how important the religious denominations are to him. And his Brownshirts are marching en masse to worship services. The churches have never been so full. . . ."

He looked over at the radio, where dance music had replaced Hitler's gurgling voice. He turned it off.

"But anti-Semitism is obligatory at the throne of this new emperor. And the church will be all too willing to pay this tribute."

"That would be the most egregious betrayal possible of all that is Christian!" Bonhoeffer had jumped up and was pacing back and forth in anger. "What's been the source of Christianity's strength for two thousand years? The fact that it has transcended all boundaries between nations and races with its charge that we 'go forth to all nations. . . .' And now, suddenly, none of that counts anymore? It's a betrayal of our faith," he repeated.

"Betrayal is cheap. The betrayal of Jesus cost only thirty silver pieces. Hitler will probably be more generous. And what are, say, thirty pastors of Jewish descent compared to eighteen thousand *Aryan* pastors? Everyone will say that it is for *their* sake that we have to expel those thirty, difficult as it may well be. I don't even know whether I myself would act any differently in their place." He looked pensively at his narrow, brownish hands. "But I'm not in a position of power. Fortunately. I am just a pastor. And a Jew."

Although these words genuinely troubled Bonhoeffer, he did not yet want to abandon his optimism, and certainly not his vision of a church that might be a home for everyone, a home based solely on God's word.

The following Sunday, his question from the pulpit of Trinity Church in Wedding was thus "Where is the church? Where do we find it?" He demanded, "Let us return to the Holy Scriptures, let us set out together in search of the church." And he recalled the words with which he and those like him had stepped up to oppose the German Christians, "The church must remain the church."

Now he varied his demand. "Not only must the church remain the church, but the church also must confess, confess, confess!"

Here, at the culmination of his sermon, Bonhoeffer gazed out at his congregation. Had these people understood what he was trying to say to them? Did *anyone* still understand what the church should be?

That was July 23, 1933. On this Sunday, the church elections were to take place.

"I'M NOT MADE FOR 'NO'"

Rays of sunlight flickered through the trees. The roof of the heavy Mercedes limousine had been pulled back. Bonhoeffer gazed blissfully—and a bit soporifically—at the golden autumn day. "Why can't we just drive somewhere and relax instead of attending this ridiculous synod?"

The green, softly rolling hills of the Thuringian landscape stretched out around them. The motor purred comfortably, with Bonhoeffer, Hildebrandt, and the somewhat older social pedagogue and Barth student Gertrud Staewen in the passenger seats, and the chauffeur at the wheel. Karl Bonhoeffer had generously put the limousine at their disposal for the excursion. Anyone who had seen them trundling along so comfortably through the countryside could easily have taken them for a merry group of young people out for a pleasure trip.

But their destination in this second half of September 1933 was Wittenberg, the city of Martin Luther and setting of the First German National Synod with Ludwig Müller as its newly elected Reich bishop.

"Of all people to have instead of Bodelschwingh!" Although Hildebrandt had merely shaken his head incredulously, Bonhoeffer was noticeably morose. "I don't know whether Bodelschwingh genuinely would have been the better Reich bishop in the long run. He's more one of our kind, yes, but still. . . ." Bonhoeffer's profound disappointment was obvious.

They had met the previous August in Bethel, where twenty-three years earlier Bodelschwingh's father had passed on to him leadership of the world-famous institutes founded the previous century.

On July 23 the German Christians had won 70 percent of the vote and with it a resounding victory in the church elections. Their opponents, the "Young Reformers," of whom Bonhoeffer was one, were resolute about countering this victory at the very least with an unambiguous "confession" that would articulate unequivocally what sort of institution the church should remain in the future.

"*You* are the one who must do that, Bonhoeffer"; that was the insistent urging of those with whom he had met and discussed the situation. Ultimately he had indeed set out with the others for Bethel, as it were under the patronage of the highly respected Friedrich von Bodelschwingh.

It was the first time Bonhoeffer had ever seen the grounds at Bethel, which was located near the town of Bielefeld. He was profoundly impressed, particularly by the worship service in which he participated shortly after arriving, crowded in among the institute's patients. The white caps of the deaconess attendants stood out among the crowd. He also saw completely healthy children from a nearby school as well as students from the university. Even a few vagrants had joined in. It made no difference here.

That *is the church*, he thought, recalling the warm feelings he had
had in the Harlem worship services. *Here people genuinely pray and
hope and believe rather than cogitate and speculate and try to maneuver
for more power.* The hymn that now commenced could just as easily
have been a spiritual. But it was the familiar "Take Thou Now My
Hand." Bonhoeffer, however, felt as if he were hearing it for the very
first time.

"Can you understand a bit better now why this place is more
important to me than the position of Reich bishop?" Bodelschwingh
had asked him after the worship service. He then tugged excitedly at
Bonhoeffer's arm, "Do you see the young lady over there in the polka-
dot dress? She's a sister of the famous Captain Canaris." He clearly
could not conceal his pride in having such an illustrious patient.

That alone put Bonhoeffer off somewhat. At the same time, he
wondered whether a man of such renown as Bodelschwingh really did
have the right to run away merely because of a few German Christian
loudmouths, and to withdraw into the secure world of Bethel instead
of putting his powerful reputation in the service of a cause that needed
him at least as urgently as did the patients here. And his uneasiness
increased when he and his colleagues set about drafting the planned
"Bethel Confession."

Bodelschwingh constantly meddled and intervened, toning things
down, smoothing things out, particularly with regard to the Jewish
question. At the same time in Berlin, the first Prussian Synod since
the church elections was convening. One of its resolutions resulted
in the acceptance of the Aryan Clause in Prussia, one more reason
Bonhoeffer thought it necessary to use the most unequivocal, explicit
wording in the confession they were composing here in Bethel. And
again, Bodelschwingh toned down the language.

"Pretty bad for our Jewish colleagues in Prussia. What are there,
eighteen of them now? Is that right?" That was all Bodelschwingh
could muster. "Of course, we will help them however we can. But
the fact that Jews will no longer be admitted to study theology, well,
that just seems to be the compromise we'll have to accept." Many in
the church were of the same opinion. Including Martin Niemöller, a

pastor in Dahlem and Bodelschwingh's assistant during the latter's brief time in office as Reich bishop.

Nonetheless, this same Niemöller ended up being one of the cofounders of the "Pastors' Emergency League," whose purpose was precisely to help protect these Jewish pastors. Its two thousand members were considerably more than anyone originally thought would join. Bonhoeffer, of course, was also a member. They had already presented a sharp protest against the Aryan Clause and demanded its rescission.

"What do you really think of Niemöller?" Hildebrandt now wanted to know during the ride to Wittenberg. Bonhoeffer had to think about it for a moment. Gertrud Staewen, sitting on the passenger's side in the front seat, quickly turned around and said, "A U-boat commander, still, just like in the war. He's just exchanged his command station for the pulpit. A German nationalist through and through. I don't trust him."

"A strange fellow, that much I'll grant. Nor do I find him particularly likable," Bonhoeffer concurred not without slight hesitation. "He doesn't deny having voted for the Nazis in March. And have you heard his most recent scheme? We pastors should all, as a block, join the party to show Hitler once and for all that we are opposed not to him, not to Adolf Hitler, but only to the German Christians."

Even the chauffeur was startled.

"But still," Bonhoeffer added reflectively, "at least he makes no secret of his views. Someone who says what he thinks, as opposed to the other sort." He again thought of Bodelschwingh, with his soft gaze that constantly avoided looking directly into the other person's eyes. "I certainly prefer someone who speaks his mind over the person who's constantly trying to harmonize everything, who has such oh-so-good intentions and yet usually only accomplishes quite the opposite." He thought of the Bethel Confession and sighed deeply.

"When will you be putting the finishing touches on the manuscript?" Hildebrandt asked. Bonhoeffer shrugged his shoulders and tried to look composed. "Bodelschwingh first had to submit the draft to various 'experts' for their opinion, and one of them," he laughed briefly and maliciously, "one of them seriously recommended that we not say anything against the German Christians, but instead against Karl Barth, who is the *real* enemy of the church. In October," he continued when the incredulous laughter of the two others had subsided, "it will probably be finished. But without me."

"You're that disappointed?"

Yes. He was that disappointed. Moreover he had the sad feeling that he had stood quite alone among his own colleagues. He together with Hildebrandt. But the latter slapped the package of flyers lying on the seat next to him. "These flyers will speak a clear enough language in Wittenberg. We'll nail one on every tree. Then everyone will know the real truth about the Aryan Clause." The resignation of recent weeks seemed to have dissipated in Hildebrandt. He was obviously once again ready for a fight. Bonhoeffer nodded and then looked out at the passing scenery.

A village on the side of the road, half-timbered houses, slate roofs, a small church. Bonhoeffer suddenly recalled his experience on the Tibidabo in Barcelona. *Ah, you seducer, if only you had offered me something like this, a modest pastorate out in the country or a nice professorship somewhere in Switzerland instead of "all the kingdoms of this world," then, I fear, you would've had an easy time of it with me.* Again he sighed.

"What's with you?"

"Oh, nothing, really. I was just thinking of London." He had just received an offer to take over two German congregations in London, at least for a time. His name had been suggested by Theodor Heckel, a consistory officer responsible for all the German churches abroad, a kind of "foreign minister" of German ecclesiastical policy who himself had that element of contented, smiling impenetrability one often associates with Renaissance cardinals in Rome. "I hope it comes through."

"Why shouldn't it come through? Heckel is infatuated with you."

"Let's wait and see what happens in Wittenberg."

Another village passed by. Then another church. Then the expansive view of a green valley with a soft bluish veil hovering over lush greenery. Bonhoeffer surrendered himself completely to the scenic beauty and then said suddenly, softly, "Franz, you wouldn't believe how all this here disgusts me. All these struggles and battles in Germany concerning things that, quite frankly, are utterly self-evident, all this constant, ceaseless 'no' to the nonsense of the others. . . ."

Hildebrandt looked at him questioningly. Bonhoeffer continued, but now even more animatedly. "I've always been a child of good fortune, I realize that. I've always—and with a good conscience and in all sincerity—always been able to say 'yes' to *everything*, to my parents, to my family, my school, my teachers—despite occasional criticism—indeed to my whole world: always, *always* this 'yes.' I almost think I was virtually *born* for this sort of 'yes.' But now . . . ."

The heavy automobile hummed along the country road. Inside the car, everyone had fallen silent. Gertrud Staewen had turned around again and looked curiously at Bonhoeffer, who was a bit embarrassed at her searching gaze. But he continued, not without a slight trace of defiance in his words. "I'm simply not made for 'no.' That's why I have to get out of this Germany."

"You have it good." Hildebrandt's laugh sounded slightly envious. "Everyone is after you. No one will have me. I already tried to find something in Holland. They didn't even answer."

"Then I'll just take you along with me to London." Bonhoeffer laughed. "I can make that happen, believe me."

"Is there anything you can't make happen, Dietrich?"

After finally reaching Wittenberg, they found the city hardly less decked out with banners and flags than was Nuremberg a short time earlier during the National Socialist Party rally. "The Victory of Faith" had been the motto there, and now the three in the Mercedes wondered out loud, "Well, then, let's see which faith will be victorious here in Wittenberg." They were prepared for the worst.

But everything turned out a bit different.

In the Castle Church, where Martin Luther was buried, Reich Bishop Müller stood in the pulpit and read—in a slightly stammering voice rather than a soaring one , as one might have expected—a kind of report, a "rendering of accounts" using expressions such as "populist community" and "Germanism reawakened," but nothing about any Aryan Clause. Bonhoeffer and Hildebrandt, listening from behind a pillar, were almost disappointed.

"When will he finally say what he really wants?" Hildebrandt whispered loudly at Bonhoeffer.

Müller finally mumbled something that sounded like "true to the species," and the two nudged each other. "Watch out! Here it comes!" But Müller had already moved on in his speech, and still nothing about Jews not being allowed to be pastors. "He just doesn't have the nerve."

They didn't know who the gaunt gentleman in the gray raincoat next to them was. They could not imagine that, as a matter of fact, the Foreign Ministry in Berlin had dispatched him to make sure the Reich bishop said *nothing* about the Aryan Clause. The instructions had come from the highest quarters: This topic was kindly to be excluded from the synod.

Why? Because the international reaction to the Berlin Synod had been an utter disaster. And the irate—and annoyed—Foreign Ministry was grimly determined to prevent *any* such recurrence now that the recent treaty with the Vatican had bestowed such a respectable patina on Hitler's Third Reich.

The friends walked out of the Castle Church. They wanted to send Müller a telegram insisting that he come out and say where he stood on the issue, and that afternoon they virtually papered the city with flyers just as planned. At the same time, however, they had a dull sense that they were merely shooting their energy out into empty space, and in front of the church Bonhoeffer lifted both arms toward the clear blue autumn sky. "*How* I wish I were already in London!" His concern that something could still derail those plans was not entirely unfounded.

"So, it seems you, too, signed this protest against the Aryan Clause. Is that right? And might one not also then assume that you will express your views on the subject abroad in a commensurate fashion?"

The Reich bishop had invited Bonhoeffer to an interview in Berlin and was now looking across the desk at Bonhoeffer with deep blue eyes set within a pinkish smooth face. His expression reflected less a sense of fanaticism than the quiet joy of having come so *splendidly* far in this world.

Bonhoeffer could not possibly take this man seriously.

He responded respectfully but firmly, "I am not a German Christian, nor will I ever be one. But that does not mean I would ever, in any place, express myself in a fashion that might cast aspersions on my fatherland. What's the line in the seventh chapter of the Augustana. . .?"

"Excuse me?"

"You're doubtless familiar with the *Confessio Augustana*?"

"Well, yes, of course. I mean, of course, yes." The Reich bishop stammered. "Of course I'm familiar with our revered church father Augustine."

"I fear," Bonhoeffer's tone of voice remained polite and deferential, "I fear the Augustana has little to do with that gentleman. It is the confession the Lutheran Church presented against Emperor Charles V in the year . . . mmm, let's see, when was it now?"

The bishop had no idea.

Now, too, Bonhoeffer exhibited amiable, smiling understanding toward the Reich bishop. "Well, you can chalk it up to my *own* weakness in such matters. But I am fairly certain it was in the year— just a moment—yes, in the year 1530." Bonhoeffer countenance took on a dreamy, almost beatific expression as he began to quote the Augsburg Confession, in Latin, of course. "Oh, you know, the part about the 'one holy church continuing forever,' *item docent, quod una sancta ecclesia perpetuo mansura sit. . . .*"

The words resonated in the room as Bonhoeffer recited them with affected emphasis and sweet, lilting emotion—he himself reveling all the while at the thought that the Reich bishop did not understand even a single syllable.

Müller finally waved Bonhoeffer off, his smooth, perpetual smile taking on a somewhat pained expression. "Yes, yes, very good, very good. There are no really serious arguments to be raised against your going to London." Clear beads of sweat glistened on his high, bald brow.

And Bonhoeffer was indeed looking forward to it all. To London. To his new work. To a life far removed from all these domestic

German church spats. "I would like to withdraw to the wilderness for a time," he had written Karl Barth. But London would be anything but a wilderness; that much he could see from his very first visit among his two future congregations. Moreover Hildebrandt would also be there.

Yes, he had indeed been able to make that happen. "We need to share the work, the apartment, and the salary. And if each of us takes only a single cube of sugar with his tea instead of two, if we can avoid constantly interrupting each other during the sermon—as difficult as that may well be for you, my good Franz—and if we do not both insist on sleeping against the wall, then it will all work out just fine." He had laughed.

The only thing that did pain Bonhoeffer a bit was having to leave his students behind. Otherwise, however, he was thoroughly enjoying the train ride taking him to the coast and to the ferry over to England. He thought about this utterly comical figure, the Reich bishop, and once again recalled his visit to the Tibidabo in Barcelona and the daydream promise that one day he himself might become bishop of all of Germany.

You hapless seducer, you, he now thought, *you really are out of luck with me. I much prefer a modest pastorate in London to being a Reich bishop like him!* And he stretched out with such a loud, self-satisfied sigh that his startled fellow passenger almost dropped his sandwich. Outside, whizzing by the compartment window, was a Germany that for Bonhoeffer would now recede to a more comfortable distance for a while.

A Germany in which, thanks to the "Enabling Act" of March 23, 1933, Hitler had acquired almost total power and authority, and where Reich President Hindenburg—the last check on that power—had become a mere shadow of his former self.

A Germany in which at the trial of the parliament arsonist Marinus van der Lubbe and his alleged conspirators the country had gotten an initial, disturbing look at how the regime would likely be dealing with its opponents from now on.

Germany in the autumn of 1933.

TEGEL, SUMMER 1943

A quiet day. No bellowing guards. No bootsteps echoing in the corridor. Bonhoeffer listens to the silence and lights a cigarette. Not the first today.

When he first got to prison, he had hardly missed smoking at all—much to his own amazement. But now, having access to tobacco once again, he has also returned to his old, familiar habit of chain smoking. Even a cigar now and then. He smokes whatever's there.

No, there is no lack of tobacco. Nor of pencils and nice, white paper. Those on the outside are permitted to send him books and soap and fresh underwear. Quite frankly, the cell has the potential of being made quite cozy.

No! Anything but that!

Do *anything* to avoid getting accustomed to all this here. *Anything* to avoid starting to regard it as normal. *Anything* to avoid losing sight of the fact that it *is* a dungeon and he a prisoner waiting for one thing and one thing only, namely, his trial. And with it, freedom.

But when, finally, will that trial actually begin?

He has in the meantime received a copy of the official indictment, essentially a repetition of Roeder's litany. Bonhoeffer is alleged to have avoided military service; to have told his draft board in the town of Schlawe that he had already been assigned to a military post; and to have tried to bring about the release of Licentiate Niesel through devious means. Same old song. And it's as if Bonhoeffer had never had a single conversation with Roeder and had never refuted each and every charge, point by point.

Well, fine. Then he will say exactly the same thing in court that he has said in the interrogations. Namely, that he had not sought to avoid military service but rather had been assigned to the intelligence service. Both Canaris and Oster would be willing to testify under oath that such was indeed the case. Although Oster had at first done an about face, initially—and surprisingly—

denying he had ever been involved in securing a military deferral for Bonhoeffer, he had in the meantime recanted that statement. That alone should secure Bonhoeffer's acquittal.

But when? When, finally, would things get that far along?

Bonhoeffer's stomach turns slightly at the thought, and everything is once again as unbearable as on that first day. The stinking pail in the cell corner, the horrible food. He who otherwise is such an enthusiastic diner, with such a cultivated palate. And now he feels slightly nauseous at every crumb he must force himself to swallow. The cigarette is the only thing that tastes the same as it did outside, in freedom.

But again—when, damn it all, *when* will the trial finally begin? And with it the end of all this sordid mess here?

He leans back, closes his eyes, hums a few bars of a melody, notices that it is "Solveig's Song" from Edvard Grieg's *Peer Gynt Suite*. He had recently heard it in the prison infirmary, where the guards sometimes allow him admittance, particularly the one guard, Sergeant Linke. Linke is well-disposed toward him— indeed, has almost become his friend.

There he was permitted to listen to the *Missa Solemnis* and excerpts from Hans Pfitzner's *Palestrina* and then the *Peer Gynt Suite* with "Solveig's Song," which, truth be told, he does not really like.

This aching, longing melody had always sounded somewhat pompous to him. Like a heavy, plush portiere opening with a rustling swoosh. Now however, here in this cell, the song touches him, and does so with utterly unexpected power.

Maria! His Solveig! Patiently waiting, as loyally, as faithfully as the Norwegian girl for her restless wanderer!

He sees her before his mind's eye, just as she had appeared several weeks ago in the military court, standing over in the door to the interrogation room. But different from the image he has conjured in the depths of his prison loneliness, in his cell. Not some meek Madonna. Instead her mouth firmly set with an element of defiance, and an element of unbridled rebellion in her countenance. *You, none of you, will be able to intimidate us.* At the same time, however, her eyes had flashed with fear. Fear for him.

He had wanted to go over to her, hold her in his arms, calm her. But something kept both of them riveted in one spot. No embrace. No kiss. Even though Roeder had tactfully turned toward the window. They had stood there stiffly, rigidly, and after what seemed an eternity had reached out and taken each other's hands, had begun to speak, hesitatingly, falteringly, utterly pedestrian things, banal things, really.

"You're doing well?"

"Yes, I am, quite well, thanks."

"Do you need anything?"

"No, no, not really."

Then toward the end—Roeder had once again turned toward them, clearing his throat and gesturing toward his watch— "What do you do in your cell all day?"

Exercise, he could have said. Knee bends. Sit-ups. To stay in shape. And a cold shower every day, naked, from head to toe. A necessity. Instead, however, he had simply said, "I write a little," punctuating his answer with an embarrassed laugh.

Yes, he writes. First it was supposed to be a play. Indeed, he has already populated it in his imagination with various characters. But then the memories come. Of grand evenings at the theater and grand performances of grand plays. Of Ibsen or Strindberg. But he cannot write as they did. So his play remains fragmentary.

So a novel. That would be more his speed. Perhaps a family novel set in an upper-middle-class milieu. Where he genuinely knows his way around. Surely he could write something like that. A story in which at the same time he returns to the world of Wangenheim Street and to Friedrichsbrunn. At this time of the year, in August, it must be beautiful there.

Bonhoeffer can almost sense the fragrance of pine trees and of fresh raspberries. He had always picked raspberries with

Sabine, and, ever the little gentleman, had always topped off her pail if it contained less than his own. That was his world, and whenever he thinks about it now he never sees it in the morning light or the midday sun, but always at dusk. A world bathed in evening twilight.

A farewell, Bonhoeffer thinks as his pencil scrapes against the paper. *This could be a farewell. From precisely this world, a world that—if ever I am able to return to it—will never again be as it was.*

He pauses. Hears steps outside in the corridor. *Please, not a guard. Not now. Or if it is a guard, then, please, not Knobloch, but rather Linke.* Linke has not only acted as a courier, passing messages back and forth between Bonhoeffer and his parents, Maria, and his friend Eberhard, he is also genuinely considerate of Bonhoeffer, always inserting the key in the cell door as gently as possible and knocking before actually opening the door itself. Only then does he enter, clearing his throat to alert Bonhoeffer, and then a "Pardon me. . . ."

The key rattles in the lock. The door opens. Someone clears his throat, says, "Pardon me." Bonhoeffer looks over to the door.

Knobloch is standing there.

Almost shyly, he says, "I hope I'm not disturbing you." Bonhoeffer can only shake his head in surprise. "It's just that I, well, had a question. . . ." Bonhoeffer nods encouragingly. "It don't really concern me, but I was just wondering. . . ."

Bonhoeffer nods again, curious now about Knobloch's visit. "The thing is," Knobloch searches for the right words, "you are, so to say, a . . ."

"I'm a what?"

"Well, you know, a fine . . . a fine . . ."

Bonhoeffer smiles. "A fine stuck-up prig." Knobloch is now horribly embarrassed. "Oh, no, no, not a stuck-up prig, no, I mean . . ." Suddenly the words just stream forth. "My comrades are always telling each other all sorts of things. Like that your mother comes from the nobility and that your father is a famous professor and your uncle is the Berlin city commandant. . . ."

Paul von Hase, yes. One of his mother's cousins.

"And now you, here, in this hole. How does someone stand it, someone like . . . you, good sir?"

Like "you," no need for "sir," Bonhoeffer is tempted to correct him, but suppresses the urge.

"Our sort, well, you know," Knobloch goes on, "I don't know nothin' else, just grew up like this, in the back alleys, with the garbage cans and everything. I get on with all this here just fine. But for you, good sir, it must be hell. . . ."

"Hell, yes, in a manner of speaking," Bonhoeffer answers, simultaneously thinking, *but hell—real hell—actually looks quite different from this.* Hell is where the trains go. The boxcars full of people wearing gold Stars of David on their chests, the *exact* destination remaining unknown, just like in Berlin in October 1941. He'll never forget those images.

"And you're not troubled or anything, sir, I mean, you don't look it at all. That's what makes me wonder and all, you see what I'm sayin'?" Knobloch has become quite animated now. "Whenever I see you come out of your cell, always so snazzy and clean and all, smiling like the sun is shining or something, I can't help thinking, just look at . . ."

"Just look at the fine stuck-up prig!" Bonhoeffer laughs heartily. But Knobloch vehemently shakes his head. "Oh, no, no; like, well, you look like a manor lord about to give orders yourself, but real friendly-like, without shouting, but everyone still does what you say. That's how you seem to me. And I'd just like to know how someone like that gets on here like you do."

"Perhaps," Bonhoeffer begins cautiously, very cautiously, trying to avoid anything that seems like condescension, "perhaps my parents are the reason, . . ."

"Yeah, upbringing," Knobloch nods, "It's there for most everything. That's also the way we Social Democrats have always seen it."

A Social Democrat. Now I see, Bonhoeffer thinks to himself, and then goes on, more quickly than before, and a bit more sure of himself. "They taught me a thing or two that has helped me here. About always watching yourself, about never just letting yourself go, about keeping your composure even when everything around you is pretty lousy. . . ."

"So you know where you come from. You know what you are," Knobloch remarks.

Bonhoeffer nods. "Perhaps you're right, yes. We have something like a foundation, we have ground under our feet, we have our place in the world." Almost word for word as in his play. Perhaps it's not such a bad piece after all.

"And culture," Knobloch now says. "They also gave you that."

He's now standing with his back to Bonhoeffer, reverently examining the books on the narrow shelf. Bonhoeffer shrugs somewhat helplessly. "Books are best friends. And whoever reads, is never alone." This platitude even annoys him. But Knobloch merely nods and runs his fingertips across the leather bindings. "You got some nice books here. Probably really old, aren't they?"

Adalbert Stifter. Jeremias Gotthelf. Theodor Fontane. Gottfried Keller. Also Wilhelm Raabe. Jean Paul. The epic writers of nineteenth-century German literature. It is this world that Bonhoeffer has discovered over the past few months. This world has taken him in, given him a home. *Indian Summer, The Hunger Pastor, Green Heinrich.* And, of course, Goethe with his novel *Wilhelm Meister.*

"Do you like Rudolf Binding, Herr Bonhoeffer?"

Maria's voice. Back during one of their earliest meetings. He had started stammering. He had once read Binding's novella *Offertory Procession* and had found the whole thing insufferably mushy and bombastic. But he had not told Maria that, and she had continued speaking. "I like him. And Ernst Wiechert, too. And the Balt, Werner Bergengruen. Are you familiar with *The Grand Tyrant and the Court*?"

He was indeed familiar with it, and found it quite dreadful, an overbearing, only seemingly critical transfiguration of the *Führer* cult in a historically transparent disguise. He had told Maria so, and she in her own turn had vehemently contradicted him. He was astonished, a girl who contradicts. Moreover a girl who likes Wiechert and Rudolf Binding.

Next thing you know, he had thought, *she'll be saying that Rilke is her favorite poet.*

"My favorite poet is Rilke, you know," she had said at precisely that moment, and Bonhoeffer had shivered at the thought of so much *feeling*. Maria had only smiled. "What do you have against feelings, Herr Bonhoeffer?"

That remark had gotten to him. He often reflected on this later as well, including amid the silence of his Tegel cell. His immediate response now is, "No, I have absolutely nothing against feelings. . . ."—but he now casts a horrified look over at Knobloch to see whether he has heard Bonhoeffer muttering to himself. But Knobloch has already left.

The next day he is back again, this time carrying a worn, slightly greasy book. "Brought you something, since you like to read so much, like you said, and then you're not so alone. Got it from the library around the corner from us. The lady there said it was something for readers with fine taste, and the lady poet is supposed to be from the nobility as well. . . ."

Nathalie von Eschstruth. *The Day of Saint John the Baptist.* An ornate art-nouveau illustration on the cover depicts a naked couple entwined in each other's arms. *Sabine*, Bonhoeffer thinks. She once read something by Eschstruth, secretly. But Susanne—impudent Susanne—had gotten wind of it and had tormented Sabine with insufferable giggling. "Oh, Sister, you're reading this kitsch?"

Bonhoeffer tries to project an appearance of gratitude.

Knobloch certainly has good intentions, better, in fact, than many people with college and doctoral degrees. He could easily be Bonhoeffer's Teddy, his confirmation pupil from Prenzlauer

Berg in Berlin, albeit not quite so impertinent. Teddy, with whom he had sung, "Brethren! To the sun! To freedom!" explaining to him then that the "sun" does not necessarily refer to socialism and that freedom is possible only in Christ.

Teddy had grinned mischievously at this, and Bonhoeffer had wanted to belt him one. But Bonhoeffer liked him nonetheless, and later often thought about him. And suddenly he feels a strong, warm feeling of sympathy for this man here, this Knobloch, this older Teddy.

Knobloch has walked over to the door and then turned around once more. "Be sure to pray real good, Herr Pastor, pray that the Brits don't get any dumb ideas."

Bonhoeffer doesn't understand.

"You know, the Borsig factory is next door here, the cannon factory. And if they start droppin' bombs on it and they don't aim so good, we're gonna get hit as well."

Christian— or National Socialist

1933/1934

"Hitler has shown himself quite plainly for what he is, and the church ought to know with whom it has to reckon."
—Bonhoeffer to Erwin Sutz, September 11, 1934

I Have My Church Again

The spectator seats were overflowing, as if the grand magician of the stage himself, Max Reinhardt, had issued a personal invitation to a grand premiere. But this was no theater production. And what was on display here was no play.

The trial of the presumed parliament arsonist, Marinus van der Lubbe, and of the four alleged instigators of that crime began here in the Leipzig Supreme Court on September 21, 1933. The courtroom was filled with diplomats, the international press, and prominent party members who had traveled here specifically for the trial. This throng included two other gentlemen as well, one older, one younger.

"Have a look, the new guiding lights of our nation!" whispered Hans von Dohnanyi to his father-in-law, Karl Bonhoeffer, simultaneously nodding toward the National Socialist luminaries in attendance in their brown shirts. Karl Bonhoeffer cast a depressed glance over at them. "Thugs," he snarled briefly. Then he looked over at van der

Lubbe squatting apathetically on the other side of the room. "You poor dog," he muttered.

He had turned in his official physician's opinion on van der Lubbe, a strictly scientific report avoiding anything even remotely akin to a "political" statement. Then, over the next three months, he had increasingly come to doubt the appropriateness of this entire spectacle here.

The trial ran its course. The self-confessed van der Lubbe, however, increasingly receded into the background. In his stead, another defendant, the Bulgarian Georgi Dimitrov, came forward, acting as his own lawyer. Bringing to bear a considerable palate of practiced dialectical skills, he mercilessly put the screws to Hermann Göring, who in insufferable, pompous self-importance had pushed his way to the forefront of the trial as a witness. So mercilessly, in fact, that finally Prussia's corpulent prime minister—only one of a half-dozen titles and offices he had accumulated during this period—stormed out of the courtroom with an enraged cry for vengeance.

Then, in December, the verdict finally came in. Death by guillotine for van der Lubbe, who was executed the following month. Acquittal for the others. But the insinuation of a "grand Communist conspiracy" had collapsed like a house of cards.

"Can one call that an orderly trial?" asked Karl Bonhoeffer, stepping out into the falling snow with his son-in-law. Hans von Dohnanyi quickly lit a cigarette, which he had had to do without inside the courtroom. "Formally, yes, even though the presiding judge certainly should have put the witness Göring in his place. But, yes, the trial itself was essentially in order. Let us hope that trials will remain thus. . . ."

His father-in-law looked up at him in astonishment. Dohnanyi tried to manage a laugh. "You should sit in on some of the meetings the Commission on Constitutional Law has been holding in the Ministry of Justice. They've been discussing the 'new' legal thinking, the new laws in the National Socialist state. You should see how this vulture Roland Freisler, Hitler's crown prince of judges, prances and plays himself up. The *things* he's trying to push through! The party *alone* would determine what's right and wrong. Of course, I'm trying my best to prevent the very worst from happening, but . . ."

He broke off in mid-sentence, as if he himself did not know exactly how one genuinely could prevent the very worst from happening. The two men walked on in silence.

"Dietrich was right," Karl Bonhoeffer finally said. "Nowadays, nothing is apolitical, not the church, not law, not science/ . . ."

Dohnanyi cast a curious, questioning glance at him. "You would assess van der Lubbe differently today?"

Karl Bonhoeffer merely shrugged and then said after a lengthy pause, "Well, at the very least the political consequences would have to be weighed differently. And in the final analysis," the next words seemed difficult for him to get out, "in the final analysis even science will end up having to bow to political expediency." He took a deep breath. "How I envy Dietrich. He doesn't have to concern himself with such things for now. Sitting pretty over there, far away in London. . . ."

But there too, even in faraway London, where on October 17 Dietrich Bonhoeffer had embarked on his first independent pastoral service in the two German congregations of Sydenham and Saint Paul's, he followed the trial. Admittedly, other things had occupied him more at the time, and he was just sitting down at the breakfast table when he was startled by Franz Hildebrandt, who pushed the morning edition of the *Times* over to him. "Read what it says there today!"

Hildebrandt had followed him to London at the beginning of November just as planned. He and Bonhoeffer had managed to set up house in a halfway acceptable and comfortable fashion in two rooms in the old parsonage. A magnificent building with a view of half of London, magnificent rooms. Hildebrandt was amazed. But Bonhoeffer quickly warned him, "Yes, but wait till the mice scurry across your feet. And take note, the icy gust that passes across your face when you're sleeping is *not* the resident ghost but a draft from the leaky windows. Not a single window here will close properly, nor a single door."

Mice and leaky windows notwithstanding, however, the two friends thoroughly enjoyed their shared bachelorhood, and the high point of each day was the breakfast they invariably managed to stretch out into late mid-morning, a period whose own highlight was then the relaxed time spent reading the *Times*.

Today, on November 15, Hildebrandt leaned over the newspaper and read: "Berlin Plenary Assembly of the German Christians in the Sports Palace. . . ."

"What else? Read on. Especially the speech delivered by that legal shyster Krause, the head of the German Christians in Berlin. What he says is absolutely an abomination, it's . . ."

And indeed, it was. Nor was it simply that Krause was demanding the full implementation of the Aryan Clause and that all high church offices be filled by loyal party members. He was also reviling the Old Testament as a mere collection of stories about Jewish cattle dealers and pimps and was demanding the liberation of the Christian faith from *all* such Jewish ballast.

Amen! Bonhoeffer slapped his hands down on both knees out of sheer enthusiasm. "Now, finally, he has shown his true colors and those of his entire organization. Not even the most German of German Christians will put up with the Holy Scriptures being reviled that way, and such nonsense will simply turn every other person's stomach," he announced, rubbing his hands together gleefully. "I bet this will cause a storm that will sweep our revered Herr Reich Bishop from his seat before he has even managed to sit down on it." The Reich bishop's official installation had not yet taken place.

But Bonhoeffer's prediction only half came true. Müller remained the designated Reich bishop even though he had to withdraw his patronage from the German Christians, and they in turn were thus no longer the key movers in the church. Similarly, at least for the time being there was no more talk of any implementation of the Aryan Clause in the church. Many people, however, were still demanding Müller's resignation. "He won't even make it to the end of the year," Bonhoeffer gleefully declared in London, but then added a note of personal yearning, "Ah, if only I could be there now for it all. . . ."

"Are you homesick, Dietrich?"

Bonhoeffer poked around listlessly in his gray porridge, fishing for the glob of marmalade in the middle of the bowl. "Well, it's just that here one is still too close to avoid taking an interest in everything but too far to take an active part oneself. . . ." He shoveled a spoonful of the insipid porridge into his mouth and said, "Not only that, but it would be nice—you know, instead of porridge and roast lamb in mint sauce—to have a proper pork knuckle or Berlin-style liver with apple rings, lots of onions, and a huge mound of mashed potatoes. . . ."

Müller remained in office. And January 25, 1934, came, the day on which a grand discussion between Hitler and all the leaders of the church was scheduled. The general consensus was that the Reich bishop would not survive the day. Martin Niemöller, spokesperson for the Pastors' Emergency League, was especially counting on that being the case, and even as all the attendees were gathering, knowing looks were already being exchanged, remarks whispered, and jokes about the bishop circulating.

Hitler entered, and many in the room who had never seen him up close were astonished that *this* man, a man who seemed more awkward than imposing, really could be the show-off who so pompously delivered all those speeches and decrees they had heard. Here he seemed almost shy, and when he shook each attendee's hand in turn, his handshake seemed peculiarly feeble and without character, as if he were fearful of being touched by others.

The door opened once more, and Göring entered, a red portfolio under his arm. He brandished it affectedly before Hitler, his feet spread wide apart as if already posing for his own monument. "I have something to read aloud that will be of interest to you and to everyone here, my *Führer*." Hitler nodded.

Göring turned to the others. "Pastor Niemöller has apparently made a very strange telephone call. . . . He's here, I believe, is he not?"

Niemöller involuntarily took a step forward.

"Yes, well, it seems you made the following statements. . . ." And Göring read with his rich, bright voice how everything had allegedly been perfectly engineered, the *Führer* conned by Herr Reich President

Hindenburg to the best of his ability, and the Reich bishop now made ready for the last rites. Niemöller's *exact* words from a conversation with a like-minded university lecturer, Walter Künneth. Insolent. Arrogant. Rude. *Word for word.*

The weight on Niemöller's chest was so heavy he could scarcely breathe. Yes, he had said all those things. But never dreamed that telephones could be tapped. Now, however, Hitler himself had begun to speak, but not at all excitedly, more with astonishment. How this was all doubtless a conspiracy against Müller and how he, Hitler himself, was apparently to become its tool. But, "*You* elected your Reich bishop, not I. If *you* want to get rid of him, then *you* need to do it."

Then an exchange of conciliatory pleasantries ending in Hitler's ringing resolution, "*I*, in any case, will do *nothing* to that end." He then added, "Taking care of the German people is quite task enough; you can feel free to leave that to me. And I in my own turn feel free to leave the care of your own church to you."

Those were his final words. Once more he shook everyone's hand, and this time his handshake was as firm and hard and tight as a vice, and his gaze so cold that a gust of icy breath seemed to pass across everyone's face.

Niemöller, of course, was the target of countless sidelong looks, some sympathetic, some accusatory, and the empty space around him in the room expanded until finally a colleague took him by the arm and walked outside with him. "Well, we'll just have to appeal to a *higher* authority, it seems. . . . ," leaving in abeyance whether he was referring to the aged Hindenburg or to a different, considerably higher, and considerably older authority.

Alas, neither the one nor the other seemed to have any objections to this Herr Müller as Reich bishop.

As it was, Müller obviously now felt in a strong position, and Bonhoeffer, in London and furious at these developments, followed as this man customized "his" Reich Church. One strapping Nazi became his "chief of staff," another his "safeguard of the law," while the shimmering personality of Heckel now advanced to the position of "bishop of foreign affairs" and was soon sitting directly across from his one-time favorite Bonhoeffer at a table in London.

Bonhoeffer—Heckel angrily pursed his lips before continuing—would forthwith kindly refrain from *any* criticism of the church government in Berlin, his connections with the ecumenical movement bordered on high treason, and he himself was but a hair's breadth removed from the "Prague émigrés"—the customary derogatory National Socialist designation for leftist intellectuals who had fled to Prague.

Bonhoeffer had left the room speechless with rage.

That is not *my church*, he thought, *but, then—where is it?* He thought of the paper that the leaders of the Protestant church had composed two days after the ill-starred meeting with Hitler. Theodor Heckel had pushed it across the table to him in scornful triumph. "The attendant church leaders have adopted a unanimous position in support of the Reich bishop. . . ."

Later on Bonhoeffer's mood finally brightened a bit. He read half out loud what the *Times*, always a dependably well-informed newspaper, had reported at the beginning of June 1934.

Namely, that during the final days of May, in the town of Barmen, the church opposition had finally come together as a "Confessing Church"—the expression had already been circulating for some time—and had issued a "theological declaration" that among other things asserted that "the Christian Church is the community of brethren in which, in Word and Sacrament, through the Holy Spirit, Jesus Christ acts in the present as Lord."

No other Lord but Christ. No other truth but the Bible. "Why, that's Barth! I recognize my Karl Barth there!" Bonhoeffer had hardly even arrived in London before Barth had sent him a long letter insisting that Bonhoeffer's place was now in Berlin, not England, and that he should take the next—at latest the second—ship back. "Back to the machine gun, Bonhoeffer!"

Where, however, could such a machine gun be positioned? In front of the desks of the bishops who were fearfully, timidly ducking away from making even the most harmless decisions?

Now, however, there was again a place for it. Now Bonhoeffer could shout for joy. "I have my church again!" And though he would have been pleased to shove the newspaper over to Franz Hildebrandt at the breakfast table, Franz's seat there was now empty. At Niemöller's urging, he had returned to Germany at the end of January to work with the Pastors' Emergency League.

No one was there with whom Bonhoeffer might share his joy. Too bad! All the more was he then looking forward to next weekend, when he would be the guest of Bishop George Bell in Chichester.

Learning from Gandhi

"Did you sleep well, my friend?"

George Bell, pink and fresh as the new day itself, looked up as Bonhoeffer walked into the room. Bonhoeffer stood, astonished, in front of the breakfast buffet in the bishop's palace.

Shimmering silver, glittering crystal. Ham and eggs on stainless-steel warming plates, radiant red strawberries arranged in small pyramids. The fragrance of braised mushrooms and fried breakfast sausages—the latter smaller than any sausages Bonhoeffer was used to seeing in Germany. An "English breakfast" in all its magnificence. But not a trace of porridge.

Nor, frankly, did Bonhoeffer particularly miss the porridge. Instead he took healthy servings of the rest of the offerings.

"Feel free to take your time eating, dear friend! If we then have some extra time before you have to return to London, I'd like to take a little walk with you." The bishop stood at the window and peered out. "The weather seems to be nice enough today. But how long will it remain so?"

Although he and Bonhoeffer had already met in 1932 at an ecumenical conference in Geneva, it was only in England that they had become something resembling friends. The tone between them was one of well-tempered cordiality and considerable mutual respect.

Bell was occasionally amused by Bonhoeffer's impetuosity and by his German—and youthful—inclination for thoroughness. In his own turn, Bonhoeffer was put off a bit by the slightly condescending paternalism with which Bell was wont to refer to Hildebrandt and him as "my two boys." At the same time, however, he sensed Bell's genuine warm-heartedness behind the occasionally snobby facade. Bonhoeffer admired the comprehensive education and literary skills of this former Oxford professor and similarly had high regard for Bell's influence in ecumenical circles as well as for his strict rejection of all "official" German ecclesiastical politics.

"Did I understand you correctly yesterday at dinner? You would like go to India for a while?" Bell asked now that they had entered the park with its undulating waves of colorful rhododendrons. The gravel path crunched underfoot.

"Yes, to India. That's always been my dream. And yesterday my grandmother wrote and told me she would not only finance the trip but would also very much like to accompany me there herself. And at ninety-two years old. . . ."

They both laughed.

"And what, good friend, if I may ask, are you hoping to gain from such a journey?"

"I can't exactly say myself." Bonhoeffer hesitated. "Earlier it was more just a childhood fantasy. I had seen this film, *The Indian Tomb: The Mission of the Yogi*; perhaps you're familiar with it yourself, the one with Conrad Veidt. . . ."

"He emigrated, didn't he? Lives in London now. Is apparently making a film here, *The Wandering Jew*. I think I read that somewhere."

"At the time he played the part of the maharajah of Bengal. And as a boy," Bonhoeffer laughed, "I absolutely wanted to get to know a maharajah like that *personally*. Today, on the other hand . . ."

He paused, unsure whether Bell would be put off. But then he decided to be honest. "I would absolutely love to make the acquaintance of Mahatma Gandhi. I know he is not very popular in this country. . . ."

"But a great man nonetheless. No one can deny that, not even we British, not even if his nonviolent resistance ends up costing us the most beautiful pearl in the royal crown." Bell smiled, having noticed

Bonhoeffer's slight embarrassment. "But what makes you so curious about him? His life of poverty? His political position?"

The hushed tranquility of the British idyllic country spread out around them as they walked along. It was as if the houses here were still being illuminated by gaslights, as if the horse and buggy were still the standard mode of transportation, and even more than in New York Bonhoeffer felt himself to be in a completely different world, a world from which his Germany had disappeared, dropped from sight, somewhere beyond the sea.

He reflected a moment on Bell's question and then said softly, "Perhaps one can learn from someone like him. How to use nonviolent resistance. . . ."

The two friends were silent for a moment. The only sound was the crunching gravel beneath their feet. Then Bell slowly remarked, "I assume you're thinking about possible resistance against Herr Hitler. . . ."

Bonhoeffer did not answer. Both of them knew well enough what the reference was.

"And you're confident," Bell continued his query, "that the German people want that sort of resistance?"

He stopped on the path and looked out over the gently rolling sea of white rhododendron blossoms. "More than a year ago—you may remember, I was in Berlin—I got a firsthand look at the enthusiasm of the German people. I even understood that enthusiasm. Finally a ray of light, a ray of hope after all the misery of the economic crisis. . . ."

He became more animated. "You will find sympathy for Herr Hitler even here in England, and not just among our own fascists. The Tories are happy indeed to see this 'bulwark against Bolshevism,' which Germany seems destined to become right in the heart of Europe. And many others . . ."

They passed by the small chapel immediately next to the palace. Bell briefly rattled the locked door. "We British are a relatively fair people, and Germany—we realize this even if we do not say it out loud—was not treated fairly by its enemies after the war, what with the Treaty of Versailles and all the other, utterly superfluous humiliations.

Not a few people here are still suffering from a bad conscience in that regard, and some doubtless are thinking, 'Well, it serves us right that the Germans now have their Herr Hitler.'" He suddenly stopped. "Does the name Winston Churchill mean anything to you?"

"The Lord of the Admiralty in the Great War?"

"Yes, that and more. He allegedly recently said that he hopes his fellow Englishmen will have a man like Hitler around should they ever get into a situation similar to that of the Germans before 1933."

"Martin Niemöller could also have said that." Bonhoeffer laughed. "Last fall he expressly congratulated Hitler on the German withdrawal from the League of Nations. And I can never quite shake the suspicion that he and his kind view themselves as the real, that is, the *better* Nazis, and view it as Hitler's bad luck that he has not recognized that yet."

Bell could not repress a smile. "And you yourself doubtless do *not* consider yourself such?"

"Hardly. Even though . . ."

"Even though what?"

Bonhoeffer hesitated, then said, "Sometimes when I see the enthusiasm of the others, even that of some of my own colleagues, I almost wish I were one of them and had their enthusiasm. As it is, however, I'm . . . well, . . ."

"You're Dietrich Bonhoeffer." Bell had again become quite serious.

"And who is Bonhoeffer?"

Bonhoeffer posed this question so abruptly and loudly that Bell could only look at him in astonishment. Bonhoeffer continued in the same passionate tone, "Sometimes I think I'm nothing but a congenital malcontent, a party-pooper, a perpetual know-it-all because I don't share everyone else's glee at this Germany and its *Führer*. That's why I'm so alone. I don't deserve any better."

"My dear friend. . . ." Bell wanted to soothe him, but Bonhoeffer had already begun speaking again. "I envy Franz Hildebrandt. He's permitted to be against Hitler because Hitler is against the Jews. But I, a German like millions of others . . ." He broke off with a small gesture of helplessness.

"And in the face of all these things," Bell asked, "you want to run away, all the way to India?"

"That's not the only reason. Even more, I believe it's only from the East, from pagans, that *true* Christianity can emerge, just as Christ himself came from the East."

They walked back to the ivy-covered palace, whose unshakable, solid gray stones had something comforting, consoling about them. "Nothing is eternal, only us," these walls seemed to be saying, walls that had indeed remained the same for centuries and centuries. Bell looked up at the sky. "The weather really does seem to want to stay just this beautiful. Perhaps even for the entire summer."

Once they were back inside, Bell raised the subject of India again. "Go ahead and visit Dr. Gandhi, my good friend! He is without a doubt one of the few truly great men of our century. But if you are hoping he can teach you how to deal with—how to oppose—a man like Herr Hitler, well . . ."

He smiled and looked over at Bonhoeffer, his blue eyes expressing equal portions of slight mockery and gentle sadness. "Gandhi has been successful because we British tend to be ashamed of using violence or force. Yes, we do use it, but we always feel uncomfortable doing so. Herr Hitler, on the other hand . . ."

His voice had gotten very soft, almost a whisper. "He is not uncomfortable with anything, believe me. Reverting to violence does not shame him in the slightest. Against his enemies as well as against his friends."

Back to the Machine Gun!

The weather did indeed stay beautiful and clear for the entire summer, both in England and over on the Continent. Toward the end of June it had already become so hot that people were flocking to the seaside and to the lakes. So also in Munich, where a whole troop in brown shirts set out for Tegernsee, a lake in upper Bavaria.

But these men were not just in a vacation mood. They swore and complained about how the party and the *Führer* had sold their souls to the bourgeoisie since coming to power in 1933, and about how Hitler had in fact come to power quite differently than these men had originally imagined. To wit, Hitler had given far too much consideration to his conservative backers. One of the men in the group at Tegernsee shouted, "What do you mean, 'the revolution is over'? It's just beginning, now, with us Brownshirts." The others nodded and grumbled their approval.

"Take it easy, men." Their group leader intervened, an exceptionally ugly man whose nose had been half torn away from his rough, large-pored face. "We're here in Bad Wiessee to rest up, to have a vacation. So off with those hot clothes, and get your asses into the water!"

The men tore off their shirts and trousers and plunged into the cold water, laughing, howling, naked. Some remained that way even after climbing back on shore. Their captain, Ernst Röhm, grinned with satisfaction.

Evening came. Someone started playing records. Tangos. Slow. The men danced together, tightly embracing. Bottles of beer and red wine made the rounds. Only gradually did things become quiet again in the Hotel Hanselhorst.

Röhm's men, most of them in pairs, withdrew to the sleeping chambers on the second floor to sleep off their intoxication. Night enveloped the hotel, then the first signs of dawn. One of the men woke up, stumbled half-asleep to the balcony, leaned over the railing, and vomited out into the darkness. Then he listened to the quietness below.

An indistinct noise seemed to be approaching. Droning, growling. Threatening. A column of cars from Munich was approaching. But who would drive out from Munich to Tegernsee at this hour? The young man on the balcony, now fully awake, listened even more intently.

The noise was now quite near. Pale searchlight beams flickered through the predawn darkness. The young man suddenly realized the danger. He wanted to cry out, wake the others, warn them. But he just stood there, speechless, transfixed. The first shots and volleys began chattering through the darkness.

That was early in the morning on June 30, 1934.

Over the course of this and the following days, a startled Germany learned that at the very last moment its Reich chancellor had rescued it from an enormous threat and had once again just barely managed to thwart a conspiracy of truly gigantic proportions. The most egregious conspirators had been shot on the spot, beginning with Röhm. Nor should anyone feel sorry for these fellows, all of whom were treasonous, corrupt homosexual drunkards.

The nation meekly nodded its approval and did not really linger over the question of whether really *all* the victims of this "Night of the Long Knives," as it came to be called, were homosexual conspirators. For example, General Schleicher and his wife, or Dr. Klausner from the group Catholic Action, or a music critic by the name of Schmidt—even the owner of the Munich tavern "The Bratwurst Bell" was among them.

Instead, the bells tolled, and on the following Sunday all the nation's pastors—whether from the "Confessing Church" or those in step with the party—thanked the good Lord for having sent them Herr Hitler to rescue them from this pernicious threat. Their congregations looked up at them with credulous faces, and very few indeed dared to whisper that this alleged "rescue" was anything other than a cleansing of Hitler's most resolute opponents. By getting rid of Röhm and certainly others as well, the *Führer* was merely getting rid of a few rivals. No more, but also no less.

Bonhoeffer, too, spoke from the pulpit on this July 8.

But he did not offer thanks to the good Lord. Instead, he chose a text from the Gospel of Luke in which Jesus alludes to political murders during his own age. Then as now, however, as Bonhoeffer explained, the question of guilt or innocence was not that important. What was important was God's admonition to reflect on ourselves, to search out our own guilt, and to atone for that guilt.

He gazed out at this congregation in the pews.

Not many had attended the service. Bonhoeffer, rarely conciliatory, often harshly demanding, was not a particularly popular preacher. He now concluded with the words: "Lord, lead your people to penitence, beginning with us. Amen."

"That was a good sermon, Herr Bonhoeffer. And a right courageous one at that."

Baron Schröder, chairperson of the church council for all German Protestant congregations in Great Britain and Ireland, suddenly stood next to Bonhoeffer, who had not even noticed the old gentleman. He quickly undid his clerical collar and almost blushed with gleeful embarrassment. "I would like to have been considerably more straightforward."

"Even more?"

Bonhoeffer put his robe on a hanger and said softly, "No one should remain silent concerning what is going on in Germany just now. We must speak out."

"You're *that* concerned about the sixty dead?"

"The number was higher. Almost three hundred."

"How do you know?" Schröder was astonished. Bonhoeffer merely shrugged. Not even to Baron Schröder—a man of integrity who had already often spoken out against the new lords in Germany—did Bonhoeffer want to divulge his source of information, namely, his brother-in-law Hans von Dohnanyi.

Schröder noticed how upset Bonhoeffer was by all these events. He wanted to calm him, soothe him. "Yes, yes, very bad, all of it. No doubt about it. On the other hand, however, the highest echelons of the Brownshirt leadership genuinely must have been a malicious bunch, morally degenerate, probably most of them homosexual. . . ."

"And? Is that punishable by death?"

Bonhoeffer said this so clearly and so coldly that Schröder was a bit unnerved. Not least because in his experience this young man had been more inclined to prudery, to being rather severe and strict concerning issues such as divorce, adultery, and premarital sex. And now, he of all people? Defending homosexuals?

But Bonhoeffer had already continued speaking. "Ethicists, moralists perhaps may well pass judgment on a person's disposition in this sense. But the issue here is something completely different."

"Namely?" Schröder looked at Bonhoeffer with expectant skepticism.

"Namely, that in the middle of Germany, an allegedly civilized country, people are simply being shot down without a trial, without sentencing, and by the *Führer* personally, some say. . . ."

"He's appointed himself the supreme judge in the land."

"The supreme henchman. That's what he is. At best. And even a henchman acts only on orders. But who's giving Hitler orders? His conscience? Does he even have one?"

The baron was a bit taken aback. Bonhoeffer sensed his confusion and forced himself to speak in a calmer voice. "Will you do me the pleasure of staying for lunch, Herr Baron? Strawberries and cream for dessert." *That syrupy thick cream,* Bonhoeffer thought, *really is the only truly tasty thing English cuisine has to offer,* and once more he longed for a pork knuckle and mashed potatoes.

They walked over to the parsonage together, which since Hildebrandt's departure had seemed peculiarly cold and empty. For that reason alone Bonhoeffer enjoyed having company at a meal, and he would have liked to speak with the baron about more pleasant things, about the worship service he had conducted over Christmas in a seamen's church, or about the new, more modern hymnal he was thinking about introducing.

But Schröder picked up the earlier discussion quite on his own. "Are you saying that we cannot simply let the concerned parties deal with the matter? After all, there was not a single Protestant clergyman among the victims. . . ."

Bonhoeffer had trouble repressing an angry laugh. "People don't even take us seriously as opponents, that much is true. However," he reached for the bowl of strawberries, "murder has been committed. And murder concerns everyone. It concerns us as Christians as well. As a matter of fact, it *especially* concerns us."

He passed the strawberries over to Schröder a second time. The baron merely shook his head, prompting Bonhoeffer to take an even more generous portion for himself over which he then poured probably more cream than was really seemly. "We now know who Hitler is. A person who shrinks from *nothing*. And that requires a completely new kind of opposition."

"My dear Bonhoeffer," Schröder tried in vain to give the conversation a lighter, even joking tone, "you of all people are already opposing quite enough, don't you think?"

"No doubt. I will fly to Berlin and get sick either on the plane itself or, at latest, in Heckel's office when he *again* hands me the loyalty oath, which I *again* will not sign. And in the meantime, the church is going to ruin."

"But come, now you're really exaggerating!" Schröder was getting annoyed.

"Am I? Hitler has wrecked faith. At least almost wrecked it. And not through any help from his Bishop Müller or any of that German Christian rubbish. Müller is much less dangerous than those who just give in and accommodate themselves to everything and are not shy about kowtowing. *They* are the real danger."

"Your opinion of the Confessing Church is *that* low?"

"It's a start, nothing more. And as long as party publications—I read this somewhere or other myself—maintain that party members can certainly also be members of the Confessing Church, then that church is actually helping Hitler more than even the German Christians themselves. Who really takes them seriously anymore, or Müller? But a church that professes the gospel and yet still curtsies before Hitler . . ."

Bonhoeffer adjusted his glasses and became as serious and severe as he had been in the pulpit earlier. "A person can only be a Christian. Or a National Socialist. But not both at the same time. That's what I've come to understand. That's what I intend to fight for. And that's why . . ."

He stopped in mid-sentence. He had not wanted to tell the baron yet. But at some point he would have to.

What had happened was that during the spring the Reich bishop had closed down the traditional preachers' seminaries, institutions established by the regional churches to provide more intense theological training in connection with the normal university course of study. Müller's "Reich Church" intended to take a different path for training preachers, one conforming more to National Socialist policies. In response, the Confessing Church established its own seminaries. One had already been set up in Elberfeld. Four others were planned, including one in Pomerania. Bonhoeffer had been offered the position as its director.

So, back to the machine gun! But also farewell, India. India would now remain the unattainable distant shore, the promised land in the shimmering Far East.

A pause followed. Schröder finally interrupted the silence. "So, you're planning on leaving us? Soon?"

"Probably not before the end of the year. I'll be staying on a little longer yet." Bonhoeffer got up. "But for now let me make us some more coffee."

"It's really a shame, my dear Bonhoeffer," Schröder called to him in the kitchen. "Your work here is important." He heard Bonhoeffer's bright laughter. "Which work? The children's worship services? The nativity plays?" Just as in Barcelona, he had introduced both innovations in his congregations.

"I'm thinking more of your engagement on behalf of German émigrés." This was one objection that Bonhoeffer did indeed take seriously, since the fate of these people was one of his major concerns. He had already often enough asked Schröder or Bell for financial support and had even mobilized his American connections in this regard. On the other hand, even though he had in all candor directed the collections initiated by Goebbels on behalf of the winter auxiliary in Germany, he had at the same—and with equal candor—also solicited donations on behalf of needy émigrés.

"Leaving isn't easy for me either," he now said as he returned with the freshly brewed coffee, "and I still do have a couple of things to finish up here. I'm absolutely intent—and here I'm counting on your help, Herr Baron—on convincing the German congregations here in England to sever their ties with the church government in Germany and to recognize only the Confessing Church, and then . . ."

Schröder took a sip of coffee, letting the cup linger a moment at his lips so as not to betray what chance he really thought Bonhoeffer had of accomplishing that particular goal.

" . . . and then I must help organize the next ecumenical youth conference in August. Heckel wants to get representatives from the Reich Church government accepted as equal participants alongside those from the Confessing Church. That *must* be prevented."

"Where this time?"

"In Denmark. On the island of Fanø. It supposed to be quite beautiful there, what with the sea and the sand dunes. . . ." And Jean Lasserre would be among the delegates.

Good Lasserre! How appalled he had been in New York when Bonhoeffer told him once that although he detested war, love for one's fatherland might nonetheless sanctify it.

Yes, that genuinely was Bonhoeffer's opinion at the time. But it had fundamentally changed. War was not something sacred. Jesus himself forbids war. And that was exactly what Bonhoeffer intended to make clear in Fanø. Jean Lasserre would be pleased.

"Not a particularly popular position in Germany just now," Schröder said. "I'm sure you've heard that compulsory military service is to be introduced again. What will you do when the state summons you to arms?"

Bonhoeffer reflected. For several minutes.

Then, with hesitation, "I only hope that God will give me the strength and courage to refuse induction."

"You seem intent on becoming a martyr, my dear Bonhoeffer. Or even a saint." The baron laughed.

Bonhoeffer did not answer. He merely smiled. Albeit with a slight trace of arrogance and yearning.

Tegel, November 23/24, 1943

The attack begins at 7:29 P.M. The "Christmas trees," the flares of the approaching bombers, dance down toward the city. It's all over at a little past 9:00. Berlin breathes a sigh of relief, and Bonhoeffer returns to his cell after being deployed as a medic in the prison during the attacks ("You're a doctor, aren't you? Well, then you should be able to do that!").

But now he is in a different cell. On the third floor. Generally considered to be safer. Bonhoeffer, dressed in a ski outfit that his parents have sent him, is standing at the window. During the day he can see the towers of two churches in the distance, and sometimes snatches of choral singing waft over. But everything is dark now, and hazy. New moon. Bonhoeffer is a bit puzzled, since word has it that the more extensive bombing raids are undertaken only when conditions offer good visibility.

The detonations of the past hour are still reverberating inside him. *God's voice. God's wrath,* he thinks, and with a smile, *Well, haven't I become properly "Old Testament" in my thinking?* He recalls his time in the preachers' seminary in Pomerania. Even then, his students had been astonished at how intensively he studied the Old Testament, almost more than the New.

A blissful recollection. Images of the time at the seminary in Finkenwalde, a very good time indeed. But then the sirens are howling again and the "Christmas trees" dancing down.

A second attack, just after 10:00. Shouts and raucous commotion in the cells. Bonhoeffer rushes out into the corridor. But he doesn't dare open any of the cells, knows what recently happened to a guard who had done that. A prisoner had crushed his skull with his stool.

Bomb explosions are thundering all around. Over at the Borsig factory, here in Tegel as well, just as Knobloch had prophesied. Plaster dust falls from the ceiling, making it difficult to see. Bonhoeffer hears more cries, tormented, terrified, near death. He searches for the wounded.

One is lying on the floor, perhaps already dead. Bonhoeffer turns him over on his back. This one is still alive. Krawuttke—one of the most unpleasant guards in the prison, coarse, obscene, perpetually cursing. Now he groans without pause, "Oh God oh God oh God . . ."

Bonhoeffer kneels over him, utterly calm. "It'll all be over in ten minutes," he says. Krawuttke falls silent. He doesn't seem to be badly injured.

But in ten minutes it is not yet over. Not until just after 10:30 have they seemingly gotten through the worst of it. The sirens howl their "all clear."

Bonhoeffer is standing at the window again, thinking about his parents. He hopes they have taken his advice and withdrawn to the Sakrow district, to the Dohnanyis' house, or—even better—have evacuated to Friedrichsbrunn. Were he himself not imprisoned here in Tegel, perhaps he too would be out there at Friedrichsbrunn. A privileged citizen yet again.

Here, however, he has no such privileges. Every bomb can annihilate him as easily as any other inmate or guard. Here his life is as intimately connected with the fate of everyone else as it otherwise would be only if he were in a military unit fighting at the front.

And what if he *were* there, at the front, instead of here, in his cell? They have just drafted his friend Eberhard. He's to be deployed in Italy. Bad times for the sensitive young man. The drills, the slang, the chicanery. He hopes it will not be too hard on Eberhard emotionally. With these thoughts, thoughts of brotherly concern for his friend, Bonhoeffer falls into deep, dreamless sleep.

The next morning he takes down Goethe's *Reynard the Fox* from the bookshelf, his favorite reading material at the moment. Just as the fox outwits the lion through slippery logic and smooth talk—could that not just as easily be the situation with him and Roeder?

But the lock in the cell door rattles. Knobloch enters, as has frequently been the case recently. Bonhoeffer waits for the customary, "I have another question, Herr Pastor. . . ." But this time Knobloch talks about the damage of the previous night's bombing raid.

The roof. It has taken several direct hits. A breach in the wall. But no one has been killed, just slightly wounded. Though the infirmary itself has been completely demolished. Bonhoeffer nods. "We urgently need a proper medical bunker to secure our care of the wounded." He's already speaking as if *he* bears the responsibility for such things here. Gradually Tegel has become something like a home to him after all.

No! No! A thousand times no!

Bonhoeffer constantly has to remind himself. Constantly. He thinks about the trial that must, finally, start sometime. A tentative date of December 17 has been mentioned. Maybe he'll be home by Christmas.

Knobloch is standing next to him. "I have another question, Herr Pastor. . . ." So, a question after all! Bonhoeffer puts his volume of Goethe aside and nods.

"I heard yesterday that you kneeled down next to Krawuttke in the corridor. And how you said that in ten minutes everything would be over. . . ."

"And?"

"And, well, it just seems that would have been your chance to give him a piece of your mind and all, about God, since he's just laying there wailing 'God oh God' and such stuff . . . and yet he's the most godless pig here, that Krawuttke. You could've converted him straightaway, right there. . . ."

He breaks off and looks expectantly at Bonhoeffer.

"God is not there so we can use him to extort faith from somebody," he says slowly, "and he's not there just so somebody can summon him to keep something bad from happening. God's not a tool. And he's not just on call, like someone we can summon. The best thing is not even to call him by his name, like the Israelites. . . ."

"Huh? The Jews don't do that?"

Bonhoeffer shakes his head. *Smart Jews!* he thinks. Especially when one considers how often God is invoked precisely when someone wants to do the *worst* sort of things in his name.

He sits there, his hands dangling between his knees, and he feels as if he's talking more to himself than to Knobloch. "God is not an object. He doesn't belong to us. We belong to him. And he alone decides whether he'll turn to us in loving care. And we can't use what we call 'religion' to force him to do that."

He pauses, then continues speaking so softly that Knobloch has to lean forward to understand him. "I believe we're moving toward a *religionless* age that will have to create a *new* religion for itself. If we can show we're capable of facing up to the world, on our own, without any sort of divine assistance, perhaps *then* God will turn to us again."

"Help yourself, then God'll help you, that's what my old man used to say," Knobloch responds. And even though Bonhoeffer had intended it a bit differently, he nonetheless feels Knobloch has understood the essence of what he's saying.

Knobloch, now standing back at the door, turns around once more. "All the things you say, Herr Pastor, it's just all really interesting. Even someone like me can understand. Sometime maybe we can talk about it all, really talk. My folks, they have a garden where we can sit and chat real comfortable-like. . . ."

He stops in mid-sentence, a bit embarrassed. "But I'm guessing it might not be proper and fine enough for you."

A fine and proper prig! Bonhoeffer, too, looks a bit embarrassed, tries to come up with an answer. But Knobloch continues speaking. "By the way, the book I once gave you, from the library around the corner from us . . ."

"*The Day of Saint John the Baptist*, by Madam Eschstruth . . ."

"Have you read it yet, Herr Pastor?"

Bonhoeffer would like to lie, to be polite. But he cannot with this man. "No, not yet," is all he says.

Knobloch looks relieved. "That's probably best, since I heard it was actually really bad kitsch or something, not really anything for someone like you. . . ."

Bonhoeffer smiles. "I'll read it anyway."

And indeed he does. Knobloch has hardly closed the door before Bonhoeffer puts *Reynard the Fox* back on the shelf and begins thumbing through the book by Nathalie von Eschstruth, smiling, gently sighing to himself. He can only *imagine* what the reaction would have been had his Finkenwalde seminarians *ever* seen this book, way back in that summer of 1935.

Back then, too, they had heard the thunder of bombers and fighter planes over at the nearby military airfield in Stettin. But those were only exercises. The real thing began five years later and is now an almost daily occurrence. Night after night after night. . . .

First, however, Bonhoeffer will read Nathalie von Eschstruth.

I Want to Be a Saint

1935–1937

"The summer of 1935 was, I believe,
the most fulfilling period in my entire life thus far
both professionally and personally."
—to members of the first seminary session, November 1935

WE LOVE HIM—WE HATE HIM

"Well, that's probably it for today. They won't be exercising anymore tonight."

The young men in their nightshirts returned to the sleeping room. The flak thunder had harshly startled them out of their sleep. After rushing out to the balcony, they had seen a heavy bomber hanging in the searchlights like a giant, fat bug above the Stettin airfield. "Imagine, that thing really does have a stomach full of bombs, and they're dropping them right over our heads," one young man had muttered.

It was a balmy summer night in 1935.

Two men had remained out on the balcony. One sat down on the railing, "'Nother cigarette?"—"The director would probably not be real pleased."—"But he himself smokes like a chimney."

They sat there. And smoked.

"You know," the one said, "it's satisfying to occasionally catch him in a moment of weakness." He hesitated. "Tell me honestly . . ."

"Tell you what honestly?"

"Are you able to think of him as anything other than the 'director'? Even though he himself wants us to address him as 'Brother Bonhoeffer'? For me, he's the director. That's it."

"What's more," the other man said, "he's no older than we are."

"But you don't notice that."

This Pomeranian "preachers' seminary" had been in existence since April 26, 1935. At first, Bonhoeffer and his twenty-three pastoral candidates had found refuge in the tiny hamlet of Zingst on the Baltic Sea.

Then, in June, they had moved on to Finkenwalde, near Stettin, to the Katte Estate, where once upon a time Prussia's Frederick II had spent the night in the house of his friend Katte. That, however, was about all Finkenwalde could brag about. What the candidates actually found was an abandoned building that local rumor suggested had recently served as a brothel run by a half-crazed madam. Only gradually did the candidates manage to turn it into a reasonably inhabitable building that, surrounded as it was by firs and birch trees, was in fact quite happily situated.

The candidates did not fare all that badly in other respects as well. Although the students were dependent on donations, the landed Pomeranian gentry was inclined to support the Confessing Church almost as an amiable obligation, and soon enough all sorts of furniture and furnishings were arriving along with groceries and even a live pig. Bonhoeffer conscientiously distributed the goods as equitably as possible. Rarely had he felt as free and happy as during this period.

And during the evenings one could hear gentle music floating through the building, *Swing low, sweet chariot* . . .

"He's playing his Negro songs again," one of the candidates quipped. Another nodded, "And beautiful songs they are. And whenever the director tells us about New York . . ." He interrupted himself. "I mean, not just to hear about New York, but to actually be there sometime. Or anywhere abroad. Anywhere but *perpetually* here in Pomerania. . . ."

The other young man put his cigarette out on the balustrade and flipped the butt out into the darkness. "Let's go swimming tomorrow!

It doesn't have to be the Hudson River. The Oder River will also do just fine. . . ."

An old rowboat was tethered to the shore in the branch of the Oder River near the seminary—everyone had agreed that they had to have water nearby. Bonhoeffer had managed to get the boat quite cheaply. This branch of the Oder was the candidates' private "swimming hole," and the next day the two young men glided into the water there, submerged, and then came back up to the surface puffing and blowing out water.

"Too bad we're not on the coast of the Baltic anymore. We didn't need bathing suits there."

"Well, you can just as easily play Adam in paradise here as well."

"Better not. The director doesn't really approve."

They swam alongside each other for a short distance.

"You mean he's a bit of a prude?"

"Well, not really a prude. I just don't think the physical body means all that much to him. Didn't you hear him say recently that early-morning exercise was not really necessary, and that mornings were better spent in prayer?"

"But he's the best handball player here, and the best swimmer. . . ."

"The best everything. The perpetual number one." They swam back to the boat, climbed in, and lay on the wooden-plank seats with their slightly pungent fragrance of tar and river vegetation. They squinted up into the brilliant, cloudless blue Pomeranian summer sky stretching out above them on all sides.

"We had somebody like that in my class at school once," the one began again, "the model student in everything. But not really ambitious, not pretentious, nothing like that; always friendly, helpful, the best sort of schoolmate. But there was just always this wall between us, like glass. You could see him through it but not feel him, so he was never really good friends with anyone."

"Like the director?"

"The way he's always making you feel like you've done something wrong. Like on the first day, when no one volunteered to do the dishes, you remember? So he did them himself, alone, and no one was allowed to help him. My, oh, my, children, we were all so *ashamed*. . . ."

His friend laughed. "And when he was about to go to Berlin and asked us what he could bring us back, perhaps cheese or chocolate, and someone quipped, '*Both.*' . . ."

"And so, of course, he did bring back *both*. And brought his library here, and his record collection, and the expensive Bechstein grand piano—which anyone can play who wants to. . . ."

"He gives *everything*. Just not himself."

A barge lumbered by. The boatman waved. The two young men waved back.

"I wonder if he has even a single real friend."

"Maybe the pastor who they say's a Jew. Franz Hildebrandt. He's in Dahlem now with Niemöller. . . ."

"And among us here in Finkenwalde," the other young man interrupted, "the director seems to be especially fond of Eberhard. I know he uses the formal form of address with him and calls him 'Brother' just like all the others, but the undertone, like when he asks him, 'And so what do *you* think, dear Brother? . . .'"

One could not fail to sense the slight jealousy these young men felt toward the favorite at the foot of the Bonhoeffer throne.

"Know what I sometimes think?" The young man looked at the reflection of the sun in the softly gurgling water. "I think the director was probably born to be a monk."

His friend laughed.

"No, I'm serious. Even his idea about establishing a 'House of Brethren' here, a kind of monastery. He says the Anglican monasteries in England really made an impression on him. And that we have to take the opposite path from Luther, namely, not *out* of the monastery, but back *into* it."

The other young man had folded his hands behind his head and closed his eyes. "Well, in the final analysis we really won't have any other choice but to enter a monastery if the church won't employ us."

"You think?"

"Does anyone even know how long the Confessing Church will be able to hang on?" He raised himself up on his elbows. "But what does *he* care, the coddled professor's son? He doesn't have to worry about his future. The golden boy, always number one, always with a silver spoon in his mouth. . . ."

His friend had now also sat up. "Sounds like you almost hate the director."

"A little. Perhaps." Then after a pause, after lying back down on his back and closing his eyes again. "And I love him. That, too."

The other nodded. "Just like all of us here."

As a matter of fact, during this period Bonhoeffer was indeed concerned with things other than the pastoral candidates' professional futures. He sat in his single room—the only privilege he allowed himself in Finkenwalde—depressed, and thought about what his brother-in-law Hans had whispered to him.

Hitler, who since Hindenburg's death was both *Führer* and Reich chancellor, apparently intended to take a harder line, especially with regard to the Jewish question. Laws were already being formulated and would be announced at the next Nuremberg party congress, laws relegating Jews to second-class citizenship—once and for all.

Bonhoeffer's fear and concern was now joined by a ray of hope, namely, that the church, which had so tenaciously avoided taking an unequivocal position on this question, would finally be *forced* to show its colors.

September 15, 1935, was the big day. Because Hitler had a bad cold, Hermann Göring read the so-called Nuremburg Laws in his stead. The telephone rang in Finkenwalde.

Bonhoeffer picked up the receiver. "Hey, Franz . . ." As always, he was always elated to hear the voice of his faraway friend. But then he became quite pale, and his hand trembled trying to hold the receiver. "What? *What?* But you can't be serious. . . ."

You Can Go or Stay

Bonhoeffer's hands were still trembling after he hung up the phone—even though Hildebrandt himself had been quite calm.

Hildebrandt had just told Niemöller he would no longer be working with the Pastors' Emergency League. Indeed, he no longer intended to

be a pastor in the Confessing Church at all. He had just heard through
the grapevine that at the next Prussian Synod—scheduled for the end
of September in Berlin-Steglitz—the church would indeed stand by
its objection to the Aryan Clause but would otherwise grant the state
complete freedom in dealing with the Jewish question.

In other words, the church was for all practical purposes bestowing
its blessing on the Nuremberg Laws.

"I'm going to be there even if no one invites me. And I'm going to
speak, no, shout out against this measure. Even if they end up burning
me at the stake like the heretic Jan Hus," Bonhoeffer exclaimed after
relating news of these latest developments to his seminarians.

"We'll all be there! We'll all raise our voices!" the seminarians'
voices buzzed in excitement.

Bonhoeffer looked at their young, excited faces. *My community of
saints*, he thought, *just as I always dreamed, and with its own, completely
new sense of shelter*. As was always the case when he thought of such
things, he could not repress a warm, grateful feeling of happiness.

The synod, which was initially scheduled to take place in Königsberg
and was then moved to Berlin-Steglitz, began on a fairly positive note
insofar as the past summer had brought what was in fact a surprising
turn of events in the larger arena of church politics.

Hitler's unalterable "Müller is staying" had turned quite
unexpectedly into an equally unalterable "Müller must go." The Reich
bishop disappeared. Ten years later, in the early morning hours in
Grunewald, and in his own way, he acknowledged this complete
loss of power and the loss of all his dreams for a uniquely German
Christianity beneath the swastika—by committing suicide with a
shot to the head.

What now emerged instead was a "Reich Ministry for Church
Affairs" with the former Prussian minister of justice Hanns Kerrl at
its head, a not entirely wrongheaded man who as an "old warrior"
nonetheless was also a believing Christian who maintained that his
goal was a unified church of the people.

Many thought this step alone would resolve all the conflicts. The
only remaining skeptics were the "Dahlemites" such as Bonhoeffer

and his ilk, so named after the Dahlem Synod, which not only confirmed the resolutions of Barmen but also considerably sharpened them.

As it was, however, Bonhoeffer now found himself in the gallery of the Berlin Synod along with his seminary students. In the hall down below, a gentleman from the newly created ministry was speaking, not Hanns Kerrl himself, but a representative. He spoke about the *great* love Minister Kerrl had for the church and how the minister was not even *remotely* thinking about creating a state-controlled church. The seminary students laughed out loud.

Bonhoeffer did not laugh. He was waiting for the discussion finally to get around to the Jewish question.

It never did. Neither in the presentation of this gentleman nor in those of any representatives of the church itself. Only a couple of words about the baptism of Jews, which could not really be prohibited. The fundamental question would allegedly be left to a later synod, a Reich Synod.

Adjournment. Putting things off till later. Nonbinding resolutions. That was the depressing yield of Steglitz. Bonhoeffer sat in the train with his seminary students on the way back to Stettin, thoroughly sober after the events at the synod. He recalled a letter he had received from Karl Barth.

As a professor of theology, Barth had agreed to sign the required oath to Hitler only with the qualifying addendum that the ultimate authority would still remain his own Christian faith. That was the end of his academic career in Germany. He received an appointment in his hometown of Basel, Switzerland, but had written Bonhoeffer shortly before that. Bonhoeffer had immediately copied the letter and distributed it to all his students.

The tone of the letter was one of utter disappointment. The Confessing Church, Barth wrote, was of absolutely no help to precisely those who needed help during this time. The church no longer spoke on behalf of those who could not speak. It concerned itself with helping only itself, spoke only for itself, revolved only around itself. Recalling these words, Bonhoeffer could not help laughing out loud, so loudly, in fact, and so bitterly, that the others in the train compartment were completely taken aback.

Had Jesus thought of himself and his disciples when he climbed up to Golgotha? And what, pray tell, does the Confessing Church really "confess"? Was the Confessing Church still even a viable entity?

Well, yes, at the front lines. Where pastors were abused and reviled by Brownshirts during their sermons, and where others had already been dragged off to concentration camps. Bonhoeffer included all their names in the regular evening prayers. He also thought of his colleague in the "Red Wilhelmsburg" section of Hamburg who was able to conduct his worship services only under the protection of strapping, muscular Communists, while outside the Brownshirts bellowed their *"Sieg Heil!"* into the air.

Indeed, Bonhoeffer sighed, the Reds have even more solidarity with us than many of our own brethren. He had heard about yet another pastor whose confirmation pupils had grilled him about his position regarding the "Jewish rabble." The very next day, members of the SS chased him through the village with a sign around his neck: "I am a wretched servant of the Jews."

Only *such* men—*only* they—were allowed to call themselves "confessors" in this sense. And the others?

Kerrl's church policies—smooth as silk—were aimed at subjecting the Confessing Church to a gentle death by suffocation by establishing the so-called church committees. These "committees" were populated by the most respected people from all the different factions—Confessing Christians, German Christians, neutrals—and at their head one found the most respected personage of all, namely, the former Westphalian church superintendent Wilhelm Zoellner, who had been persuaded to come out of retirement to accept the position.

The respect people had for Zoellner, who was over seventy years old, was so great, that his vote in favor of this committees' declaration for a "National Socialist populist movement on the foundation of race, blood, and earth" did not really strike anyone as odd. Bonhoeffer's assessment, however, was that "the church committee is the folding screen—just like the one on stage, in the theater—behind which the Confessing Church is to be stabbed to death." He could not imagine at the time how right he was.

Then came December 2, 1935.

This Monday began just as did any other. It was not until the evening that Bonhoeffer called everyone together. "Did anyone see the Stettin newspaper?" No one had. But that question alone was puzzling, since none of them was ever particularly interested in this staid, provincial newspaper. And now Bonhoeffer was calling them together because of something in this paper?

Bonhoeffer had already spread the paper out. "A new implementation of the 'Law to Restore Order in the German Evangelical Church' has just been decreed, the fifth." Then he read from the newspaper in a soft, monotone voice. All ecclesiastical authorizations by independent church groups were forthwith invalid. This was to include especially—here he paused—"any authorization of examinations and ordinations."

"They're proscribing *us*? Forbidding *our* ordination?" someone cried out.

"Yes, that's exactly what they're doing. For all practical purposes this amounts to a prohibition." Bonhoeffer had closed his eyes. "This means—let us be perfectly clear about the implications here—this means that none of you has any assurance of ever being appointed pastor anywhere or even of being recognized as having been ordained. Your future—I must tell you this plainly—will be both difficult and uncertain."

He now—something he very rarely did in public—took off his glasses and rubbed his eyes vigorously. The others, horrified, now saw a gray, distorted, childlike face.

But he quickly gathered himself. "You can go or stay, as you wish. Feel completely free to do what you think best. But if even a single one of you does stay . . ."

He put his glasses back on. His voice took on a confidential, somewhat metallic tone. ". . . then I will also stay." Outside, the winter's first snow had started falling.

Is This What a Saint Looks Like?

The procession of those who on this January 15, 1936, were paying their respects to the deceased Julie Bonhoeffer was long. At its head, directly behind the casket, her grandson Dietrich followed in his clerical robe.

He had been preparing himself for this moment since at least the previous December, when the ninety-three-year-old had caught a virulent case of the flu. And yet her death still seemed to have torn part of his world in half.

Along with you, Grandmama, he thought—simultaneously recalling the taste of ginger cookies—*we are also accompanying another age, another time to the grave. And our duty is now to ensure that the values of that age, its understanding of courage, propriety, and truthfulness, will not also disappear.*

These were the same thoughts Dietrich articulated at her graveside in his funeral oration. During his talk, he recalled her actions in front of the Department Store of the West. "Her final years were clouded by the great suffering she endured because of the fate of the Jews among our people, which she bore and suffered in sympathy with them," he spoke with a raised voice, ignoring the horrified looks of surprise on some of the faces in front of him. His own eyes sought out his brother-in-law Leibholz, who nodded back with a slight smile.

Immediately after the service, he withdrew into the small attic room that his parents had put at his disposal in their house. That house was now located on the Marienburg Allee, where the Bonhoeffers had moved the previous year, a smaller but even more handsome house. "And this room here," his mother had said as she opened the door to the attic room, "will always be your kingdom, Dietrich. Here you will always be at home, no matter where you may otherwise find yourself."

A knock on the door. Eberhard came in. "Am I disturbing you?" Bonhoeffer never ceased to be touched by the gentle Saxon accent of his friend, who had been born in the city of Magdeburg.

"No, no; you never disturb me. And you don't even need to knock. This is your room as much as it is mine."

Eberhard had accompanied his friend to Berlin for his grandmother's funeral, and Dietrich's parents had put an extra bed in the attic room for him. Such would remain the case for the next few years as well. They viewed their son's friend as their own son.

And a strange friendship it was.

The first time Bonhoeffer had sat together with the other seminarians, hardly any of whom were really all that much younger than he, he had actually felt like one of them himself. Only gradually, and painfully, had he then come to see that he was not really like them after all.

Neither a friend nor one of the "brethren." Just the "other," the teacher, the director. At first he had casually tried to downplay these differences. In vain. And once—during the previous Whitsun festival—he had surprised several of his seminary students in a tavern in a quite merry and not entirely sober condition.

He had wanted to join them, have a beer with them, laugh and joke with them. But the horrified respect with which they had all jumped up when he arrived had already created too much distance. And he, more annoyed at his own narrow-minded reaction than at anything else, had wrinkled his brow with pedagogical severity and said, "I fear, dear brethren, that this may not be entirely the right way to greet the Holy Spirit."

Only with Eberhard were things different.

He was funny and lively and candid and had a youthful sense of humor that in many ways resembled that of Dietrich's friend Franz Hildebrandt, albeit without the latter's slight inclination to cynicism. And just as was the case with Hildebrandt, there were no barriers between Dietrich and Eberhard. No affectation, no artificiality, almost like brothers—with the younger Eberhard even managing to loosen up the occasionally rather morose Dietrich with a dose of his own, lighter personality.

Now I finally have the younger brother I've always wanted, Bonhoeffer concluded, simultaneously thinking about his own older brothers and about how worshipfully he had looked up to them. Now someone else, someone younger, was looking up to him. At least Bonhoeffer hoped that was the case.

"You're working on another book?" Bonhoeffer nodded. It was no secret among the seminary students that their director spent every free minute working on what was becoming a rather formidable and lengthy book. "Do you already have a title?"

Bonhoeffer leaned back in his chair. "What do you mean 'already'? *Discipleship*."

Eberhard chuckled. "Your eternal theme."

He was right. Ever since his time in New York, Bonhoeffer had never quite been able to shake the idea that Jesus must genuinely be resurrected anew, as it were, in every believer, and be recreated in the church community itself. And that every believer would in precisely this way enter into true discipleship, and would do so according to the Sermon on the Mount: Blessed are the pure of heart, those who suffer, the merciful, the meek, the peacemakers, all those who are persecuted for righteousness's sake. . . .

"So is your real goal to found a new religion?" Eberhard had once teased in Finkenwalde. Bonhoeffer had put his pencil down and stared straight ahead for a moment.

He finally turned and answered. "No, not a new religion. Just the old one, but this time freed from all the ballast that merely distracts us from real faith. Concentrating solely on the essentials, and so simple that anyone can understand it and follow its commandments." He paused. "But we need to hurry up before the others beat us to it."

At this very moment he envisioned the gray, sad tenement blocks in Wedding, and all the residents there with their dull longing for even a *little* happiness in life. "Communism is promising a paradise. That's not so dangerous. There *is* no paradise. Everyone eventually sees that. But the new lords in the land, they're much, much more dangerous. They're promising *salvation*."

He became animated. "Yes, National Socialism—it's becoming ever clearer to me—is far more than just a political party. It intends to be a religion—the new gospel, and far more dependent on feeling than on reason."

He thought of the frequent "messianic gaze" on Hitler's face, of his gestures—gestures of benediction and invocation, of his predilection for beginning sentences with "But I say unto you . . . ," and on the ecstatic behavior of his believers. Hitler's speeches—Bonhoeffer could not help grimacing and feeling repulsed at the mere thought—were like . . . well, they were like perverted Sermons on the Mount. And Dietrich had once even remarked to Eberhard, "Everyone thinks they can convert Hitler. But they're wrong. It's Hitler who's converting us! Or at least trying to. And, quite frankly, he's already been quite successful to a point. Unfortunately."

He saw the look of horror on Eberhard's youthful face and quickly sought to assuage his fear. "But perhaps there's something positive in that. We Christians are finally being forced to reflect on our own faith. On what each of us, every individual among us, needs to be and become within that faith. You, me, all of us. . . ."

He broke off with a smile, and Eberhard smiled as well. "So, you see yourself in discipleship to Christ. . . ."

"I see everyone like that. That's what I said." Bonhoeffer was a bit embarrassed.

"But you see especially yourself that way."

The two friends were silent for a moment.

Eberhard finally broke the silence, but spoke in a quiet voice. "I think I'm finally beginning to understand. You're not just creating a new faith, you also want to create yourself anew at the same time. . . ."

"Create myself anew? Why?"

Eberhard flashed the kind of oh-so-wise smile one can have only in one's mid-twenties. "Because it's not enough for you simply to be Dietrich Bonhoeffer."

Bonhoeffer started for a moment. "And so who am I really?"

"Perhaps," Eberhard hesitated, "perhaps a saint."

Bonhoeffer looked like a child caught with his hand in the cookie jar, not least because Franz Hildebrandt had already once cynically teased him: "Ah, you'll not rest, old adversary, until you have been sainted and we must then all kneel before you. Isn't that right?"

Bonhoeffer tried to laugh but could not quite make it come out the way he wanted. "Well, perhaps this is not such a bad time to become a saint. Even though. . . ." He hesitated and finally, shyly, took off his glasses, "Is this what a saint looks like?"

And once again, a small, sad, childlike face emerged.

Red Card for Heaven

Eberhard had once said something else to his friend as well. "You're too hard, Dietrich. On yourself. On others."

I have to, Bonhoeffer thought. *Would our Finkenwalde seminary even exist otherwise despite being prohibited by the state?*

Again and again he found himself sitting across from those in Finkenwalde who wrung their hands and hemmed and hawed about maybe not wanting to remain in the seminary after all. Not many, just certain individuals, really. But every such case pierced Bonhoeffer's heart. Not least because he understood these young men, at least to a certain extent.

No future, no prospects of acquiring a respected place in society, a nice parsonage somewhere, a decent salary, a wife and child. There were indeed many reasons for *not* staying at Finkenwalde, and really only *one* for remaining. But that *one* reason, in the final analysis, was also the most important, namely, the one faith, the one *true* faith.

That faith alone was valid. Everything else was heresy. And "those who knowingly separate themselves from the Confessing Church in Germany are separating themselves from salvation."

Those were Bonhoeffer's exact words in a lecture. And the exact words that, at the insistence of his seminary students, he had published in the June 1936 issue of the journal *Evangelical Theology*. The uproar this assertion caused ultimately ended in the accusation that what Bonhoeffer had *really* meant was that no one would get into heaven without a "red card"—the "red card" being the membership card in the Confessing Church.

One person, however, had *always* known that this Dietrich Bonhoeffer could not be trusted, and that was Bishop Theodor Heckel in the Church Foreign Office. He thought of the trip to Sweden that Bonhoeffer had taken this past spring with his seminary students in order not just to *tell* them about foreign countries but to *show* them such a country as well. The trip had been a great success.

But not in Heckel's eyes. He had issued an explicit warning against this Bonhoeffer, a pacifist and enemy of the state whose activities would doubtless *not* be serving Germany's best interests. When Bonhoeffer undertook the trip despite being discouraged from doing so, the bishop immediately reached for the telephone.

Heckel, who had hitherto managed to weather every coup, including Müller's fall from power, and who would even weather the earth-shattering collapse ten years later, in 1945—during the 1950s he emerged as one of the "expelled bishops" none the worse for wear as far as status and reputation were concerned. This Heckel had his hands on all the strings of ecclesiastical power and kept up contacts in every possible quarter.

After returning from Sweden, Bonhoeffer learned that his authorization to lecture at Berlin University, where he had previously held weekly classes, had been revoked. The charge was that he had failed to secure proper permission for the trip abroad and was now also known to be the director of a prohibited preachers' seminary.

Bonhoeffer did not understand. He understood neither this measure nor all the uproar over his assertion that salvation was to be found solely in the Confessing Church. "I was just repeating what I've always said."

"Dear, dear Dietrich," Franz Hildebrandt laughed, "you're making pronouncements that otherwise only the pope in Rome presumes to make, and then you're expecting people to love you for it? But, then, I've always suspected," he laughed again and pointed a threatening finger at Dietrich, "that you were secretly a papist. At the very least, you certainly have the skills to be an inquisitor."

Bonhoeffer did not find his friend's remarks particularly funny.

They were sitting at Hildebrandt's place in Dahlem, and Bonhoeffer looked pale and exhausted. He had already had a bad case of flu that winter, was tormented by depression, and generally weary of life. "What can we do now, Franz? Try to keep the seminary afloat even though things are crumbling and collapsing at every turn? Why? To what end? To produce yet more starving clerical paupers?" He interrupted himself and put his face in his hands. "Sometimes I think I'm staring straight into the face of the 'beast' from Revelation. It looks like a distorted Luther and is sticking its tongue out at me."

Unusual words from someone who was otherwise always so optimistic and always ready to tackle even the most formidable projects. Hildebrandt looked at him sympathetically and then gave him a packet of paper. "Have a look at this. Read through it. Perhaps it will cheer you up a bit."

Bonhoeffer paged through the manuscript, at first apathetically, but then with ever-widening eyes. "The memorandum? It's finished?"

"Yes, finally."

A memorandum to Hitler. Three committees had drawn it up. Hildebrandt was on one of them and had sought his friend's opinion on several occasions. Now, finally, the memorandum was finished.

This document enumerated in a precise, neat fashion everything that the Confessing Church—and not just the Confessing Church—found distressful in the present situation. And not just the increasingly evident "deconfessionalization" of all spheres of life and the increasing "de-Christianization" of the people. The authors also very much wanted to know what the expression "positive Christianity" was really supposed to mean.

But they also spoke about hatred of the Jews, about state-organized anti-Semitic activities, and they made unequivocal statements about alleged election fraud, about concentration camps, the Gestapo, and the rampant presence of spies among the population.

"If Hitler even reads it."

"He'll read it. It's to be delivered to him tomorrow in the Reich chancellery."

Bonhoeffer was horrified. "But what if it falls into the wrong hands? I mean, outside the Reich chancellery itself? Do you realize how much damage a couple of well-intentioned newspaper articles in Sweden did to our cause? How we were allegedly being persecuted as Christians and how our trip there was a veritable triumphal procession of the Confessing Church?"

"Don't worry, Dietrich." Hildebrandt carefully packed the manuscript up again. "There are only two other complete copies of this thing besides the copy for Hitler, and both are in completely secure places. One is in the church of the Swedish legation, the other with our good friend Dr. Weissler." Friedrich Weissler, who as a Jew had been dismissed from his position as the director of a regional court, was now the head of the chancellery of the Confessing Church. He was viewed as an absolutely trustworthy man, more overly cautious than not.

The memorandum was delivered on June 4, 1936. Then silence. Six long weeks of silence. No reaction from the Reich chancellery. Then the telephone trilled once more in Finkenwalde. Again it was Hildebrandt at the other end. And again Bonhoeffer turned white as a sheep.

"*What?* But how on earth did *that* happen? The memorandum published in Switzerland, in the *Basel News* . . . ?"

A Martyr—A Jew

And indeed it was. The memorandum to Hitler, splashed across the pages of the Basel newspaper, word for word, the entire text. And not just there.

The *New York Herald Tribune* followed suit a few days later. The *New York Times* dedicated a long, lead article to the matter. Even before that, an extensive reference in the British *Morning Post* had alluded to it.

The stir this incident caused could not have been greater, and the excitement in the Confessing Church itself was initially considerably more vehement than in the state agencies, whose reaction—at least at first—was remarkably reserved.

After all, the Olympic Games were about to be hosted in Berlin. Fifty thousand foreign guests were expected. The signs declaring "Jews Not Allowed" had disappeared from the swimming pools and park benches, and Julius Streicher's coarsely pornographic political smear sheet, the *Stormer*, had similarly disappeared from store windows. Anti-Semitism in Germany? Hostility toward the church? Nothing but cheap propaganda against the magnificent new, indeed renewed Germany!

Hence the last thing the state wanted was a scandal that might threaten this image of a peace-loving country open to the entire world! Accordingly, it was in no particular hurry to hunt down those responsible for having smuggled such a memorandum abroad.

The officials took their time. After all, one does not host the Olympics just every year. Let things just ride along and then decide what to do later. In the meantime, Bonhoeffer received numerous reports and rumors about how such a thing could have happened.

Ernst Tillich and Werner Koch! Bonhoeffer knew both of them well, Tillich from the youth conference on Fanø. And Koch as one of the Finkenwalde seminarians who had participated in the journey to Sweden. Then there was also gentle Dr. Weissler with the memorandum hidden away in his drawer.

Tillich had visited Weissler, had pressured him to turn over the manuscript. But only for a short time, just overnight, and only for a brief communiqué that would be dispatched to the foreign press. Weissler had sighed and squirmed a bit . . . and then turned it over. "Well, okay. But really, only for a single night."

Tillich nodded. And then copied out the entire memorandum that night. Word for word. Every line. Bonhoeffer, however, could imagine Tillich's friend Werner Koch whispering, "This is great, Ernst! The foreign press needs to know about this! Then Hitler won't have any choice but to react!" Our good Werner, Bonhoeffer thought. A talented writer who had already taken over the press analysis during the trip to Sweden and who imagined himself gifted with all sorts of journalistic savvy. The copy went out.

There was another version of the "leak" as well, at least for the publication in New York. In this version, a completely different person—a certain Herr Kötzschke—had played the memorandum into the hands of the foreign press, and not necessarily with the support of the church. More likely it had been with the smug satisfaction of the Gestapo, which had long maintained that the entire Confessing Church was being manipulated and directed by the foreign press.

Bonhoeffer groaned.

He had been in Berlin during the Olympic Games, had seen—despite all the Olympic sunshine—what was in the display window of one bookstore: "After the Olympics, we're going to beat the Confessing Church to a pulp. . . ." So, someone out there was just waiting for the chance to strike. Just waiting for the right occasion.

Just waiting for this damned memorandum, for example.

Autumn came. "Jews Not Allowed" was once more the order of the day for park benches and swimming pools. The *Stormer* was once more displayed in the stores. And Werner Koch, who in the meantime had become an assistant pastor in Barmen, traveled to Berlin to see his friends Tillich and Weissler.

"My husband? You mean you don't know yet? They arrested him yesterday. . . ."

Both Tillich and Weissler had been arrested on October 9, 1936. Koch's turn came on November 13. Interrogations, but still lenient enough. Interrogators at that time were still inclined to go easy on pastors. Then in February 1937 all three were transferred to the concentration camp Sachsenhausen. They passed through the gate with the derisive inscription, "Work makes you free."

"Well, good. At least we'll get out into the fresh air a bit," Wessler had tried to strike a lighter tone. Then the shouts of the guards, sharp orders, blows with a truncheon. The three new arrivals had to crawl through the mud and garbage and filth. "So, you're pastors? Great; just what we've been needing here." Prison clothes with a red triangle on their prisoners' stripes to show they were "political prisoners." Then their heads were shaved bald. Weissler whispered, "The worst is probably over."

"Let's go, Jew."

They dragged him away. "They're taking him to the bunker," someone whispered. His horrified eyes made any questions superfluous. "Not exactly his lucky day, your friend there," another prisoner grinned. It was February 13, 1937, a Friday.

These three were not the only ones from church circles arrested around this time. Bonhoeffer's prayer intercession list became longer and longer, for the net around the Confessing Church had grown ever tighter, the restrictions and regulations ever more rigorous, and later, in Tegel, Bonhoeffer often wondered why he had been arrested only so late rather than right at the beginning like so many others.

For there had certainly been excuses and reasons enough to do so, not the least of which were his continued work with the prohibited seminary, his contacts abroad, his connections with Hildebrandt, with Martin Niemöller and the Pastors' Emergency League, to name but a few.

Bonhoeffer, in his cell, often saw Niemöller's sharply featured face before him with his dark, opinionated eyes. Yes, Niemöller was someone who had early on genuinely tried to be a resolute Christian *and* a National Socialist and had ended up being an equally resolute Christian but an unequivocal anti-Nazi, unwavering on either side.

Bonhoeffer admired that.

He himself, however, had found that his highly disciplined intellect always immediately provided an alternative. He found it difficult to think and act with unequivocal clarity and strict straightforwardness. And even those times when he did manage to wrestle his way to such thinking and action, one could always sense the strained, affected, laborious effort behind it. A bystander always had the sense that here, in Bonhoeffer, was someone who had to *resolve* to be radical, someone who was *not* radical by nature.

Niemöller was different.

Once having chosen a certain path, a temperament like his— sometimes obstinate, sometimes incomprehensible—tended to follow that path all the way to the bitter end, *even* if it turned out to be the wrong one and his friends could only groan, "Brother Niemöller, did you have to say it like *that*?" He had it harder than Bonhoeffer, but also easier.

But when had Bonhoeffer last seen him? In Tegel Bonhoeffer could no longer even recall.

No, it wasn't on July 1, when he and Eberhard had wanted to visit their colleague in Dahlem. After they knocked on his door at 61 Cecilia Street, Eugen Rose—one of the seminarians from Finkenwalde—had opened. "They arrested Brother Niemöller this morning." Frau Niemöller, remarkably composed, as if a long-anticipated disaster had finally happened, waved them into the dining room, where Franz Hildebrandt was already sitting. "They'll be here soon."

And they were. A long column of black cars. They searched the house for eight hours, with the four people there under arrest. Finally a triumphal cry from Niemöller's study, where thirty thousand marks were stored in a safe, the emergency reserves of the Pastors' Emergency League. "Well, no doubt the money from your Jews, right?" That was another rumor that had long been making the rounds. Namely, that the Jews were financing both the Confessing Church and the preachers' seminaries.

The Gestapo left toward evening. Bonhoeffer, Eberhard, and Hildebrandt were all allowed to leave.

"Do you still have your passport, Franz?"

"Yes, fortunately they didn't find it."

"Then take it and get out of here! As fast as possible. Away from Germany!"

"But where?" All his worldly wit and savvy seemed to abandon him, leaving behind an anxious, despairing man.

"Anywhere. Maybe France. Jean Lasserre told me that the French Protestants like Prussians because they had done so much for the Huguenots. Or go to England. Uncle Glocke will be glad to take you under his wing." *Glocke*—the German word for "bell"—had become the cover name for their patron George Bell.

"But I have to conduct worship here on Sundays."

A pulpit without a preacher—an unbearable thought for a man such as Hildebrandt.

"It'll be fine without you. It *has* to be fine without you. Or do you want to end up like poor Weissler?" Last February they had heard that Weissler had hanged himself in Sachsenhausen.

Significantly, however, no one was allowed to open his coffin. At the same time, there was talk about an SS man who while being dragged away by his colleagues, had wailed something to the effect of, "Well what do you want? How was I to know the Jewboy was connected with the church?" The man disappeared afterward, and talk had it that he, too, had committed suicide.

The American firm holding Weissler's life insurance policy had insisted on an autopsy. But that, too, had been denied. And at his funeral, a Gestapo official had come up and remarked to Pastor Asmussen, "I am sincerely counting on this funeral not turning into a demonstration."

It did not. But many pastors had attended, most of them in clerical robes. One had whispered to another standing next to him, "I suppose we really ought to call Weissler a martyr now."

The other had nodded.

"Who would have thought? The first real martyr for our cause a Jew."

The other shrugged. The wind rustled their robes.

TEGEL, EARLY MAY 1944

The visit is over. Bonhoeffer is again sitting in his cell, but more agitated than is usually the case after a visit from Maria. Each time he sees his fiancée, he then must retrieve the image he has formed of her during the endless hours he has spent alone, without her, cut off from her.

He searches among his papers and comes across the manuscript of his novel. He's not worked on it for some time now, indecisive about whether he should even continue it at all. And now he is totally, completely uncertain.

No, he is no great novelist like Theodor Fontane or Thomas Mann. And now the middle-class world of his novel, its milieu and all its characters and conflicts, suddenly seems far too distant, far too unreal to him. He now realizes, a bit to his own astonishment, that that world has become peculiarly alien to

him. Suddenly he can no longer find *himself* in that world. Nor
Maria.

Yes, he had wanted her to make an appearance in that novel as
well. Beautiful, strong, clear. The natural housewife, predestined
to be a mother, the highest calling for a woman. That is how he
had wanted to portray her. Fundamentally different from any
of the little ladies he had gotten to know in his sister Susanne's
circle of friends, with their cocktails and longing looks "made
in Hollywood." Bonhoeffer shivered. That other type made
him shiver as well, those half-men in their gentlemen's suits, a
cigarillo in the corner of their mouths.

But is Maria really the way he has tried to portray her in
his novel? Someone "who had experienced the happiness of a
good family life from early childhood and now carried it within
herself as an inalienable possession"? Well, yes, Maria certainly
did carry this happiness within her, certainly. But did that also
mean—as he had written in that same sentence—that she was
"born to be a mother"?

Bonhoeffer envisions her the way she had just sat before him,
over in the gray visitors' room. And envisions her in Pomerania
earlier, during his time in Finkenwalde, he the pastor and
seminary director, she the youngest Wedemeyer on one of the
landed estates nearby with its beautiful manor and beautiful
rural scenery and not inconsiderable domestic staff, probably
just like in his own parents' house so long before.

The little princess. But free of any of the precious "little
princess" behavior.

How old must she have been at the time? Hardly ten, maybe
eleven? She had clung to her grandmother's skirts, and that
grandmother—Frau Ruth von Kleist-Retzow, from an old line of
Pomeranian nobility of the purest sort—had at first impressed
Bonhoeffer far, far more than had her little granddaughter.

A smart woman. Resolute, quick to act, and full of curiosity
about Bonhoeffer's own work. She knew her Barth, whose
writings she virtually devoured. She had heard of Bonhoeffer's

own plan for a book and never tired of asking him about it. A woman of boundless curiosity and imposing understanding. "I'm just wondering why, Madam, you are not a pastoral candidate at our seminary," he had once said in jest. She, however, had taken him quite seriously.

And then there was the little one, her little granddaughter.

Bonhoeffer had once asked her what her favorite subject was in school. "Math," she had said, and he was not a little startled. A girl? Math? He had sooner expected "drawing" or "sewing."

"And what about religion? Perhaps religion too?" he asked further, unexpectedly annoyed by the sound of his own voice, a voice like that of an uncle which he seemed to be "putting on" as a sort of protective shield against this little . . . well, this little feminist.

"It depends," the little girl had quickly responded with not the slightest trace of insecurity or hesitation; "If the teacher is nice. Like you." Bonhoeffer had tried to laugh as heartily as had all the others. But he had not *quite* managed to. Then her grandmother had intervened.

"You can assure me that you and no one else will be the one to confirm our little Maria, can't you, Herr Bonhoeffer?" she had asked. Maria's grandmother was greatly looking forward to the confirmation instruction, which she herself had every intention of attending and every intention of spicing up with her *own* questions and opinions. In his own turn, Bonhoeffer had merely wrinkled his brow in a more fatherly frown, *again* annoyed at the weighty, affected tone of his voice. "But isn't she a bit young for confirmation instruction, only twelve years old?"

He would never forget the look Maria shot back at him with her blue eyes. Not disappointment, nor even anger. Merely astonishment. Her two eyes clearly asking, "So who am I to you? What do you even *know* about me?"

His gaze drifts over to the window now. A bouquet of dahlias had stood there last autumn. Maria had brought them, a bright, colorful greeting from October outside the prison walls. The bouquet had reminded Bonhoeffer of some lines written by Theodor Storm in his poem "October Song": "And though things go ever so crazy outside, Christian or not, the world, our beautiful world, can ne'er be undone."

Well, probably more un-Christian than Christian at this point, Bonhoeffer had thought. The old agnostic from Husum—the "gray town" on the north German coast, as Storm himself had called it. Yes, the old agnostic was certainly able to turn spontaneous emotions into equally spontaneous language—and to do so as naturally as if he were breathing the words out onto the paper. *If only I,* Bonhoeffer thought, *could allow such feelings simply to flow, unfettered, unhindered.*

At their farewell earlier in the visitors' room, Maria had stood up. He had taken her hand as always and drawn it up to his lips with a stiff, slight bow. She had smiled, knowingly, but a bit sadly as well. "Must you always, always keep yourself under such control, Dietrich?"

Whereupon—as he now realizes not without painful anxiety—he had blushed a crimson red, a man of almost *forty* before a young woman half his age, then stammered, "In your family, you learned how to express your feelings. We did not learn that in the Bonhoeffer family. . . ."

This exchange had reminded him of a day during the Great War. Their father had directed the twins—Sabine and him—to select several toys from among their things. "Not toys you already want to throw away, but something you still really like as well."

They had then gone to the Charité Hospital, to the children's wing. The little patients there had immediately sat up in their beds and gleefully called out in a cacophony of chirps and shrills, "Uncle Karl! Uncle Karl!" Little arms had reached out for Karl Bonhoeffer. He in turn had sat down on the side of the bed next to one child, taken another up in his arms, pressed a fat kiss on the face of yet another, all the while radiantly smiling.

Sabine and Dietrich, still holding all the toys they had come to distribute, had only looked at each other, puzzled. *Why does father never act this way with us?*

How utterly different was their mother, Paula, who could laugh and weep to the point that her son sometimes even felt slightly embarrassed, such as the day she had vehemently hugged him and waved the "red card" in the air—she had just become a member of the Confessing Church—with the resounding cry, "Now I'm one of you, Dietrich!" He had gently extracted himself from her embrace.

"Are you maybe afraid of women, Dietrich?" When brother-in-law Hans had wanted to know why there was still no woman in Dietrich's life, he had looked at Dietrich as searchingly and as quizzically as if he were trying to solve an especially sticky legal issue.

Afraid of women? Is that why, ultimately, Bonhoeffer had fallen in love with Maria? With someone who was, really, still but a child, nineteen years old at the time of the engagement? Rather than with a mature woman?

What Bonhoeffer will still have to learn—and not without some pain—is that Maria is no longer a child. And has not been for some time now. Nor was she ever really such in the sense of childishly naive innocence.

In any event, she is now a young woman. Alert, intelligent. But also critical. Almost too critical. Where he expects confirmation and affirmation, he hears objections and opposition. Gentle but firm. Will their marriage be the same way? Will Bonhoeffer no longer be the "director" as he was to his seminarians?

Bonhoeffer is not particularly inclined to think of marriage. Not here in Tegel, not just now, not when the much-anticipated trial has *again* been postponed to some indefinite time in the future because his brother-in-law, over in the other prison, has gotten seriously ill. Not now, when freedom is still not even remotely visible.

But he does now think of Maria. Of her in the visitors' room, earlier that day.

After his remark about having never learned to show feeling, she had come over to him—no, had *flown* over to him—utterly disregarding the guard who was present, had thrown her arms around his neck and kissed him so long and hard on the mouth that his lips could *still* feel the sensation. He passes his fingertips lightly over his lips.

But no bouquet of dahlias this time. A kiss. Someone like Theodor Storm would immediately transform that kiss into an appropriate poem.

Perhaps, Bonhoeffer thinks, he, too, should try his hand at poetry sometime.

"You oughta write something really nice sometime, Herr Pastor. Something that can help these poor devils here, something to comfort them." Knobloch. His words just after a jarring air assault last November. Bonhoeffer had then composed three prayers; one for the morning, another for the evening, a third for persons in particular distress. "O God, great misery has come upon me. My cares are about to crush me, and I do not know where to turn. . . ."

Nice lines. Insightful and sensitive. But now he needs to expand them into a proper poem.

No, he's no Theodor Storm. Just Dietrich Bonhoeffer. And he alone, Dietrich Bonhoeffer, is to be the subject of these poems, *his* most personal, private emotions and feelings, which at this moment, here and now, in thought, he sends out to Maria.

He will learn to show those feelings. To her. To everyone.

He tries: "And thus did you depart, beloved happiness, sorely beloved pain. What shall I then call you? Distress, life, bliss, part of myself, my heart—the past?"

He stops, listens. Somewhere a door closes. He writes further, "The door slammed shut. I hear the steps disappearing in the distance. . . ."

No Time for Saints

1938/1939

"O God, in the coming weeks
please grant me clarity
concerning my future"
—diary from his trip to America, June 18, 1939

THEY ARE BURNING ALL THE MEETING PLACES OF GOD IN THE LAND

On the evening of September 8, 1938, the Leibholzes—Sabine and Gerhard—returned to Göttingen from a visit in Berlin. To the considerable delight of their two daughters, however, they were not alone. Bonhoeffer and Eberhard had accompanied them, and the children were especially excited about a visit from Uncle Dietrich.

He was always confident, always in a good mood, always ready with a whole inventory of jokes and teasing. It had been a long time since the two young girls had seen their parents in such a merry mood.

Their mother seemed smaller, their father paler when Brownshirts paraded by in the distance, singing, "To the gallows with the Jews! Up 'gainst the wall with the Jews!" The daughters often heard their parents whispering together, and what they said with fearful glances always sounded dreadful, terrible, frightful.

Such as when their mother had remarked, "I cringe every time the doorbell rings. I always think: They've come to get us." And indeed, others in the city had genuinely been taken away, in the middle of the night, chased through the streets in their nightclothes.

"But that can't happen to us, can it?" seven-year-old Christiane had whispered to Marianne, her older sister. But Marianne knew only that no children ever came to visit the Leibholzes anymore, not for a long time now, despite their beautiful garden with all the trees laden with sweet fruit.

They saw their father pacing back and forth in that garden, always in a circle, as if in a prison yard. "And the worst part," Sabine had told her brother in Berlin, "is that this incessant, never-ending smear propaganda is now rubbing off on Jews themselves. Gerhard recently stood in front of the mirror and asked in all seriousness, 'Do I really look so frightfully Jewish?' Or he looks at his hands and says, 'Are these really greedy, money-hungry Jew claws?'"

On this particular September 8, however, the parents had seemed a bit more cheerful, their mother hectically running around, busily assembling all sorts of luggage and such. "Tomorrow," she had called out, "early tomorrow morning we'll be taking a wonderful excursion, so put on as many clothes as you can!"

They had set out in two separate cars. The girls had been allowed to sit in the backseat of Uncle Dietrich's car. He had sung and laughed with them and finally turned and said, "Okay, pay attention. I'm going to teach you a new song. . . ."

"You best pay attention to the road instead," Eberhard had groaned next to him. Bonhoeffer's driving skills were notorious, and in New York it had taken him four tries before he passed his driver's test. "Because in America you have to bribe the examiner," he had sheepishly asserted. Not even Eberhard believed him.

On the hills just outside Giessen, they had stopped to rest and to have a picnic on the side of the road. Although the children cheerfully sang their new song, all the adults had serious, sober expressions on their faces. "Wait a couple of days in Switzerland, then write Hans in Berlin and ask whether you might come for a visit," Bonhoeffer said. "If he telegraphs back 'Now is not a good time,' you'll know that you need to stay in Switzerland. . . ."

The Leibholz family drove on, the girls waving until they could no longer see Dietrich. Dietrich himself stood there for several minutes looking after them even after he could no longer see the car. "I wonder if we'll ever see them again." His friend forced out a laugh. "As soon as the nightmare here is over along with the whole 'thousand-year Reich' thing, then yes, most certainly. And that 'thousand-year Reich,'" he stopped laughing, and instead looked pale and sad, "well, according to the latest calculations, it will last at most another 995 years." They walked back to the car together.

Eberhard drove back to Berlin. Bonhoeffer remained in Göttingen for the time being. Sitting in the Leibholzes' study, he thought he could almost see the physical shadows of those who had just been expelled from their world. He felt like an intruder.

Bonhoeffer thought of the last words the dying Cardinal Mazarin had spoken upon seeing his art treasures for the last time: "I must leave all this!" Bonhoeffer now looked at the beautiful Baroque furniture, the paintings on the walls, the heavy Persian rugs. What would he himself leave behind if he suddenly had to leave?

Actually, nothing, he thought with quiet elation and relief. *I don't have anything. Only myself.* He turned back to his work.

He had in the meantime finished his book *Discipleship*. Now he was working on a new book. It was to be called *Life Together* and would tell the story of Finkenwalde, of the seminary, the House of Brethren, would describe life there, a life strict after the fashion of a monastery but *not* cut off from the larger world. A life, ideally, lived in concrete discipleship to Christ, ever ready to go out into that larger world and proclaim the faith.

Bonhoeffer wrote about the daily routine, about the precious experience of confession, and about the necessity of regular meditation (during which, to be sure, many Finkenwalde students just as regularly nodded off). He often wondered whether that life might be a model for the future or was already nothing more than a nostalgic glance backward.

My best time, Bonhoeffer thought again, *perhaps at that time alone was I truly, completely who I am.* Namely, someone who while standing outside yet stood wholly inside, a brother among other brothers and yet the one at the front, the director, the head.

But all that now belonged to the past.

Himmler, head of the SS, had prohibited the Confessing Church from continuing its educational and training institutions, and Finkenwalde had been shut down, its doors sealed after a visit by the Gestapo. Bonhoeffer himself had not been present when all this happened, had heard about it only by telephone. He could not help thinking about the day Franz Hildebrandt had telephoned to tell him about the church's "blessing" of the Nuremburg Laws.

For his own part, Hildebrandt had not followed Bonhoeffer's advice to leave Germany as quickly as possible after Niemöller's arrest. Instead, he had continued to preach in Dahlem, never forgetting to include the persecuted and incarcerated in his prayers for intercession. But they had picked him up as well. By some miracle, however, he had been freed again after two months. Now, however, even *he* had to acknowledge that someone like him could not remain in Germany much longer.

He had been able to flee to England. George Bell, who in the meantime had become a peer in the House of Lords, offered him the chance he had been hoping for, and Hildebrandt was now a pastor in London. His friend greatly envied him. The mere thought of simply being gone, being far away, anywhere . . . in London or Barcelona or New York . . . or India . . . still that dream of India . . .

Gandhi himself had written him. Dr. Bonhoeffer was certainly welcome to come if he was also willing to share the simple life of the others. Bonhoeffer was all too ready, and he read Gandhi's lines to his "Dear friend" over and over: "You will be staying with me if I am out of prison. . . ."

He put the letter aside and once again turned his attention to the German present.

The seminaries were to be kept going despite the prohibition. The Confessing Church was not entirely without recourse to various tricks and feints of its own, and a place had been found in the most remote backwaters of Pomerania. There superintendents suddenly needed a surprising number of young assistant pastors—and those assistant pastors were all to be drawn from the seminarians and their teachers who now assembled at the most inconspicuous locales for further study.

Bonhoeffer, too, was now an official "assistant vicar," a rather modest designation for someone who once seemed destined to become a bishop. He found accommodations in Schlawe, a tiny village that still had real city gates and such, not far from the small Pomeranian town of Köslin. "Well, it seems we're underground fighters now, theological 'irredentists' of a sort, aren't we?" Eberhard had once asked, alluding to the Italian freedom fighters a century earlier.

"Yes, I guess we are," Bonhoeffer had responded. He and Eberhard were just now hiking in the Harz Mountains, spending their vacation time together in Friedrichsbrunn. They stepped out of the dark forest of fir trees and into a bright, colorful meadow full of flowers. Bonhoeffer squinted over toward the mountain precipices, veiled in blue, across the meadow. "Perhaps we are also a bit like the early Christians in ancient Rome."

" . . . waiting to meet the lions in Nero's coliseum?" Eberhard laughed.

No, not Nero. Nor any lions. The lords and emperors today had other means. The church committees, Minister Kerrl's attempt to reunify the church, no longer existed, and the elderly Wilhelm Zoellner had resigned after various abuses in the city of Lübeck, a German Christian bastion. He no doubt sensed, not without a touch of melancholy, that he himself had become a mere figurehead, a pawn in a game of completely different powers.

The new man's name was Friedrich Werner, a jurist, now the virtually omnipotent chancellery head of the church government. And he was always ready—with either sugar treats or a whip, depending on the needs of the moment. Arrests here, enticements there. And he wanted to give his *Führer* a particularly nice present for his birthday on April 20, 1938, namely, the oath of allegiance to Hitler of every pastor in Germany. Those not prepared to take that oath would simply be dismissed.

The Confessing Church promptly snapped to and told its pastors they were free to take the oath. Most did. And the shame was complete when Hitler's minion Martin Bormann coarsely informed the church administration that, quite frankly, the *Führer* couldn't care less about this sort of birthday present.

Bonhoeffer could not help indulging in considerable schadenfreude.

He, the "Dahlemite," was already positioned in the "radical" corner in any event, an outsider subject to not a few disapproving glances. Does Brother Bonhoeffer *always* have to be so full of himself with all his protests against everything and everyone and *always* at the cost of others? For the rest, as an "assistant vicar" he was not directly affected by the oath in any case.

All the more, however, was he affected by other things. For example, by the notice from the authorities in Schlawe that he report for induction into the military. And by all the rumors of war circulating during this summer of 1938.

Bonhoeffer climbed on his motorcycle—which had cost him considerably more than he had wanted to pay—since there were neither train nor bus connections here in the Pomeranian hinterlands. Puttering from one secret educational institution to the other, he wondered whether, should things get that far, he would be able to refuse military service.

That is, would he be that courageous—or that foolish?

He had to think of Werner Koch. After being released from the concentration camp, he had sat across the table from Bonhoeffer, haggard and gaunt, his face now bony and pointed. "They called me the 'shrew,'" he tried to grin. And he spoke about the block over which prisoners were strapped before being beaten, and about the day a guard had thrown Werner's cap into the "death zone" between the fences. "Go fetch it, pastor!" He would have been shot in the back "trying to escape" had he gone after it.

He himself did not know how he had endured it all and then even been set free after two years. Bonhoeffer had merely nodded and listened.

Would they incarcerate him in such a camp as well if he were to refuse military service? Or did they simply put people like him right up against the wall?

For the time being, the decision was put off. Bonhoeffer's father had spoken with the commandant of the Schlawe induction center, a certain Major Kleist, an old friend of the family. So, at least for now there would be no "soldier Bonhoeffer" and no such decision to confront.

Europe, too, seemed to be granting itself one last chance to catch its breath.

Autumn came, and peace seemed to have been rescued once more. England's prime minister Chamberlain returned home from the first airplane flight of his life, climbed out of the plane, winded and huffing and puffing, and gleefully waved the papers to the army of waiting journalists—papers that would ensure peace. Yes, indeed, in Munich the German *Führer* himself had promised not to raise any more territorial claims.

That had occurred precisely when in Berlin Hans von Dohnanyi had advised his brother-in-law Gerhard Leibholz not to remain in Germany any longer. Why? Because soon, very soon, all Jewish passports would be confiscated and new ones issued with the stamp "J" on them. And if despite the agreement in Munich war *did* come, all the borders would immediately be closed, and closed once and for all. . . .

So the Leibholz family did indeed set out, emigrating from Germany by way of Switzerland and France on to England, where Bishop Bell had in his accustomed fashion graciously taken them in. When morning tea was brought to Sabine in her room in the bishop's palace, she was utterly ashamed. The previous evening she had already eaten the cookies that had been set out on the bedside table. How her brother would have laughed!

Otherwise, however, the autumn of 1938 offered little reason to be merry. Bonhoeffer, riding cross-country on his motorcycle one foggy, dreary evening in November, could not help thinking of the previous spring, when Hitler's troops had marched into Austria, and how enthusiastic the Germans themselves had been—everyone, even most of the pastors in the Confessing Church, even Eberhard. But not Dietrich.

Why not?

His thoughts from earlier returned, from the early Nazi period. Why had he never given the Nazi salute? Never shouted *Heil*? He had not done so when the Rhineland was occupied, nor when the Saar region was regained, nor after any of the other triumphs the regime had celebrated, triumphs that had made even the most resolute opponents a bit uncertain at least for a *few* moments.

Sometimes, amid all the enthusiasm and excitement, he seemed like an outcast to himself. And, indeed, that was exactly what he was, someone who cast *himself* outside the community of all the others.

But in the final analysis, were these others right, and he wrong? Was he simply incapable of sharing the enthusiasm of the majority, ultimately because it was, quite frankly, the majority and he the eternal prince who wanted absolutely nothing to do with a peasant such as this Hitler? And how on earth—Bonhoeffer's next thought—was it that precisely this peasant, this prole, was successful at everything he tried? How was it that an entire people—yes, an entire people— cheered him on the way they did?

He pictured this man who now called himself the *Führer*—the great "leader"—of the Germans. He had come like the messiah, had performed miracles like the messiah. But the messiah himself—no, that could not possibly be him. And then a thought washed over Bonhoeffer with such horrific suddenness that he slammed on the brakes of his motorcycle as if in shock.

What if this Adolf Hitler were indeed no messiah at all, but the messiah's counterpart, the *devil* himself in messianic form—he, too, a follower of Christ, but perverted and distorted and contorted into the deepest abyss of evil?

Bonhoeffer had always yearned for, always sought the *visible* God, the *visible* good. What if, however, absolute evil had now become *visible* in this one man? Bonhoeffer looked up into the grayish dark night sky, as if heaven itself might provide a sign, an answer. Nothing but clouds passed overhead, however; dark, restless clouds. And it began to rain. Bonhoeffer set out again on his motorcycle.

The motorcycle clattered over the cobblestone streets of Schlawe. At the parsonage on Koppel Street, the superintendent's housekeeper met him in the doorway. She handed him a towel. "Have you already heard, Herr Vicar?"

"Already heard what?" Bonhoeffer rubbed his hair dry with the coarse towel.

"Over in Köslin. It burned down. The synagogue."

Nor was it just the synagogue in nearby Köslin that was burning. All the other synagogues in Germany were in flames as well. And rocks were being thrown. Windowpanes were shattering into a thousand pieces. And many in Germany were shaking their heads. "But one simply doesn't do such a thing!" The anger of the people at large toward the Jews, however, was at least a tiny bit understandable, considering how that Jewish lout in Paris had just shot down some legation secretary or other. For his own part, Dr. Goebbels reacted with a broad grin to the rumor that this "people's anger" was perhaps not *quite* as spontaneous as one might think, quipping with a wink, "Well, let me tell you how that anger *would* have looked had I *really* organized it. . . ."

It was the night of November 9, 1938.

Bonhoeffer sat in his room in Schlawe. "Speak up for those who cannot!" Karl Barth had once demanded. And in a discussion of medieval liturgy, Bonhoeffer himself had spoken the sentence that would often be cited later: "Only those who speak up for the Jews are allowed to sing Gregorian chants." He could still see the horrified faces of the others.

But he did not speak up now. He only picked up his Bible, thumbed through it, looked for Psalm 74. "They are burning all the meeting places of God in the land." He marked it in pencil, along with the lines, "We do not see our emblems; there is no longer any prophet, and there is no one among us who knows how long. . . ."

Just get out of this country, he thought.

Who Has Chosen the Better Part?

"It was right for you to have stayed quiet, Dietrich."

"Do you really think so, Hans? Some of us did protest, like Karl Immer from Barmen, and Gollwitzer...."

"Yes, certain individuals. But what can one solitary individual accomplish? And loud protesters only end up endangering themselves. They never pose any real threat to those against whom they mean to protest."

"But..."

"Think about your colleague Karl Barth, with his foolish admonition—he had barely even gotten back home to Switzerland— his admonition that Switzerland barricade itself as fast as possible against Hitler's Germany, and his equally foolish challenge to the Czechs to rise up and defend themselves against Germany. The only effect was that he harmed everyone, especially the Confessing Church ...." Even among Bonhoeffer's own seminarians, Barth's appeal had generated considerable bad blood.

The slender man in the dark suit, his tie impeccably tied as always, had gotten up and walked over to the window. "Heroic posturing, however well-intentioned, accomplishes nothing. Anyone who has any intention of *really* changing anything in this country needs power. And needs the armed forces above all else...."

Bonhoeffer and Hans von Dohnanyi had been sitting across from each other in the house on Marienburg Allee. Both had come to visit Bonhoeffer's parents. Dohnanyi had come from Leipzig, where the past October he had become Germany's youngest judicial counselor at the Reich Supreme Court. His brother-in-law, on the other hand, was about to embark on a trip to America as a guest lecturer at his former institution, Union Theological Seminary, carrying with him a "certificate of nonobjection" from the military induction center in Schlawe.

Bonhoeffer felt a sense of eager anticipation.

He would be leaving the day after tomorrow, June 2, 1939, from the Tempelhof airfield, traveling first to London. Then everything here would be behind him—at least for a while—including his anxiety over the fate of his colleagues and his worries about his own fate.

He would no longer be a proscribed lecturer in Berlin, nor a disguised "assistant vicar" vagabonding around East Pomerania as if he were smuggling contraband. The kowtowing of his own Confessing Church would no longer vex him, and everything here in Germany—people like Heckel or Kerrl or Friedrich Werner—would be a matter of indifference to him, at least for a while.

Dohnanyi was still standing over at the window, looking out into the garden. "Your parents really have built themselves a beautiful house here. And now with the Schleichers living right next door . . ."

Bonhoeffer nodded and heard his brother-in-law laugh softly. "Always nice together, we little princes from good families. A tight caste. Sometimes I do indeed understand why some people don't particularly like oh-so-fine prigs like us. Arrogant, vain. And we are. But still," he fumbled in his pockets and—being an even worse chain-smoker than Bonhoeffer—lit up one of his unavoidable cigarettes, "we little princes still know what is proper, what is fitting." He looked around for an ashtray. "Things like this 'night of the broken glass' last November—it won't do, it's just unacceptable."

Bonhoeffer pushed a copper ashtray over to his brother-in-law and lit up a cigarette himself.

At one time, these two men had viewed each other not without a bit of skepticism. Dohnanyi: too rational. Bonhoeffer: too emotional. Ultimately, however, these opposites attracted each other, and the two men, almost to their own astonishment, had become something resembling good friends. Indeed, the older man had in the meantime come to trust the younger to an extent that sometimes unnerved Bonhoeffer himself.

He knew about the dossier Dohnanyi had prepared outlining with impeccable care all the legal transgressions and misdeeds of the new lords in Germany. He suspected that Dohnanyi's regular visits to Berlin were primarily to see Colonel Oster, someone who was directly associated with military intelligence circles around the mysterious Admiral Canaris. And he had sensed, instinctively, what Dohnanyi had meant when he had asked Bonhoeffer about the biblical assertion that all who take the sword perish by the sword.

And about what he, Bonhoeffer, thought about that. Might killing another person might be justified despite the fifth commandment?

"Probably," Bonhoeffer had answered, at first still rather innocently. He did not really listen more closely until his brother-in-law continued speaking as if Bonhoeffer knew exactly what the real issue was. "Of course, I would prefer a proper trial to an assassination. The guilty party could be declared mentally incapable, something an international authority could attest to, someone like your father, for example."

"Father would *never* agree to do that." Bonhoeffer had taken a step back, horrified. Dohnanyi, however, had remained wholly composed. "Oh, really? And are you sure?"

"Did *you* ask him?"

"He said yes." Since the trial against Marinus van der Lubbe, Karl Bonhoeffer had undergone a change of thinking about which his son had not the slightest inkling.

During these years, however, no attempts were ever made against Hitler's life, nor was he put on trial. Instead, he had enjoyed a virtually unstoppable victory march that included the invasion of Czechoslovakia itself in the spring of 1939—with hardly any serious resistance at all.

Dohnanyi also mentioned this on this day in May 1939, saying, "The only thing that will rescue us at this point is a war." When his brother-in-law cast a horrified look his way after hearing this declaration, Dohnanyi quickly added, "A war would finally prompt the opposition in the military to forget their Prussian obedience and put an end to this whole sordid brown-shirt bewitchment. They'd have the people on their side, absolutely. No one wants war except Hitler himself."

"Do you believe he genuinely wants war?"

Dohnanyi laughed. "Do you want to know what he said in a circle of young officers recently? That every generation needed its own war, and that *he himself* would see to it that this generation had one as well."

He returned to his easy chair and swung himself into the seat with a slightly theatrical gesture. "But even if Hitler were the most peace-loving man in the world, he'd still risk it. He has too." He watched a smoke ring dissipate in the air. "Why was he elected in the first place? Hardly because of his idiotic ideology. It was because he had promised bread and games—especially bread. And everyone—all of us—wanted the misery in Germany to end, didn't we?"

Bonhoeffer thought of the young boy without shoes and about his confirmation pupils in Wedding, and nodded.

"But then, as early as 1934," Dohnanyi continued, "behold! Already another major crisis—and Hitler's reputation as a miracle worker was taking a beating. And behold again! Fate—or he himself—dropped this alleged 'Röhm coup' right into his lap. And once more, he could play the role of savior. But now, five years later," his voice became increasingly urgent, "his distorted economic policies have run aground once and for all, and now yet *another* crisis is lurking just around the corner, but much worse than the one before. And the only thing that can spare him having to admit what is happening— is war."

"And you came to that conclusion yourself, Hans?"

Dohnanyi, a bit embarrassed, looked down at the tips of his fingers, yellow-stained from years of smoking. "No, no. Canaris did." Then added reflectively, "The most interesting person we have."

"Not Hitler's man?"

"Certainly not. And you know what he recently said? That when war breaks out—he's figuring it will happen in the fall—he would ask that I be assigned to the intelligence services. That I would be more useful to the cause if I were there rather than in Leipzig." He did not wait for Bonhoeffer to ask just *which* cause that might be, continuing on instead, "So both of us would be spared having to serve in Hitler's gleaming armed forces. I by being in the intelligence services, you by being in New York. But I envy you. You've probably chosen the better part."

He sighed softly as he stubbed out his cigarette and immediately lit another one. "Yes, indeed, I envy you. I also envy you for not being tied down, no wife, no family. . . ." He unexpectedly looked up at Bonhoeffer. "How is it that there's still really no woman in your life?"

This unexpected turn into Bonhoeffer's private life took him by surprise. It took him a moment to collect himself. Then, very softly, he said, "There was one, but that's over with."

"The thing with Elisabeth, your cousin?"

Bonhoeffer nodded. Yes, she probably could have become his wife, back in the early 1930s. Also a theologian, and smart, a kindred soul. In fact, he had almost abandoned his England plans for her sake. In the meantime, however, she had become someone else's wife.

Bonhoeffer felt no resentment when he thought about her, only quiet tenderness, even today, even as his brother-in-law, a relentlessly tenacious lawyer, observed him with unabashed curiosity through the thick veil of cigarette smoke.

"Are you maybe afraid of women, Dietrich?"

Bonhoeffer started slightly. He envisioned his mother, and thought of Paula Bonhoeffer's quiet devotion to his father. Despite his considerable love for his mother, a companion like her would indeed oppress and stifle him with her servile humility. *And in that sense, yes, you're right, Hans—I'm afraid of that.*

But he said, "A life like mine requires sacrifice. Like doing without a wife and child." And then, not a little bit startled at the boldness of his own comparison, "Do you think Jesus Christ would have allowed himself to be nailed to the cross if he had had a family at home?"

"Well, perhaps precisely because of that, yes, since in that case his family *would* have been the world for which he could have been nailed to the cross." The brother-in-law chuckled. "But I do understand you. Your only real companion is, well—your faith. . . ."

"Just as yours is law." Bonhoeffer, too, laughed. "And every speck of dust on it vexes you as if *you* yourself were being personally wronged. And the law itself, well, it's your version of theology."

The room was quiet. Outside the house, a heavy, sweet May evening held court. Here, inside the house, however, the two men looked at each other as if each had just guessed the other's deepest secret. Then

Dohnanyi got up. "Give my regards to New York. Enjoy the luxury of being there just for yourself. And take your time coming back."

"I'll be back here at latest in a year."

Dohnanyi looked at Bonhoeffer in astonishment. "Really? A year?"

"Unfortunately the induction center won't agree to a longer period."

"Well, but I'm guessing the induction center doesn't have much to say about such things in New York." His brother-in-law smiled. "Things are probably considerably quieter on Broadway these days than on Kurfürstendamm in Berlin. Here in Germany," behind his glasses, his eyes suddenly became wide and sad, "I'll probably have a lot less time for such tranquil leisure."

"And you think it really is right to leave all this behind here, at this moment?" A wave of anxiety suddenly washed over Bonhoeffer. His brother-in-law shrugged. "Each of us in his own place. Only you can really answer that."

Bonhoeffer climbed the stairs up to his attic room. "Dietrich?" Dohnanyi was standing at the bottom of the stairs, looking up at him. "You know the nice story about the two sisters who visited with the Lord?"

"Martha and Mary, yes, certainly."

"Well, Martha rushes back and forth in the house scrubbing the floors and cleaning and what not; in a word: she acts. But Mary just sits there, living for her faith, and Jesus tells her exactly what I told you earlier. You've chosen the better part."

He laughed, but it sounded more like a sigh. "Well, who is *really* choosing the better part now?"

A Crazy German—
Mister Bonhoff or Something like That

Several weeks later Bonhoeffer would find occasion to recall his brother-in-law's words with particular vividness. It was in New York itself, on the evening of June 19, 1939. He had left the stillness of his room at the seminary and, restless, had been drawn out into the noisy activity of Times Square, where he had then wandered about aimlessly, once inadvertently bumping into a stranger rushing by. "*Entschuldigung,*" he had said. Pardon me, please. But only later did he realize that he had spoken German instead of English.

Tomorrow, he thought, *I really do have to make a decision.*

Standing in front of a movie theater, he was tempted to flee into the darkness of the theater and let himself be distracted by Hollywood celluloid, at least for a couple of hours. It didn't matter what film it was. But he resisted. Not least because he knew only too well that after those two hours, all his thoughts and worries and anxieties would doubly befall him.

He put his hands in his pockets and trudged on.

During the journey here aboard the *Bremen*, he had still felt free and easy, had enjoyed the sumptuous meals, had gone swimming, played tennis. Or had sat in the salon, at the piano, had played his favorite piece—the waltz from *Der Rosenkavalier* by Strauss—or some modest popular tune or other, "Oh, I Wish I Were a Chicken." He had hummed along, and daydreamed.

The pianist *Dietrich Bonhoeffer* returns to America after a world tour. . . . Professor *Dietrich Bonhoeffer* back from a European lecture tour. . . . *Dietrich Bonhoeffer*, internationally renowned theologian and author, will be accepting a guest professorship at Harvard University for. . . .

And he was twenty years old again. The whole world lay before him. He had merely to choose; to reach out for it all. And standing at the railing with his brother Karl-Friedrich, who was also going to the States, he gazed at the Manhattan skyline rising up on the distant evening horizon.

Everything was just as before. Nothing had changed. Including Union Theological Seminary.

Bonhoeffer walked through the halls, responding to a thousand "hellos" with a "hello" of his own—without extending his hand or saying the person's name—and almost greedily breathing in the unmistakable smell of the rooms. He was staying in the seminary's beautiful, spacious guest room, the "Prophecy Chamber," with its magnificent view of the Hudson River.

I've arrived, he had thought. *I belong here, in New York's freedom, with its amalgam of cultures and races. Here, finally, I've found my place. No longer a prince. No longer the recalcitrant zealot butting heads against the inevitable, no longer the perpetual troublemaker. Simply the world citizen Bonhoeffer. Nothing more. Okay?*

But how peculiar. The first time he had been here in America, Europe had faded away behind a veil of mist, far away in the distance. This time, however, just the opposite seemed to be the case. This time it seemed much closer than before, almost menacingly close, omnipresent even. And Bonhoeffer was constantly catching himself glancing at his watch, silently calculating. *So now it's 8:00 in Germany—Now it's 10:35 in Germany—The brethren are just now sitting down to their evening meal; right now they're bowing their heads in prayer.* . . .

At such moments, one could imagine Bonhoeffer himself sitting there, head bowed slightly forward, moving his lips as if in prayer alongside the others.

One year, he began thinking with increasing frequency. *I can hold out here at most for one year.* And he was astonished at how enormously, painfully homesick he was. That had never been the case before—neither here nor in Barcelona nor in London.

But still, it was right to have left. For himself. But for the others as well, for he knew only too well how relieved some of them were after his departure.

Bonhoeffer has left! *Finally!* If he really had followed through on his resolve to refuse military induction, we here in the Confessing Church would again—yet *again*—have had to endure the most unpleasant, messy, unseemly scandal, with everyone pointing their fingers at us. "Look at that pathetic pack of pastors! Cowards, all of them! No appreciation, no feeling for the fatherland! Big mouths, but too feeble, too slack to take up arms."

No, Bonhoeffer belongs somewhere else, anywhere else, somewhere far away over on the other side of the ocean. And let's hope he has a good, long stay there. Preferably forever.

During these weeks, rumors of war were becoming increasingly loud, and Bonhoeffer could certainly have felt a sense of relief at being far, far away, here in New York, in a relatively safe place. Instead, however, he became increasingly uneasy. And sometimes, in the middle of the night, he would wake up, trembling from nightmares in which he thought he could hear his brother-in-law's voice. He would put his head back down on his pillow and nod his head toward an indistinct spot in the surrounding darkness. "No, Hans. You're the one, not I, who has chosen the better part. I'm in the wrong place here."

Working on his lectures, he suddenly realized that even though he could speak fluent English, the language was thwarting, blocking his ideas, as it were. And then he felt like one of those émigrés whose English is an insult to every New Yorker.

He went to parties and listened to people chat about raising children or about the most recent premieres on Broadway or whether Leopold Stokowski was a better conductor than Arturo Toscanini. He listened, smiled, and was politely queried about his own opinion. He usually just shrugged and remained silent.

He accepted an invitation to visit some friends in the rural countryside, saw giant fireflies buzzing amid cicadas, and was astonished—but at the same time yearned for the smell of fir trees in East Pomerania and for the brilliantly radiant meadows of buttercups in the Harz Mountains.

Then he sat in a worship service and heard the pastor talk about God as the "valid horizon of every Christian," then could not shake the image of a big, fat, garish red morning sun rising against the backdrop of this horizon. God as a spectacle of nature. Perfect for a gaudy, tacky postcard.

He had wanted to jump up, to protest, to speak out. But he remained in his seat. Let the Americans have it. Let them figure out how to free their theology from all this emotional baggage.

As if for a bit of consolation amid such thoughts, he had gone over to Harlem again, had clapped and sung along with the choir of blacks in church, "Oh when the saints. . . ." The preacher had stepped forward and spoken about two sisters of faith who had been lynched down south. "Let us pray that someday things like this will never again be possible!"

The entire congregation had then knelt down, including Bonhoeffer. He had prayed along with them, simultaneously thinking, *Shouldn't I be praying at a completely different place for completely different people? At a place where the Jewish question is no longer a joke?*

That evening he wrote in his diary, "O God, in the coming weeks please grant me clarity concerning my future." Then he went to see a movie with his brother.

The film was terrible. Long and garish and loud, preceded by a stage show, platinum blond girlies with exposed legs and almost naked breasts in the kaleidoscopic lighting of the clavilux console. Karl-Friedrich grinned. He seemed to like it.

"Not quite to your taste, little brother?" he had asked later. Bonhoeffer shook his head.

"I thought it was quite nice. Like most everything here. But, no, I could never actually live here." Karl-Friedrich sighed. "Too bad about the nice professorial position in Chicago!"

Bonhoeffer recalled how proud his brother had been after receiving the offer. "You're declining it?"

"Yes. I'm going back to Germany."

"I am, too."

Bonhoeffer said that so quickly and naturally and effortlessly that it surprised even him. And relieved him, as if he had finally loosened an oppressive, recalcitrant knot.

Poor Paul Lehmann, now a lecturer at Elmhurst College. He still considered Bonhoeffer to be the person best qualified to reform American theology. He had been indefatigable in trying to find a position for his friend at various American colleges. Then there was also the offer from Henry S. Leiper, ecumenical secretary of the Federal Council of Churches.

"I have an extensive and important task for you, Dietrich. The spiritual care of émigrés here. Who is in greater need of assistance than those who have lost everything, their language, their homes, their culture—in short, everything that has hitherto grounded them?"

It was just a week ago that Leiper had made this offer to him over breakfast, and for a brief moment—he took a sip of coffee and was looking forward to the first cigarette—the prospect swept over Bonhoeffer with a slightly intoxicating effect. He, again, would be one of the privileged, someone constantly in demand, someone who merely had to appear to have all doors open to him, even here in America!

Even in Times Square, the day before he was to tell Leiper whether he would accept the position, that same intoxicating feeling came over him—but then vanished again just as quickly; and he saw the faces of émigrés, different faces than when he was in London.

Those in London had still held out hope that the "brown episode" over there in Germany would pass soon enough. And such hope had provided strength for everyone. But what hope could he give them *now*, when war was imminent, and when ultimately this Hitler—the same Hitler who had already enjoyed virtually nothing but success—would win?

Wouldn't these faces now turn pale and reproachful? Wouldn't they immediately ask, "What are *you* doing here anyway, you who didn't even *have* to flee the way *we* did? What are *you* doing sitting here and preaching to us when others—those in Germany itself—need your words so much more urgently?"

Who are you, anyway?

No, not a citizen of the world. Just the rather peculiar German with the rather peculiar views. A "Mister excuse me, what is your name again?" Otherwise nothing.

But he was Bonhoeffer. Dietrich Bonhoeffer. He needed to become that again. "I'm choosing the better part."

Leiper reacted with annoyance when Bonhoeffer declined the offer. How on earth could anyone exchange this magnificently free country of America for a dull, dark continent like Europe? Paul Lehmann, who had rushed over at the last moment, was also unable to understand his friend's reasoning. But Bonhoeffer remained firm. The ship bound for Germany left on July 7. Bonhoeffer was on it. Lehmann stood on the dock and waved.

Once again, the two brothers leaned on the railing. Once again, Bonhoeffer gazed at the Statue of Liberty as it disappeared in the distance.

Of the thousands of possibilities that had seemed to await him upon arrival here in America, only one really remained now, namely, *to be Bonhoeffer.* He went below to the ship's parlor, sat down at the piano, and played "Oh, I Wish I Were a Chicken." And hummed along.

Back at Union Theological Seminary, the next guest was just moving into the Prophecy Chamber. He looked around in annoyance. "What on earth happened here?" Cigarette stubs everywhere, entire packets of notebook paper scribbled full as if someone had desperately tried to tether down in writing his confused, rushing, chaotic thoughts.

The newcomer, this time from Asia, turned to the young black woman who was scrubbing the floor. "Who lived here before me?"

"A crazy German. Mister Bonhoff or something like that."

A CARPENTER GETS SERIOUS

The small, dark man with the clubfoot had drawn the curtains, sat down in the plush seat, and was now smiling assiduously. "Another impressive event, my *Führer,* and what you said about England . . ."

The other man stared out the window as gloomy, autumnal Germany slid by. "Impressive, yes. Just too brief. I would like to have chatted a bit with my old comrades. But duty . . ."

"Duty," the other man obediently echoed.

It was November 8, 1939. Adolf Hitler, accompanied by Joseph Goebbels, was on his way back to Berlin in a private train from Munich, where, just as he did every year, he had just delivered a speech to his old comrades in the Bürgerbräu Keller. Though this year his speech had been shorter.

"You said you wanted to discuss our future policies with the church, didn't you, Goebbels?" Hitler had crossed his legs and gave no sign that he was particularly interested in hearing such elucidations just now.

Goebbels leaned forward so far that he was really only half sitting on the edge of the seat. "We must unfortunately assume that Minister Kerrl's church policies have failed. His concept of a peacefully united Protestant church—something I never really believed possible in any event—is simply not getting off the ground."

"Too bad." Hitler stared out the window again. "When I appointed Kerrl, I told him I was counting on him to make the unification work. He was supposed to tell the pastors that as well." Hitler's voice now became as deep and guttural as if he were back on the podium. "They had their chance, and they didn't take it. From now on I have resolved to dispense with any and all tolerance toward all this petty bickering and squabbling in the church."

He slapped his knee in annoyance. "These insufferable Protestants! I've always despised them, and especially their pastors, these squirming cowards incessantly wringing their hands and falling on their knees the minute any *real* authority appears. Now, Rome and the pope—that's something entirely different." A touch of envy drifted in among his words.

"And anyway, they could easily enough have found out exactly what I think about them," he continued. "It's all right there in *Mein Kampf*. But none of these gentlemen read it, none of them. Dead Jewish prophets are more important to them."

Goebbels nodded as if with profound sympathy and regret, not letting on whether he himself had ever gotten past the first hundred pages of his *Führer*'s book.

"I confess that, for a time," Hitler began again, "for a time, I held out hope that I might turn the Protestant church into a willing tool, or even into a kind of sustaining power for our entire Reich. I even agreed with Kerrl when he suggested we might create a *new* Protestantism that would be a kind of weapon in the struggle against Rome, just as during Luther's day. But I was mistaken. Unfortunately. But, then, I am not one to linger over mistakes." He leaned back as if that had settled the question for good.

Goebbels was not to be deterred.

"The only logical consequence, my *Führer*, is to *cleanse* German life, to cleanse it of the church and of Christianity, and to do so more thoroughly and fundamentally and intensively than has hitherto been the case—and to do so exactly as our party comrades Rosenberg and Bormann and the Reich SS-*Führer* have long been demanding. And, I might add, just as I myself have been demanding."

Goebbels, who had now become quite excited, pulled out a piece of paper. "This, for example, would involve, first, placing church finances under the *strictest* control. That will strike those clerics at their most sensitive spot, their purse. And, second, religious instruction, if allowed at all, would be conducted *only* in church buildings. And, third, all church youth groups would be disbanded once and for all."

Hitler hardly even seemed to be listening. His thoughts were apparently far, far away. But Goebbels's enthusiasm was still riding high. "No one should be allowed to enter the church until he is twenty-one years old, and then only after presenting *thorough* reasons for doing so—something unlikely for anyone who has previously gone through the Hitler Youth, military service, and the whole course of party indoctrination."

He gazed victoriously at Hitler as if he had already literally grinned the church out of existence. "The final goal should be a harmless sect called 'Protestant Church' that would be restricted to its houses of worship just as the Jews were once restricted to their ghettos. . . ."

A long, pealing locomotive whistle interrupted him. For a while the compartment was silent except for the dull, regular rattling of the wheels on the tracks beneath them. Hitler cleared his throat and seemed as if he were just awakening from a daydream.

"Well, yes, yes, all quite good, Goebbels," he began, "but let us not forget that there is a war, and the church *still* represents a moral power. Only after victory can we really have at it. Until then," he sighed deeply, since nothing—nothing—was more difficult for him, "we must be patient."

"Even toward this Confessing Church? Tolerate even the Confessing Church?" Goebbels was noticeably disappointed.

Again a prolonged whistle. Hitler seemed to smile slightly. "I will tolerate it. And I will annihilate it. The two are perfectly compatible. What is the purpose of war, anyway, with all its *special* possibilities?"

His gaze, now utterly void of anything even remotely resembling a smile, was now directed fully at Goebbels. "Most of these pastors are young—the age of compulsory military service. All of them—every single one—are to be drafted, without exception, and sent to the front, but *not* to where they might *not* be killed."

The train had reached Nuremberg. It lurched slightly and stopped. Hitler jumped up from his seat, visibly annoyed. "What's going on? Why have we stopped? We're supposed to be going directly to Berlin—those were my explicit instructions." But the door to the compartment had already been pulled open. An adjutant rushed in, out of breath, his face flushed. He could only stammer. . . .

"My *Führer*, my *Führer* . . ."

"Yes, what is it?"

"In Munich . . . in the Bürgerbräu Keller . . . an explosion . . . a *bomb*. . . ."

"Impossible!" the two men exclaimed as if from the same mouth.

"Yes . . . and apparently eight people killed . . . and many more wounded . . . probably fifty, sixty people. . . ."

Hitler had just left the Bürgerbräu Keller and was already on his way to the train station when the bomb had gone off. "A conspiracy," he said, "of Jews or Communists. Or the British. Yes, the British. Find out who's behind it and have them arrested immediately!"

But there wasn't any group behind it at all. Just a single person, a carpenter from the state of Württemberg. And not even really a politically engaged person at all, more an amiable but private, occasionally melancholy man—Johann Georg Elser, who was arrested a few days later at the Swiss border.

He had wanted to end the war. That, allegedly, was his only motive, something he maintained throughout the entire war. They allowed him to live in anticipation of a show trial after Germany's victory. Only at the very end of the Third Reich was he murdered in the Dachau concentration camp—on the very same April 9, 1945, which was to be so fateful for Bonhoeffer as well.

"An individual, one person, got serious," Dohnanyi said to his brother-in-law in November 1939. He could not help thinking about the generals the summer before, about their hesitation. Then Hitler's lightning victory in Poland had stifled any resistance before it could even get started.

"A fool, perhaps, but a fool with courage and character. He didn't waste time debating. He simply did what he thought he had to do. Perhaps," Dohnanyi sighed, "perhaps such individuals are our only hope now."

Bonhoeffer had already been back in Germany for three months. There was a war going on. And a larger war—a world war—was not far behind. Indeed, it was inevitable.

Tegel, late May 1944

May is the worst, especially the evenings. Pale blue sky, a luscious moon, gentle stars. Bonhoeffer stares out the window at the top of the cell wall, stretches greedily toward the bit of sky just barely visible at the top, and drinks in the tepid air like a person dying of thirst.

Just to be outside there. Anywhere. In a forest. By a lake. Or just on a park bench, sitting next to another person. Reaching for that person's hand, squeezing it, sensing the soft, warm skin. . . .

Maria!

Isn't that the way engaged couples are supposed to act? Content, in love, with eyes for no one else, nothing else? Yes, that would be the normal thing. But what is normal in their relationship in any case? Although he and Maria have been engaged for over a year now, they have never spent even a single full hour alone together.

A relationship in letters. In thought. But can that possibly be enough? Maybe for him, almost forty years old, someone who even in younger years never experienced the bittersweet feeling of being in love for the first time. Nor, really, ever missed having experienced it. But for a girl of hardly twenty?

The poem he had begun after her visit lies over on the table. It has become very long and very difficult. "The Past." That's the title he's chosen. His bold attempt to take Maria and his feelings for her as a symbol, a metaphor for everything out of which he had been so abruptly torn at his arrest.

> *Do you sense how I now grasp for you,*
> *clutch you, with claws, so fiercely*
> *that it must hurt you?*
> *How I tear wounds in you*
> *such that your blood gushes,*
> *simply that I might be sure you are near me,*
> *you corporeal, earthly, full life.*

Wild lines. Rebellious, despairing lines. Would Maria understand them? Or would she not sooner shrink back in horror, unnerved, and withdraw her feelings from him? He suddenly feels that these words—*his* words—would expose him, naked and full of anxiety, and that she might shrink back from that nakedness, disgusted, repulsed, horrified.

He jerks himself away from such thoughts and reaches for a slender book up on his shelf. He begins to read.

No, not Goethe. Nor Adalbert Stifter's *Witiko*, which has bcome his favorite reading material. This is not even a literary work. In dry, laconic words, here the reader is taught what a medic must know, and Bonhoeffer is cramming like a high school student. During the last air raid, an injured inmate died in his arms. He's determined that will not happen again.

He immerses himself in the book. But his thoughts constantly drift back to Maria.

What does he mean to her? Is he an idealized figure? The transfigured "Herr Pastor"? Smart, cultured, the way he appeared to her when she was a child? "And did you like my sermon, my child?"—"Yes, it was quite beautiful. You said 'God' exactly sixty-four times."

This saucy little tart! Impudent. Enchanting.

And he? Is he merely another father figure for her now that her own father is dead, killed in action? And then again, when he is actually in her presence, is he really not much different than any other older gentleman, a rather prosaic-looking person utterly without any youthful radiance around his rather roundish head? Can she really love such a person? But then why would she have said yes so quickly, so clearly, so unequivocally, without a trace of shyness or hesitation?

Did she even *realize* to whom she was saying this yes?

Again the poem. Again these pressing, despairing lines that he has rewritten and rewritten and rewritten.

> *It is as if pieces of my flesh were being*
> *torn out with fiery pincers*
> *when you, my past life, hasten away . . .*

No. He makes his decision. He cannot send these verses to Maria. Not yet. Eberhard will get them first. He can then consider whether Maria should also read them. Then perhaps . . .

Bonhoeffer sees Eberhard's youthful, impertinently contented face before him. His little brother! Now he needs him as an adviser, a spiritual counselor. In Eberhard's presence, Bonhoeffer becomes a schoolboy afraid of his own feelings, someone who—*but only a little, don't misunderstand me, Eberhard*—is pleading for help.

The door opens. Bonhoeffer smells the strong fragrance of lilacs. Knobloch is standing in the door holding two enormous bouquets, one white, one purple.

"'Scuse me, Herr Pastor. I know it's a bit funny for one man to bring flowers to another, but you just like flowers so much and all, and 'specially lilacs, like you said recently, and so I thought, well, what the heck. . . ."

Embarrassed, he places the two bouquets in a container shaped something like a vase.

"Thank you, Herr Knobloch."

"You shouldn't be always saying 'Herr Knobloch,' Herr Pastor. 'Knobloch' does just fine."

"And 'Bonhoeffer' for me. No 'Pastor.' I'm Bonhoeffer. That's enough."

I am Bonhoeffer. Fine. But who is that?

He asks himself that often these days. And especially now, in May, in the springtime, when his expulsion from the world of others is doubly painful. *I have my cell here,* he then thinks. *My fellow prisoners behind these walls. The guards outside in the corridor. That is my world. And I have myself.*

But who am I?

Well, that could be the first line of a poem. And he has already written those words down, in large letters. A call, a question. But what is the answer?

Knobloch has finished arranging the flowers and is now gazing at his handiwork—the white and purple burst of flowers. Satisfied, he tips his hat and is about to leave.

"One more question. . . ."

"Is anything wrong?"

Bonhoeffer hesitates. Will this man understand him? Or will he not be wounded, hurt?

Then, finally, still hesitating, "Who are you, Knobloch?"

"Huh?" Knobloch seems to suspect that the Herr Pastor might just be playing a little trick on him.

"No, I'm asking in all seriousness. Who really knows what he is? Do you really know that yourself?"

"What I am . . ."

"Yes, that's exactly what I'm trying to ask."

"Please, Herr . . . ?"

He still cannot bring himself to say simply "Bonhoeffer," nor will he ever, not even at the end.

"Me? Who am I supposed to be? A guard here in Tegel. . . ."

"And otherwise? When you're not a guard?"

Bonhoeffer imagines Knobloch at home in his parents' garden. Or at the kitchen table, where his mother serves him a bottle of beer, which he lifts to his lips and drinks. Or in a movie theater, looking quite dapper in a dark suit. Or at a dance, on the weekend, buoyant, a girl at his side. Who is Knobloch at those times?

"Nothing special, Herr Pastor, um, Herr Bonhoeffer. . . ."

Knobloch leaves. The lilac fragrance fills the cell. Nothing special. Fair enough. And what is Bonhoeffer?

Always something special, even as a child. First the little prince. Then the brilliant young man capable of enchanting someone like Harnack or Karl Barth. Specific roles, yes. Also in Barcelona and New York. But not yet Bonhoeffer himself.

Not even as an ambitious young pastor who had decided to study theology in order to be something *special* among his brothers. Someone whose career choice was supposed to make his father look up from his newspaper and raise his eyebrows, half in admiration, half in surprise. And that ambition extends even further.

"You're intent on becoming a saint."

That was Eberhard's remark at the house on Marienburg Allee after Dietrich's grandmother's funeral, and before that also Franz Hildebrandt's opinion, and before even that Baron Schröder in London. Ultimately, all of them are right.

Saint Dietrich. An almost sensual notion.

Perhaps it was for that reason, too, that Bonhoeffer had returned from America. Because over there he could never have become a saint. There is no need for saints abroad. But here perhaps, in this present-day Germany, at odds with itself, torn asunder internally, embroiled in a murderous war, and replete with its seething cauldrons.

"For heaven's sake, why on earth would you want to go back there? To add one more corpse to the piles already on the battlefield? Just be glad you're here. . . ."

Paul Lehmann. His friend. Who at the very last minute had traveled to New York to prevent Dietrich from leaving. "I have lecture offers for you all the way into next winter. After that, you are sure to be offered a professorship."

A professor in America. A good salary, a good life. Perhaps a wife and children. A nice house somewhere in the mountains. Fireflies in the evening. And no longer having to fight or struggle, or having to work in half-secrecy, constantly having to put up with new failures, new disappointments—like during the time in Finkenwalde, the time in Schlawe.

At those times he had often been tired, very, very tired.

Nonetheless. Standing on the ship's deck one last time with Paul Lehmann—a dull, bleating horn signaled "Passengers on board!"—he had noticed for the first time how much during those past weeks, how intensively he had missed Germany. Especially, indeed precisely all that. The struggles. The contradiction. Who, after all, was he supposed to contradict in America?

"It's like what happens to soldiers in the field," he had told Lehmann softly, not really expecting his friend to understand him. "They go on leave, are elated to be leaving the field of battle, elated to be back home. And then, soon, after only a little while, they feel something pulling them, drawing them back to the front." It was something he had seen happen to his own older brothers in the previous war. And now he felt it himself.

Again the horn warning the passengers. The ship had cast off, headed for Europe. That was the summer of 1939.

The fragrance of the lilacs is so thick now that it's almost intoxicating. Where on earth had Knobloch found them? In his parents' garden plot? Or had he stolen them somewhere?

Bonhoeffer should have asked him with a slightly severe undertone in his voice. Herr Bonhoeffer, the manor owner who watches over his people and over their morals as well, the manor lord responsible for all his servants.

Manor lord. That's how Knobloch had referred to him during their very first conversation. As someone from the sunny side of life, where there are only victors, no losers. People who give orders. People who direct. That, then, is his role here in Tegel.

But that poem—the one beginning with the question "Who am I?"— would enumerate everything hiding *behind* the mask and the roles—the fears, the anxiety, the melancholy, the precipitate anger at every, even the smallest injustice, the overwhelming flights of self-pity—yes, those too—and the pathetic moments of egoistic, whining worry about himself, and simultaneously the yearning for peace, both internal and external peace, and the hunger for beauty and love and for the fragrance of flowers and the singing of birds.

Things *every* human being knows. The feelings we *all* have. He, too. A person just like so many others. Nothing special. Not a born leader or a ruler or a lord. And even were he born to be such, the world out there, on the outside, would have no use for such lords.

> *Who am I? This one or the other one?*
> *Am I this person today and a different one tomorrow?*
> *Am I both at once? A hypocrite before others*
> *and a despicably pathetic weakling before myself?*
> *Or is what is left within me like a vanquished army*
> *fleeing in disarray before the victory that has already*
> *been won?*

Only one person knows the answer. God. But he's saying nothing. To the extent there even *is* such an answer, the man in the cell in Tegel will have to find it himself.

He looks for the heavy cigar his father had brought him during his last visit. A precious treasure. Being saved for a special hour. Like this hour right now, this May evening, this evening full of questions, full of thoughts.

He comes upon some photos. Those, too, his father had brought along. An infant lost in deep, gentle slumber. Bonhoeffer passes his fingertips across his lips and presses a kiss on the photo.

Eberhard's son. "Dietrich," just like he himself. His godson. Last May, exactly a year ago now, and a month after Dietrich's arrest, his friend had married Renate, Bonhoeffer's niece, Ursula and Rüdiger Schleicher's daughter, not even eighteen years old yet. And Dietrich had felt slightly pained, slightly off, for his friend was now a generation removed from him, and this little boy here, this little Dietrich, is already his great-nephew.

For his baptism Bonhoeffer had written a letter and spoken about the blessing of a good home and good parents, things that would *always* abide with a person—even if everything else were to collapse in ruins, the whole, unspoiled, secure middle-class world.

What kind of world, Bonhoeffer wonders, *will this infant live in someday?* What kind of world will Bonhoeffer himself enter once all this here—this cell, this stench, this period of physical incarceration—is behind him? Who will he be then? Again a "special person"? Or rather nothing special at all? Simply Dietrich Bonhoeffer? But *who*—again and again and again the same question—is that Dietrich Bonhoeffer?

Bonhoeffer inhales the fragrance of the cigar smoke, a delectable aroma for him, more beautiful even than the lilac. The pale gray smoke hangs heavy in the cell.

What if, at their last meeting, Paul Lehmann had prophesied that this cell, this room might be one of the stations—quite possibly even the final destination—in Bonhoeffer's return to Germany? Would that have been enough to keep Bonhoeffer from leaving America?

No, he thinks. Nor does he understand one of his fellow prisoners who during a recent walk in the exercise yard had groaned about how all this here, this whole mess, was just a horrible, frightful waste, a loss, lost time, lost life.

No. Nothing is lost. Not a single minute during all the years since he started his tightrope walk, the double game in his new, double life. "I have no right to participate in the reestablishment of Christian life in Germany after a war if I myself do not share the tests and trials of this time."

That, too, he had said to Lehmann in New York. And even now, even here, even as this gentle May evening recedes painfully away from him into the distance, out of reach, Bonhoeffer nods his affirmation.

Invitation to a Tightrope Act

1940

"People take whatever actions they must,
out of inner necessity.
Many people believe that resistance
is a question of will;
often, however, one is not in a position to choose at all."
—Emmi Bonhoeffer, wife of Klaus Bonhoeffer, ca. 1990

THE INTELLIGENCE SERVICE NEEDS YOU, BROTHER-IN-LAW

Naked. Nothing but a body. Fresh meat for the front. That's how Bonhoeffer felt on this June 5, 1940, standing in line with the others who had reported for their military medical examination. Young men, hardly twenty years old. Standing among them, Bonhoeffer felt painfully old at thirty-four.

Knee bends. Bending from the hips. Genital examination. "Cough, please!" Bonhoeffer grimaced. "Come now, don't be so squeamish, Herr Pastor!" The physician, owl-eyes peering from behind his wire-rimmed glasses, was fatherly and jovial. "You could probably stand to lose a few pounds, Herr Pastor. But, then, that will happen quite on its own once you're at the front." Then the piercing cry, as if it were his own, personal accomplishment: "1-A."

Fit for active duty.

Like a brand burned onto the head of livestock, Bonhoeffer mused. He was now standing in front of the red brick building housing the Schlawe military examination offices, squinting into the sun, hope still in his heart. *God knows where he will put me now.*

Where, indeed? At the front along with the other Finkenwalde students? Almost every one of them had already been drafted. One had already been killed in action, Theodor Mass, a quiet young man who had already been in prison once because of his faith.

He had been killed in September, in Poland. In the seminary newsletter to the others, Bonhoeffer had remembered Theodor. "God deemed him worthy of suffering for the sake of the gospel." Bonhoeffer had found his own words unspeakably hollow, so he added, "We should not try to fill with human words the gaps that God himself chooses to create."

When, he had simultaneously thought, will a gap, an empty space be left behind when he himself has to take up arms, or—his firm resolve—when he *refuses* to do so?

At a different time, in a different age, perhaps Bonhoeffer could have reconciled military service with his Christian conscience. But he could never have reconciled this new element—an oath to that man who at the moment was striding godlike through Europe, from one victory to the next, unstoppable, invincible.

Lightning victory in Poland. Invasion of Belgium, Luxembourg, and the Netherlands. Assault on Denmark and Norway. Beforehand the pact with Stalin, neutralizing any danger from the East. Anyone who now doubted the miraculous omnipotence of the *Führer* was nothing but a grumbler and a malcontent. And now this Adolf Hitler was even advancing toward France.

"I just can't stand to hear those insufferable, bawling fanfares before every victory announcement anymore. They honestly make me physically ill." Eberhard sighed, refilling his coffee cup from the pot that Bonhoeffer had pushed aside. The two friends had spent the past two weeks traveling around East Prussia doing "visitations" in one church community after the other. The Confessing Church had dreamed up this job for its awkward returnee from America after the preachers' seminaries had been prohibited once and for all in the spring of 1940.

Eberhard and Bonhoeffer had reached the town of Memel on this June 17. That afternoon they had gone out across the sandbar and were now sitting in a crowded outdoor café. "Very nice, very impressive, all the minesweepers in the harbor. And those bigger vessels are something like motherships for the submarines, I suppose," Eberhard had just remarked when, again, the fanfares bleated from the loudspeakers. Eberhard groaned.

Special announcement! Victory! France defeated!

Shouting and rejoicing and clapping erupted all around the café. Everyone jumped up out of their seats, some even stood on their chairs, every arm raised in a salute: "*Deutschland, Deutschland über alles . . .* ," the national anthem. Then "The flag on high, the ranks tightly closed," the *Horst Wessel Song*, the anthem of the National Socialist German Workers' Party. Eberhard turned and was about to take another bite out of his apple strudel. Someone violently poked him in the side. "What are you doing? Come on, stand up. Sing along." It was Bonhoeffer!

He, too, was standing up like everyone else, at attention, his arm raised in the Hitler salute. And he, too, was singing. "SA marches with firm, courageous pace!" Eberhard could not believe his senses. His Dietrich!? His face flushed, with wide, radiant eyes. The only thing missing was a brown shirt and the swastika armband. Then he would have been a picture-perfect Nazi.

The singing had finished. Bonhoeffer had sat down again, his eyes mere slits behind his glasses, his lips pursed, as if unwilling to divulge their secret now.

"Are you crazy, Dietrich?"

Bonhoeffer stared into the distance. "We shall have to run risks for very different things now, but not for some salute, or for some stupid song."

Somehow Eberhard no longer found the apple strudel quite so tasty.

They stayed overnight in the parsonage and, as was usually the case, shared a room. But their customary familiarity with each other had been replaced by a frosty politeness, as might be the case between two strangers who had met quite by accident in a hotel or a sleeping car.

"Sleep well. Good night."

Eberhard lay awake that night, the image of his friend before him, singing, at attention, his arm raised in salute. Bonhoeffer, too, seemed not to sleep, tossing and turning restlessly. Suddenly his voice spoke in the darkness. "You don't understand me, do you, Eberhard?"

"No, not really, Dietrich."

"Hitler has been victorious. And history is initially always on the side of the victor. And perhaps," Eberhard heard his friend sigh deeply, "perhaps in the final analysis this victory over France is something like a sign from God."

"You mean, God is on Hitler's side?" Now Eberhard was even more shocked than earlier in the outdoor café.

"Well, at the very least he is not opposing him."

"For me he's still the devil."

"The Antichrist." That was what Bonhoeffer had written Bishop Bell from America. And that is what he said under his breath now as well.

"For you, too? You also consider him that?"

"No. Not anymore. This house painter from Braunau doesn't deserve that much credit." Bonhoeffer had turned over on his back, his hands behind his head. He could still feel the rain on his face from that November night on his motorcycle when, for the first time, he had first thought that this Hitler might well be the incarnate devil himself.

"Satan is no doubt using him," he now said, "but he's too stupid to be Satan himself. Or at least not much smarter than the rest of us." He groped in the dark for one of his indispensable cigarettes. "Wait till the victories stop coming. Then we'll see what's left of him. Unfortunately, that will take some time, maybe an entire generation." The match flared up in the darkness.

"Don't go lighting up yet again, Dietrich!"

Bonhoeffer paid no attention to his friend's reproach. "The world will never again be the way it was. That has been our consistent mistake till now. We have always worked toward having things just as they *once* were. But no more. All that is dead and gone. We're going to have to get ready for a completely different age—even though we still have no idea how it will look. And that, Eberhard, is why for the time being we need to be as crafty as snakes, and why our mouths need to say something different from what is in our hearts."

The room fell silent. The two friends lay there staring into the darkness. Only the tip of Bonhoeffer's cigarette occasionally flared up brightly. He finally put it out and, with a deep sigh, pulled the covers up to his chin. "I'm really looking forward to the retreat in Bloestau. There we will be among friends, our own kind, just people from the Confessing Church. And our mouths *won't* have to speak differently from what is in our souls. . . ."

And that is exactly what Bonhoeffer did, with his customary candor. And the young pastors who had assembled in Bloestau near Königsberg listened to him talk about the mistreatment of prisoners of war, about the mistreatment of women and children in the occupied territories. "They are not our enemies. They've done nothing to us." The other listened intently, nodded, sometimes looking at each other in horror at what he was saying. Some took notes. One young man in particular did so, and with particular diligence.

"And now let's all go sit out in the sun for a while." The young men all walked to the meadow outside and lounged about on the grass, laughing, chatting. Only the one fellow seemed to be in a hurry, mumbling something about having to call his mother and then disappearing on the road to Dorfkrug.

"Yes, he said all this, word for word. And bragged about being registered in Pomerania but intending to preach all over Germany." The Königsberg Gestapo was at the other end of the line.

"Interesting, what you're saying there. Excellent that we were able to smuggle you in there." The Gestapo official hung up the phone and turned to the man sitting next to him. "Well, it looks like we have some business to attend to, Herr Colleague."

Bonhoeffer was still sitting with the others when the Bloestau police marched up, a couple of gentlemen from the Gestapo mixed in inconspicuously among them. "I take it this is some sort of denominational assembly?"

Bonhoeffer looked up. "And? Is that forbidden?"

"As a matter of fact, yes, it is indeed. As are church youth retreats. That's something you surely know, Herr Pastor Bonhoeffer."

The other young men's faces went pale. In the end, however, only personal information was taken down, nothing more. And Bonhoeffer himself would have forgotten the whole incident had he not been rudely reminded of it later.

"You're forbidding me from speaking publicly in the entire country? Because of 'seditious statements'? And I'm supposed to report regularly to the Schlawe police? Like some criminal?"

As early as 1938, after the Gestapo broke up a pastors' meeting of the Confessing Church in Dahlem, a prohibition had been imposed on Bonhoeffer—he was no longer permitted to set foot in Berlin. His father had managed to secure permission for him at least to visit his parents. And such was indeed now the case. After his return from East Prussia, Bonhoeffer was living in the house on Marienburg Allee. As was his brother-in-law Dohnanyi, who had been assigned to the intelligence services the previous year and had in the meantime attained the rank of major as the confidential assistant to the head of the Secret Service, Wilhelm Canaris, and his closest colleague, Colonel Hans Oster.

Now, behind the veil of smoke from his omnipresent cigarette, Dohnanyi observed his brother-in-law pace back and forth restlessly.

"What can I do now? They won't have me as a field and military-hospital chaplain. Those positions are reserved for people who participated in the Great War." Bonhoeffer had applied for a chaplain's position last autumn. The denial had arrived in February. "Now all I can do is sit and wait till they send me to the front."

"We'll have to do something to keep that from happening." Dohnanyi's delicate smile suggested that he already had a plan. But Bonhoeffer paid no attention to it.

"Two in our group have refused military service. They disappeared and are probably dead. I'll probably soon be the third."

"Not if you're one of us, Dietrich."

"In the intelligence service? What good can a modest clergyman do anyone there?"

"More than you might imagine." Dohnanyi stubbed out his cigarette. "Your reports about Soviet troop concentrations along the Baltic border were very, very useful to us." Bonhoeffer had indeed made some observations during that trip and then passed them on to his brother-in-law. Now, however, he merely shrugged his shoulders.

"Well, I only wanted to show my appreciation for the passport you had secured for me. I could wave it under every Gestapo official's nose, 'I'm on a mission for the intelligence service, secret commando thing, as you can see.'" Bonhoeffer laughed. "I felt like Mata Hari herself. But at one point or another it won't work. And then the game is over."

"Who's talking about a game?"

Dohnanyi had gotten up and walked over to where Bonhoeffer was sitting. "The intelligence service *needs* you, Dietrich. Seriously. And," he bent over toward his brother-in-law and almost whispered, "in fact, we need you doubly, so to speak."

WE CANNOT LEAVE IT TO GOD TO DO THE WORK

"Where can he be?" Hans von Dohnanyi repeatedly checked his watch. "He's always so punctual."

On this particular morning he and Bonhoeffer were waiting for Colonel Oster in the house on Marienburg Allee, and Bonhoeffer was actually quite looking forward to this reunion. He had made Oster's acquaintance years before next door in the home of his brother-in-law Rüdiger Schleicher and had immediately taken a liking to him.

And not just because Oster was the son of a pastor and had already confided in Bonhoeffer that he would have much preferred to become a theologian than a military officer. Hans Oster, who had already served as an officer in the Great War, held some very interesting views. For example, that soldiers—especially soldiers—should be the strictest pacifists precisely because they are capable of fully comprehending the horrors of war.

Bonhoeffer also sensed a political kinship, since both he and Oster believed that the murder of Ernst Röhm signaled the *true* beginning of Hitler's reign of terror, and that anyone who would commit *such* acts was certainly capable of other things as well, more horrible things. One could also add the book burnings from the previous year. Here Oster would cite the poet Heinrich Heine, "Wherever one burns books, one will ultimately also burn people." Heine's books, too, had landed in Goebbels's bonfires. Bonhoeffer could only agree with the prediction.

The two men thus found common ground in their profound and resolute aversion toward the regime—albeit a regime that at the time Oster still appeared to be loyally serving. On Easter Sunday 1940, however, the two had had an unexpected conversation that indeed frightened Bonhoeffer and that Bonhoeffer immediately repressed. Today on this bright, late-summer morning, amid wilting leaves and the anticipatory feel of autumn in the air, that earlier encounter almost seemed like something threatening to Bonhoeffer. He could hear the words Oster had spoken. "I must confess something to you, Herr Pastor, something that may very well horrify you and that may well be something you would call high treason. . . ."

But what, exactly, had he said? A bright voice interrupted Bonhoeffer's thoughts.

"Am I disturbing you?"

Eberhard, who was again spending some time with the Bonhoeffers as a house guest, came in. Dohnanyi turned to him. "No, no, not at all." He, too, was fond of his brother-in-law's closest friend, with his youthful, contented countenance. "You're certainly welcome to stick around when we snatch this gifted young man from the jaws of the battlefield at the very last minute."

Eberhard himself had been constantly threatened with induction into the military at any moment before Dohnanyi had secured a temporary exemption for him the following year as well. He grinned understandingly at Bonhoeffer, who was, however, slightly pained at his brother-in-law's lighthearted remark.

What right did he have, he wondered—he of all people, unlike millions of others—to escape an unpleasant fate out there at the front? Had his two colleagues—those who had been executed in a concentration camp as "subversives to the military"—had that same chance? Was he *again* the privileged "prince" with a comfortable, safe seat in life?

Outside, a car door slammed shut.

"They're here." Dohnanyi stood at the window next to the door and looked out toward the garden gate. "But why is Oster bringing Gisevius with him? Him of all people?" Hans Bernd Gisevius was a jurist like Dohnanyi and similarly a special officer in the intelligence service. But Dohnanyi's disinclination toward him did not come from any professional considerations. He simply instinctively mistrusted this man without being able to articulate any real reason. For just like Dohnanyi himself, Gisevius was part of the hard-core Hitler opponents in the circle around Canaris.

The men came inside. Brief greetings. Oster got right to the point.

"Let us be perfectly clear about the fact that things are quite urgent for our friend Bonhoeffer. The induction centers are greedily looking around for eligible pastors from the Confessing Church. Hence you, Herr Bonhoeffer, must acquire a deferral one way or the other. 'Deriving from the person's importance to the war effort,' as the magic formula goes. And you can defer only if we request your services. The application has already been made. But the bureaucratic hurdles take time."

He looked over at the others. They nodded. Dohnanyi sighed.

"What do you think?" Oster turned again to Bonhoeffer. "Is there any way to get through this period until our application is accepted, before anyone gets the bright idea of having you dispel your boredom by serving on the front lines? Can't the church give you some sort of assignment until we can incorporate you officially into our service?"

"What assignment?" Bonhoeffer laughed out loud. "What is there for a preacher who is prohibited from preaching?"

"Perhaps something where you write instead of speak," Gisevius offered, "something like a lengthy scholarly piece requiring lengthy scholarly preparation."

"That might be possible." Bonhoeffer nodded. "There are certainly enough topics for something like that. . . ."

" . . . and you should work on it somewhere where you can still take care of your requirement to register with the police—but can do so inconspicuously and not constantly be under the scrutiny of the Gestapo. Any ideas where you might find such a place?"

Bonhoeffer thought about it for a moment. Finally Eberhard spoke up. "Dietrich, I'm sure Frau Kleist-Retzow would take you in on her estate in Klein-Krössin."

"Yes, I'm sure she would. No doubt about it." The image of the courageous elderly lady with her inclination for Karl Barth and hairsplitting theological debates made Bonhoeffer smile. "She is smart and hospitable and gracious and . . ."

" . . . and has a very charming granddaughter," Dohnanyi added smugly. Bonhoeffer blushed, annoyed with himself, though also annoyed that he had ever mentioned the sixteen-year-old Maria to his brother-in-law.

"Later, after you have become one of our secret agents," Oster was speaking again, "we probably should not engage you here in Berlin right under the eyes of the Reich Central Security Office. They already get upset enough whenever we in the intelligence service engage agents in *political* matters instead of restricting ourselves to the military. What do you think, Gisevius?"

He nodded. "Munich would clearly be better than Berlin. Is there any place there you might stay, Herr Bonhoeffer?"

"My aunt, the graphic artist Countess Kalckreuth, would no doubt provide a room for me. She has a large house and is always glad to have guests. But do finally tell me, gentlemen," Bonhoeffer looked almost pleadingly from one man the other, "what in heaven's name am *I* supposed to do for you? Believe me, I'm the most *ill-suited* person in the world for being a secret agent or confidential courier or whatever it is. Eberhard here," he smiled at his friend, "he's always saying that a person can tell 'ten miles away and against the wind' exactly what I'm thinking."

Eberhard thought about the day in Memel and preferred to remain silent.

"That's exactly what we are counting on, dear Bonhoeffer." Gisevius cracked a slight smile, his gaze remaining cool and inspective. "Quite apart from your international connections—which extend all the way to Gandhi, if I understand correctly—and your language proficiency—you do speak English, Spanish, and French, as your brother-in-law maintains?"

"Only English really well. The others I just get by."

"Well, disregarding that for the moment, your honest directness itself is your greatest asset. Including for us. People will believe you when you say you do not support someone like Hitler."

"Who's supposed to believe me?"

"Well, your friends in the ecumenical movement, for one. Influential gentlemen who will trust you and . . ."

"I am to conduct espionage for you in the ecumenical movement? *Never!*" Bonhoeffer would have jumped up and left had Eberhard not put his hand on Bonhoeffer's arm, calming him. The other men smiled, almost as if Bonhoeffer's indignation amused them.

"Officially that is your assignment. That is precisely why we requested you." Hans von Dohnanyi now took the floor, "Unofficially, however, . . ."

He pulled his chair forward. "Dietrich, we've already discussed several times how our original hope—that a war would automatically be the end of Hitler—was a delusion. Now, after the victory over France, he is more popular than ever, and even his most resolute opponents on the general staff have developed grudging respect for him. But if we . . ."

He hesitated, reached for a cigarette, flicked his lighter until a flame shot up, then let it burn, having seemingly forgotten the cigarette between his fingers. "If we're ever going to cleanse Germany of this plague—yes, this *plague!*—we're going to have to start thinking in much broader terms."

He finally lit the cigarette.

"And above all," Oster added, "we cannot leave it to God to do the work. We have to do something ourselves. And the first step is to stake out the field in every possible quarter. One of those is the ecumenical movement. And that, Herr Bonhoeffer, is where your assignment will begin. To this point the ecumenical movement has been of the well-intentioned but unfortunately painfully naive opinion that one should first wait for peace and only then get rid of Herr Hitler, so to speak at leisure and with all due propriety. . . ."

"Utter nonsense! As if you could get rid of him like a stain on a jacket!" Bonhoeffer startled even himself with his overt gruffness. "He's got to go. Forever. Then peace will come quite on its own."

"I see you're beginning to understand us." Oster smiled. "Please persuade the gentlemen in the ecumenical movement that they should share your opinion. And then persuade them to persuade their *own* governments—especially the British—that they should conclude an honorable peace with Germany. Because there is a Germany *other* than that of Hitler and Germans *other* than Himmler or Heydrich. Germans like you."

"Then," Gisevius added, "you can leave Herr Hitler to us."

"And this Hitler will be no more, after the war, when we have peace again?" Bonhoeffer thought of the millions of people who saw Hitler as their *Führer*, the millions of people who wanted him to lead them into a glorious future. He thought of that day in Memel, *"Deutschland über alles . . ."*

And it is against these millions—Germans just like me—that I am now to work? Work toward establishing peace even against their will, a peace that at best will be an amiable understanding with the enemy? Peace, even though they themselves want "total victory," a triumphant response to the shame of Versailles? And then after this war, he—Bonhoeffer—would be expected to stand before them again as their pastor? To look into their angry, rejecting eyes? *You* cheated us out of victory, they will say. You're a traitor, Bonhoeffer!

I'm not made for 'no'. Had he himself not spoken exactly these words? Long ago? And yet his fate seemed to be precisely that he was always saying no, until finally, sometime, somewhere, something would emerge again to which he could say yes. But would he even still have the breath to say it then? Bonhoeffer felt a lump in his throat.

The room was quiet. The others just looked at him, having left his question unanswered. Bonhoeffer finally stood up. "Well, gentlemen, I hope that I won't disappoint you. Or myself."

The conversation was over. Dohnanyi accompanied Oster and Gisevius out to their car. Bonhoeffer stood in the main hall in front of the Bonhoeffer family tree, which his brother Karl-Friedrich had once—far back in days of their youth—so lovingly painted. "I still don't completely understand what it is you're supposed to do for the intelligence service." It was Eberhard.

"Commit treason. That's basically it." And someday, he thought, I'll stand here as the traitor Bonhoeffer among all the others, the businessmen, goldsmiths, senators. Eberhard sighed softly and then climbed up the stairs to the attic room.

"Satisfied, Dietrich?" Dohnanyi had returned.

"I don't know, Hans. . . ."

Bonhoeffer was acutely aware now of the conversation he had had with Oster the previous March. Of the way Oster had—seemingly quite by accident—asked him about his book *Life Together* and about the possibility of confession among Protestants. And of how this conversation had unexpectedly turned into a confession, and not an inconsiderable one at that.

Oster had confessed to having betrayed the German mobilization plans to the Netherlands just before the assault on Belgium and Holland, with Canaris's concurrence. "I do realize that this probably cost many of our countrymen their lives. And doubtless not those who were responsible for this assault. . . ." His usually optimistic, bright face had suddenly become gray and dull.

He added slowly, hesitatingly, "I don't care what people may think about it. But, Herr Pastor Bonhoeffer, what do you believe *God* thinks about it?"

Bonhoeffer had had to swallow hard and think about the question for several minutes. The offspring of a family for which the love of one's fatherland was still something sacred and for which treason was essentially the most despicable of all transgressions—such a son first had to overcome some substantial barriers within himself if he were to come up with even a halfway persuasive answer.

Finally, hesitatingly, he began, "These days it seems that the tragic choice for us Christians is either to will the defeat of our own nation and thus save Christianity, or to pray for the victory of our nation and with it the destruction of civilization." He then had to take a deep breath, so difficult were his next words. "I myself, yes, I would probably opt for the first."

At the time, he had no idea how quickly, how soon he himself would in fact be called to make that very decision—to be either a traitor or a nominal supporter of power.

Just now, however, his brother-in-law slapped him amiably on the shoulder. "Come now, don't look so gloomy, Dietrich! I have a surprise to cheer you up!" Bonhoeffer feigned cheerful curiosity. "I was able to get two tickets for *Hamlet*."

This particular performance of *Hamlet* with artistic director Gustaf Gründgens in the title roll had been the headline performance—and one that was invariably sold out—for five seasons now at the Prussian State Theater. On this evening, the brothers-in-law sat in the parquet of the Schinkel Building on Gendarme Square and, fascinated, followed the intrigues of the Danish prince as he searched for the murderer of his father.

Gründgens—tall, blond, in black tights, an angel of death at the Danish court with a singing, metallic, buzzing voice—played the role clearly and severely, utterly without self-pity, more like someone who has resolved to deceive the entire world—excepting himself alone—full of malicious pleasure in his own double game when playing the confused fool before others. Even the scene at the end of Act 1, when Hamlet is planning a performance of the parable of regicide with the other actors: "The play's the thing wherein I'll catch the conscience of the king."

"Fantastic. Even better than his role as Mephisto," Bonhoeffer whispered. Dohnanyi, sitting next to him, laughed softly. "Word has it he's performing Hamlet just so he can show off his perfect legs in tights." But Bonhoeffer's admiration was undeterred.

"A tightrope walker. That's what this Hamlet seems to me." They strolled through the foyer during the intermission.

"A tightrope walker just like everyone else during horrific times. Probably like Gründgens himself." Dohnanyi nodded, then lowering his voice, "It's no secret he's helped hide his share of people who otherwise would end up in concentration camps, Jews, Communists, homosexuals like himself. While on the outside he's the Reich marshal's pet, the regime's favorite actor, and a state official. So, a tightrope walker—with a double identity. . . ."

They were standing in front of a display case with a photograph of Gründgens. Dohnanyi leaned over to get a closer look. "You know, he looks a little like you, Dietrich."

"You think so?"

Bonhoeffer also leaned over. And indeed. A similar mouth, similarly notched chin, the same, agelessly smooth skin. Broad, open patches in his face, as if ready to take on any mask.

"Perhaps you're right, Hans."

A shrill bell. Guests started moving back to the interior of the theater. The intermission was over.

"Have you given any thought to what sort of piece you'd like to write if the church is able to free you up?" Dohnanyi asked just as the hall darkened.

"Yes, something I've actually been planning for some time now, a kind of continuation of my book *Discipleship*. A piece on ethics. I'll be writing about how the reality of God as revealed in Christ can acquire genuine form in the world. . . ."

The curtain went up on stage. Members of the court were about to stumble into the "mousetrap" that the prince had so cleverly set. Bonhoeffer's thoughts, however, were still lingering with his brother-in-law's question.

One chapter, maybe even the most important one, will be called "Ultimate and Penultimate Things." "Penultimate things" include something like giving bread to the hungry. "Ultimate things," on the other hand, include proclaiming God's grace. . . .

Bonhoeffer's own thoughts were sweeping him along while onstage Gründgens had just entered to applause. Bonhoeffer fell silent and leaned back in his seat. *Perhaps*, he thought, *perhaps my* Ethics *will turn out to be something like my last will and testament.*

The striking of a gong up on the stage drowned out his thoughts.

NO—NO DON QUIXOTE

Bonhoeffer had never been particularly fond of mountains. The Harz Mountains had always been sufficiently high for him. So it was almost with a slight feeling of distaste that he now gazed up at the chain of Alps around Garmisch. *Walls*, he thought, *insurmountable walls.* He turned around and trudged back through the wintry evening. Hard snow crunched underfoot.

He had been a guest in the Ettal Monastery since the beginning of November. Josef Müller, attorney and intelligence agent in Munich, had arranged for him to stay there.

"He's our best man down there. You can give him your absolute trust," Dohnanyi had said, relating then how at his behest Müller had traveled to Rome during the spring to establish contacts—through the Vatican—with the British embassy to assess the possibility of negotiating a peace after Hitler's fall. Bonhoeffer had picked up allusions to this trip and had seen his sister Christine typing up a memorandum her husband had composed for the generals on the basis of Müller's reports.

"Whatever became of all that?" he had asked after introducing himself to Müller in Munich.

Müller frowned. "Nothing. Our grand generals said nothing and instead merely gloated in their *Führer*'s victory over France. Right now it's difficult to convince the British that there is *any* real opposition to Hitler in Germany that can be taken seriously. Perhaps you, Herr Bonhoeffer," he made a vague gesture, "will have more luck with this. Whom are you thinking about contacting first in the ecumenical movement?" Now it was Bonhoeffer's turn to shrug his shoulders vaguely.

His military deferral had not yet been secured, nor was he really incorporated into the military intelligence service yet. "Then you shouldn't wait for all that here in Munich; find a nice place to stay elsewhere, somewhere farther outside. Your aunt's apartment will suffice as your official place of residence," Müller stated.

Bonhoeffer agreed. Although the animated goings-on at Countess Kalckreuth's house with all the artists from Munich's Schwabing district were certainly amusing enough, they were not really conducive to serious theological work. Müller suggested the Ettal Monastery.

"The abbot's my friend," Müller said. "You can live in the monastery hotel and eat in the monastery. The food there is not so bad. Benedictine monks *also* know how to eat well. And in the library you'll have complete peace and quiet to get your new book going. And what again is its topic? A new Christian ethics, if I understood you correctly."

Bonhoeffer nodded. Müller laughed heartily. "Well, God knows we can all certainly use that!"

Bonhoeffer had begun the book during the previous autumn in Pomerania, at the estate of Frau Kleist-Retzow in Klein-Krössin. The elderly lady had been *very* disappointed that her guest was disinclined to read his newly penned material aloud each evening so that she might *energetically* object to whatever it was he had written.

But Bonhoeffer was simply not that far along yet. First he had to clarify things in his own mind. For his own part, he was quite disappointed that during these weeks in Klein-Krössin he had seen very little indeed of the granddaughter Maria. Unfortunately, the girl was attending a boarding school near Heidelberg at the time.

So here he sat. A Protestant pastor in a Catholic monastery. And why not? His most secret vision of a real, *lived* ecumenical movement had always been to have both churches under a single roof.

"So, I'm finally making your personal acquaintance!" the Ettal abbot, Angelus Kupfer, had said on meeting him.

"How do you know anything about me?" Bonhoeffer had asked, rather surprised.

"Well, we certainly *should* know about the author of *Life Together* considering someone reads aloud from his book *every* evening at dinner." The abbot tried unsuccessfully to suppress a wry smile.

Bonhoeffer had immediately felt at home here in Ettal, albeit with a slightly bad conscience.

For what had he said after returning from America? That he wanted to share the trials of his countrymen? Well, was he really sharing any trials sitting here in the paradisiacal tranquility of this monastery, while others were out there in the field, at the front, and while the first air raids were raining down bombs on German cities?

Shortly after he himself had arrived in Ettal, his sister Christine also arrived with her two young boys, Klaus and Christoph, along with about a hundred other evacuated schoolchildren. "Berlin is pure hell now," she had told Bonhoeffer when she first saw him. "And the worst part about it is that *we ourselves* have generated that hell." *Indeed. And only we*, her brother now thought, *can find our way out of it again.*

In front of the monastery's hotel, "Louis the Bavarian," Bonhoeffer stamped the snow off his shoes. He then went up to his room and gently opened the door.

"Christoph?" he called softly into the darkness. Silence. The only sound was the soft breathing of a child. Bonhoeffer turned on the light.

Of course! The boy lay crosswise on the bed, his arms splayed out as if he were about to lift up and fly off. Once again, he must have left his own bed and climbed into the larger one the moment his uncle had left the room, making himself quite comfortable indeed. The rascal!

Bonhoeffer gingerly picked the boy up, carried him over to his own bed, and lay him down gently. He pulled the cover up over him and felt his forehead.

Hot. The fever was still there. The boy had come down with the flu here in Ettal, and Bonhoeffer had offered to take him into his own room and take care of him there. Nor was it merely concern for his godchild that had prompted Bonhoeffer to make the offer to his sister.

Truth be told, sometimes it was awfully, awfully quiet here in this monastic seclusion, and Bonhoeffer had often caught himself looking up and listening to every noise, even the slightest breeze, hungry for any sound he himself did not make. The company of this bright boy, the idea of being there for someone *else* rather than only for himself— indeed, Christoph's mere presence in the room, even if he were only sleeping and his uncle merely listening to his steady breathing—all that was very, very salutary for Bonhoeffer.

He turned out the overhead light, turned on the small lamp on the desk, sat down, and looked at the thick packet of paper with its dense writing.

So, his *Ethics*! His major work! The work that someday would still be here to speak to others even when he himself was not. Next to it lay a large, fat book, a well-worn and slightly discolored edition of Cervantes's *Don Quixote* in Spanish. Bonhoeffer could still perfectly remember the day when he had bought it from a junk dealer in Barcelona.

That day it had been very hot on the Ramblas, and dusty, just as it always was. Bonhoeffer had stepped into the dull mustiness of the small store, had thumbed through the worn copy with its greasy spots and dog-eared pages, become infatuated with the wonderful copper engravings . . . and then paid the asking price almost without haggling. The junk dealer was sorely disappointed to see this willing customer leave so soon.

In Finkenwalde, the book had then promptly disappeared, since every seminarian there could borrow any book from Bonhoeffer's library treasures. As he was about to leave for Munich, however, it showed up again unexpectedly. He packed it up with everything else and now thumbed through it again until he found his favorite illustration—Don Quixote with a rusty lance storming the windmill sails—was that not Bonhoeffer himself?

Christoph turned over on his other side in the bed, mumbling unintelligibly in his sleep. Bonhoeffer pulled the covers up to his shoulders again and gently stroked his head.

No, I'm no Don Quixote, he thought. *That's one thing I'm certainly not.*

The knight with the sad appearance came from a different world and fought with the wrong weapons. Bonhoeffer, on the other hand, stood smack in the middle of this reality here, sharpening his own weapons with the book over on the table, a book that was to show how *worldliness* was decidedly *not* something apart from Christ, nor the existence of a Christian something apart from *this* world, *our* world.

Christ died for the world. And only in that world, here and now, not in some faraway eternity, is he a symbol for all humanity. *That* was the fundamental idea in his *Ethics*. Everything else would follow from that one idea, an understanding of the world that might later offer support in an age *without war* and *without* Hitler.

The child across the room again mumbled several disconnected words. Should Bonhoeffer awaken the child and take his temperature? No. Just let him sleep. That's the best medicine. So he sat back down at the desk and listened to the nocturnal silence.

Christ in the garden of Gethsemane, he thought, *the night before Golgotha, the only one awake.* But is that not the same situation in which *all* Christians find themselves, in *all* ages? Indeed, are we genuinely Christian only when we do *not* allow the individual to remain awake alone? And instead all share that anxiety and loneliness in the deepest, darkest night? "My father, if it is possible, let this cup pass from me. . . ."

That had been Jesus' prayer at the time. It was not answered. Or was it? The Lord had indeed "allowed the cup to pass" by having his son drain it to the dregs on the cross of Golgotha. What a terrible thought. Bonhoeffer shuddered.

In the final analysis, he thought, every *true faith is terrible in this way.* Neither consolation nor comfort, but instead a perpetual and perpetually new challenge. But how can one express that in words? Without arrogance and pedantry? Difficult. Enormously difficult. Perhaps—the thought suddenly washed over him—perhaps he would never finish this book here. Perhaps what he had to say would never be said.

Christoph's breathing was now quiet and steady. His uncle sat at the desk awhile longer and then turned out the light. He was now staring into the darkness.

Christmas approached. Visitors came to Ettal. Eberhard, with

Damocles's sword still hanging heavy over him—namely, the prospect of abruptly being called up for induction. Dohnanyi, reunited with his family. And then also Franz Gürtner, visiting his son who was attending the Ettal Monastery boarding school. Gürtner, the minister of justice, was the only person in Hitler's cabinet who had been brought along from the earlier period of the Weimar Republic. He was also Dohnanyi's mentor, his good friend, and for years now his superior.

Gürtner, usually strict, firm, and optimistic—for many people a kind of guarantee that despite all appearances, Germany was still a nation governed by the rule of law—had just come from occupied Poland. He seemed sickly, distraught, and worn out from lack of sleep. After his surprising death the following January, Bonhoeffer reproached himself for having persuaded the ailing man, who was pushing sixty at the time, to take a walk with him around the monastery on a particularly cold day.

But he wanted to speak with him about the obviously intensified call-ups of pastors of the Confessing Church into the military, wanted to ask him to try to persuade Kerrl, the minister of church affairs, to put a stop to it.

"Yes, certainly," Gürtner had wheezed between violent fits of coughing, adding with a half-choked voice, "Let's hope that Kerrl wields enough influence to bring that about." It seemed to Bonhoeffer, however, that Gürtner's thoughts were wholly elsewhere.

"I'm not permitted to tell you what I saw and heard in Poland," he suddenly blurted out, standing motionless in the deep snow, "Absolutely *horrific*. It makes you just want to run away, far away, and hide. But that's exactly what we *cannot* do, Bonhoeffer."

He looked Bonhoeffer in the eye. "Every one of us must remain at his post. For the chance that we might prevent this or that crime from taking place, or save this or that poor devil." He walked on with laboriously slow steps, supporting himself on the younger man's arm. "I'm an old man now. I don't have much more time. But men like you and your brother-in-law—you are my hope. I only hope I'm not decei— . . ." A fresh fit of uncontrolled coughing cut him off in mid-sentence.

Christmas had arrived, and they were all now sitting together—

the abbot, his colleague from the nearby monastery in Metten, some gentlemen from the Vatican, others from the Munich branch of the military intelligence service, Josef Müller, Dohnanyi, Eberhard, and Bonhoeffer. Bonhoeffer had been to Munich in the meantime to shop for Christmas presents. In a stationary store he had found postcards with Altdorfer's painting *Silent Night*, showing the holy family in a hut in the middle of a desolate, devastated landscape.

He found the scene quite appropriate, so he immediately bought a hundred of the postcards and sent them to all the Finkenwalde alumni as a Christmas greeting.

His Finkenwaldians! Scattered to the four winds now, on every front of the war, and yet on this Christmas Eve closer to him than ever! And it was precisely the most recalcitrant, stubborn, and unmanageable of his former students who now wrote him the most affectionate, grateful letters. It was of these students that he now thought while the others discussed prospects for peace.

"I see no possibility at all. Not for a long time," Dohnanyi said straight out. "Things are more likely only going to get worse, much worse."

A long pause in the conversation.

"Russia as well?" someone finally asked, hesitatingly.

"Russia as well," Dohnanyi nodded.

Bonhoeffer went back to the hotel before the others. Again the surrounding mountains, again oppressively close, and above them the spectacular, crystal-clear winter sky laden with stars. Bonhoeffer looked up at the snow-covered peaks.

Don Quixote would storm you like the wall of an invincible fortress, he thought, imagining himself again back in Barcelona, up on the Tibidabo, the tempter right beside him. "All these I will give you. . . ."

"Oh, tempter, tempter," Bonhoeffer sighed, "what on earth am I supposed to do with all your kingdoms when in the final analysis the only thing I'll end up with is a small hut in the midst of devastation and ruins? Just like the Altdorfer holy family."

A shooting star blitzed across the sky. Bonhoeffer did not really know what he should wish for. . . .

Tegel, June 30, 1944

A visitor. Not his parents, always a bit embarrassed and shy, as if asking Dietrich's pardon for not being able to do more for him than bring packages with clean underwear, books, tobacco, and food. Nor Eberhard, with that pained look of concern in his eyes for the welfare of his friend. Nor Maria, with her affectionately cheeky, slightly audacious personality. This time there are heavier footsteps, the brush of leather. The guards respectfully raise their hands to their caps in salute.

Paul von Hase. Major general. City commandant of Berlin. Uncle Paul. Standing there in the Tegel guardroom, legs wide apart, hands on his hips, face beet red. He laughs his loud, resonant officers-club laugh. "Well, I just had to come by and check and see how my oh-so-treasonous Herr Nephew is doing here in the slammer. So, do bread and water still taste good? Do the rats still squeak inconsiderately at night? Do the chains rattle too loudly? And do all of you at least have a *couple* of dungeon whores on the premises here, hmm?"

His hand fell on Bonhoeffer's shoulder with a dull slap. "Well, you look very good indeed, boy. A bit slimmer, but nice and tan in your face. Like you just came from summer vacation. So, how was it in Biarritz? Or was it Ahlbeck this time?"

As a matter of fact, the walks in the outdoor prison courtyard had indeed tanned Bonhoeffer's face, and the meager diet had indeed taken a few pounds off his otherwise somewhat pudgy body. He had been recently photographed together with some others and was astonished when he saw the pictures and understood Knobloch's earlier references to the "manor lord."

No elements of intimidation or anxiety in that picture. His face comes across firm and clear and open, his smile warm and natural. An inner calmness seems to exude from him, like someone who has finally come to peace with himself. *Perhaps,* he thought upon seeing the picture, *perhaps I have used this time in Tegel to become Bonhoeffer.*

To his uncle he merely responds, "Yes, I'm doing well. And the others?"

"Not so well. Especially your brother-in-law Hans." He leans forward, speaking softly, "Did you know he's sick?"

Bonhoeffer nods. "His legs. Varicose veins. The old Dohnanyi family ailment."

"And now," his uncle sighs, "it seems diphtheria has been added as well. It's going to be a while before the trial can take place."

"I wish it were finally here." Even back in April, his attorney, Kurt Wergin, a friend of brother Klaus, had tried to prepare Bonhoeffer for the possibility that the trial would not begin in May, and that they would probably have to anticipate a lengthy delay.

"Just don't get too impatient, Nephew." His uncle wrinkles his brow. "It's actually not a bad thing—for everyone—if the trial is, well, postponed awhile. You've got to understand that military intelligence can't do much for any of you now. Since your arrest, Oster has been transferred to the armed forces *Führer*-reserve and is for all practical purposes under house arrest. Canaris, however . . ."

He again leans over and whispers, "Surely you've heard that he was relieved of his post in February and the office of military intelligence transferred to the Reich Central Security Office under our friend Himmler?"

Yes, that, too, his father's letter had related to him, a letter Knobloch was able to smuggle past the prison censor.

"Quite a few things have gone wrong lately, so much so that suspicions have arisen that it can't just be a coincidence. Canaris, however, does seem more interested in his two dachshunds than in the ultimate victory of our beloved *Führer*." Bonhoeffer's uncle shrugs, as if resigned. Then he brightens up. "But let's celebrate our reunion here today so you can see what a fine old uncle you have. I've brought you something quite fine. Champagne."

Real champagne. Several bottles. His uncle uncorks the first and fills the glasses he has brought along. "Cheers, Dietrich!" And, "What shall we drink to?"

"To peace," is what Bonhoeffer impulsively wants to say, but he stops, hesitates. "To the first day *after* this time here in Tegel. To the first steps out into freedom, hoping that it won't be too difficult for me and that the world out there will still be recognizable and bearable for someone like me. . . ."

"Do you have any doubts?"

They sit there in the guardroom, holding champagne glasses as if celebrating some Bonhoeffer family occasion over in the house on the Marienburg Allee. Power sitting next to powerlessness; the high military officer von Hase next to the diminutive prisoner Bonhoeffer. Bonhoeffer looks down at the floor, his words come very softly and very slowly. His uncle has trouble understanding him.

"I believe I've become a quite different person here in prison. No more of that burning ambition like earlier."

He pauses and considers for a moment. "Yes, that's how I was. Burning ambition. Ultimately that's primarily why my opposition to the state was so resolute. Because the state offered my ambition absolutely no nourishment. Because I had to satisfy that ambition somewhere else. In rejection. In protest. In opposition."

He empties his glass with a healthy, greedy drink, then laughs as he passes his hand over his lips. "All the things I could have become! A grand churchman, of course, the bishop of Berlin or the poor people's pastor in Wedding, at the very top or at the very bottom—but nothing in between. Ultimately even a saint or at least a penitent who takes all the sins of this world on his own shoulders just as the Christ took up the cross on his way to Golgotha."

His uncle refills their glasses. The champagne has not only loosened new ideas and thoughts in Bonhoeffer's head; it has also loosened his tongue. Almost to his own amazement, since in earlier days he would never—*never*—have opened up this way to this particular uncle, never have revealed to him his most intimate emotions like this.

"Perhaps it just depends . . ."

"Depends on what, my boy?"

"On *not* becoming something great, *not* being so intent on making something special of oneself. But just on being *oneself*, and then just throwing oneself into God's arms, just as one is. Naively, like a child, no qualifications—and no looking in the mirror to see how *grand* one looks in the process. In the final analysis, *that's* the only true faith."

Although his uncle is listening intently, it's impossible to tell whether he is genuinely able to follow his nephew's words. Bonhoeffer becomes even more animated.

"That's how I want to return to the world after all this is behind me. As a completely ordinary person. Perhaps a very good pastor, perhaps not so good, but that's not the point . . ."

"And where might that be?"

"Anywhere. In the Lüneburg Heath perhaps, or in the Harz Mountains or in Eastern Pomerania. . . ."

"With a pastor's wife, of course, and the customary ten pastor's children . . . ?" His uncle smiles wryly and pours yet another glass.

"Well, maybe not ten, but children in any case for sure." Bonhoeffer is astonished at his own words. Previously he had *always* put aside all thoughts regarding his own progeny and had never really seen himself as a father in any case. That would have seemed like a betrayal of his own childhood, a childhood that he had never entirely turned loose as long as his parents' house had remained his home and the fixed point in his life.

But the idea of his own house, his own gaggle of children, his own fixed point, belonging to him alone, the center of his own, small world. It has only been here in Tegel that he has finally entertained such thoughts, finally overcome his shyness at even allowing such thoughts. And now precisely these thoughts have become increasingly natural for him—and increasingly attractive.

At most he wonders whether Maria could ever get used to the role of the upright pastor's wife. But the thought of having children with her like Hans and Christine's two little boys—Klaus and Christoph—or the two Leibholz girls—Marianne and Christiane. Or knowing that he had a rosy bundle of joy at home like Eberhard's infant son. . . .

"Why the smile, Nephew?"

Bonhoeffer starts and quickly extends his glass. His uncle opens the next bottle.

"In any case, I want to be something completely normal. Simply Dietrich Bonhoeffer."

His uncle grins slightly. "I fear you Bonhoeffers utterly lack the talent for that which is 'normal.'" Bonhoeffer sighs and nods.

"But still. I intend to try." Angry defiance rises up in Bonhoeffer. "But I have to get *out* of here. *Out*."

"Patience, Nephew, patience!"

"But for how *long*? I'm afraid I'm going to completely forget what the world there on the outside looks like, smells like, tastes like, feels like, or whether it even still *exists*. But maybe that's exactly what our enemies want. Maybe that's why they keep postponing the trial. . . ."

"Are you sure it's your enemies?"

Bonhoeffer stares at his uncle. Has he just suggested, just hinted that *friends* are behind all the postponements? That *friends* have been consciously delaying things?

Paul von Hase's gaze reflects a cool, penetrating superiority, as if he understands only *too* well what he has just said. "They just acquitted Josef Müller from Munich—and yet are *still* keeping him in custody, allegedly on Himmler's personal orders. And you're probably already familiar with the fate of your colleague Niemöller."

He, too, had been acquitted six months after his arrest—and yet Gestapo officials had been waiting for him on the very steps of the courthouse as he emerged. And now he was languishing in some concentration camp as a "personal prisoner of the *Führer*."

"Patience. Just try to have patience, Nephew. I can't urge you strongly enough." His uncle stands up and looks around. "It's not so very bad here in any case. And certainly better than in a concentration camp." He walks over to the door, checks to see if anyone is eavesdropping, then comes back over to Bonhoeffer.

"It won't be very much longer." He smiles. "Just one more step, and then we'll look back on all this like a bad dream, and we'll drink our next bottle of champagne someplace completely different and will toast something completely different than we have here today."

He fills the glasses and gives Bonhoeffer one. They toast. Silently. There is no need to say what they are toasting or what they are thinking.

Cheers!

Silent Witnesses
to Evil Deeds

1941/1942

"I pray for the defeat of my country,
for I believe
that is the only possibility
of paying for all the suffering
which my country has caused in the world."
—Dietrich Bonhoeffer, 1941

What Have They Turned This Man Into?

In his apartment in Basel, located on St. Albanring, Karl Barth stood at the window for several minutes looking out at the foothills of the Black Forest, then turned to his wife and said, "Nelly, you won't believe the phone call I just received."

Nelly Barth looked up full of curiosity.

"The police were just on the phone, the office of aliens. Bonhoeffer—you remember him—has just entered Switzerland. At the border our customs agents asked him for the name of someone who could vouch for him. . . ."

"And?"

"He gave them my name."

"And you vouched for him?"

"Of course I did. But I'm feeling a little uneasy. How can someone like that, someone who, after all, is opposed to virtually everything going on over there in Germany," Barth sat down with a slight groan, "how can someone like that get a passport and the funds to travel to Switzerland? Something doesn't add up here. . . ."

Nelly Barth went back to her sewing. "You're not saying he's become a Nazi, are you?"

Barth chewed nervously on his lower lip. "How can you know? Someone who's looking for a leader. That's what I said about him before. Well, perhaps he's found that leader, that *Führer*." He sighed. "After all, we've certainly already had enough surprises in this regard. But Bonhoeffer? Him of all people?"

Barth's face, always morose, became even more so. "What on earth could they have tuned this poor fellow into? And I was the one urging him to stay in Germany, to tough it out. Now I don't know what I should feel toward him—anxiety or a bad conscience. . . ."

He looked back up at the mountains. "Quite honestly, I would prefer not to see him again."

And indeed, their reunion was initially one without any particular warmth. Their conversations revolved almost exclusively around purely theological issues, and Bonhoeffer sensed the other man was observing him with skepticism and scarcely veiled suspicion. In fact, these feelings almost ruined the four weeks he had been granted in Switzerland for his first assignment.

"What on earth does Barth have against me?" he asked Erwin Sutz, his classmate from New York days who was now a pastor in Rapperswil.

Sutz could only shrug his shoulders. "You probably unnerve him a bit."

Bonhoeffer did not understand. "But why should I unnerve him?"

"He doesn't quite know what to make of you. He had trouble enough with that during more peaceful times, and now . . ." He interrupted himself and forced a laugh. "After all, you could be a dangerous Nazi agent."

"*Me*? Of *all* people? A Nazi agent?"

That was incomprehensible for Bonhoeffer. He was indeed an agent; that much was true. But not a Nazi agent. Now he was so obsessed with assuaging Barth's suspicion that he forgot the warning his brother-in-law had given him about being cautious ("Trust no one, not even yourself!"). At their very next meeting, Bonhoeffer related to Barth the entire background of his identity as an agent for military intelligence.

"*Careful*, my friend," Barth himself admonished Bonhoeffer. "Then again," he continued, "it is, of course, good that you've confided all this to me. All the mistrust between people, the impossibility of really being able to discern who is one's friend—that's perhaps the most evil poison of any dictatorship. But, now, do also tell me exactly what it is you are hoping to accomplish."

To be perfectly honest, Bonhoeffer himself did not really know the answer to that question, and occasionally he succumbed to the same suspicion that Roeder would later drive into the ground, namely, that his brother-in-law had in fact merely wanted to keep Bonhoeffer out of the military—no more, no less—and never really had any intention of engaging Bonhoeffer as a genuine "agent."

"So, tell me what it is you want me to do for you," he had pressed his brother-in-law. Dohnanyi had smiled, a bit condescendingly, Bonhoeffer thought. "Nothing directly political, Dietrich. We have other people for that sort of thing, people who understand more about politics than you do."

Connections with the ecumenical movement were another matter. They had gotten considerably more lax since the mid-1930s and were now to be cultivated anew. The most important thing for the moment was for those involved in that movement—the non-Germans—to be informed that a German opposition movement *did* in fact exist. Bonhoeffer had obediently nodded and had then traveled from Basel through Zurich and on to Geneva, where he planned to meet with the emergent World Council of Churches and its general secretary, Willem Visser 't Hooft.

Bonhoeffer had already become acquainted with this Dutchman in 1939 during a layover in London before traveling on to New York, but had been too distracted by his own problems at the time to assess him fairly. He now found that Visser 't Hooft was an extremely pleasant,

intelligent conversation partner, and Bonhoeffer was immensely
enjoying being able to discuss theological questions again amid all
the other concerns.

The two men went walking together on Lake Geneva, where
Bonhoeffer then outlined the vision he had entertained for so long,
namely, that of a great unity of faith and world. "That is presumably
also the subject of your book on ethics, is it not?" Visser 't Hooft had
politely asked. "Yes, it's one of my main themes." Visser 't Hooft
squinted as he gazed out over the glittering surface of the lake, toward
the bright red sail of a boat running before the wind. "I am genuinely
looking forward to reading it."

Bonhoeffer laughed sadly in response. "Well, you'll need
considerable patience. In the first place, I don't really know if I'll ever
finish the book. Then on top of that, my 'friends' at home have just been
so kind as to slap me with a prohibition against publishing *anything*."
A letter was already lying on his desk in Munich prohibiting him from
engaging in any literary work because of "seditious activity."

Visser 't Hooft smiled comfortingly at him. "Keep your composure,
my friend. They can forbid writing but not visions."

No. No one could do that. Not the visions Bonhoeffer had—but
unfortunately also not the visions others had, people like Adolf Hitler,
who during these very same days in March 1941 had stepped before
his assembled generals and declared to them that his "iron resolution"
to invade Russia was irreversible.

France had already been completely defeated, and England as good
as defeated. Russia, as the *Führer* put it, was the only threat remaining
that counted for anything—and at these words his gaze seemed to
wrap itself around each individual in the room like an iron clamp.

Out there, in those broad expanses comprising the Soviet Union,
it was not a matter of merely conquering an army. The goal was to
annihilate an entire system with whose representatives there could be
no possibility of establishing any sort of relationship. This was Hitler's
introduction to his generals. He continued, "Neither beforehand
nor afterward are Communists capable of being our comrades in
any form or fashion." And whoever among them is a "commissar,"

belonging to the intellectual elite, is accordingly to be shot on the spot, without judge, jury, or sentence. "And that, gentlemen, will be your assignment!"

These "gentlemen," as one could read years later in several of their published memoirs, were profoundly shocked at these statements— but somehow skillfully managed to keep that shock concealed from the *Führer*. Instead, they merely sat there, stone-faced, staring at the man who had just degraded soldiers into hit men. Not a trace of opposition in the room.

Nonetheless, some of them suddenly found that the almost submerged and forgotten idea that one might—sometime, somehow, somewhere—get rid of this man no longer seemed *quite* so outlandish. And in the canteens and officers' mess halls, officers increasingly put their heads together and talked of conspiracy, some even mentioning the possibility of assassination—but many also spoke about the sense of honor of the German officer, about Prussian obedience, and about the oath of loyalty they had all—*all* of them—sworn to the *Führer*.

For the time being, however, the campaign Barbarossa proceeded as planned—the assault on Russia. And Bonhoeffer almost howled with glee, "This is the beginning of the end!"

He was once again in Geneva, once again sitting across from Visser 't Hooft, who looked up in perplexed astonishment. "Does a German victory really please you so greatly?" And indeed, at this time the Russian campaign seemed to be turning into the same sort of lightning victory the Germans had enjoyed in both Poland and France.

"Well, what do we really mean by 'victory' here?"

Bonhoeffer had leaned back and was looking up at Mont Blanc through the window, its snow-covered imperturbability towering up into the deep blue sky. "Hitler will come to ruin in Russia just as everyone before him—Sweden's Charles XII, Napoleon. And then," he now turned back to Visser 't Hooft, "then *our* task will begin, namely, to win the Allies over to an honorable peace. Or rather, our task has already begun."

"Well, I fear the time is not particularly favorable for that right now." The other man sighed. The time for such eternal compromises in the face of Hitler's power politics was, Visser 't Hooft maintained, over now that Winston Churchill had succeeded Chamberlain. The new prime minister and minister of defense had for decades been intent on entering into the history books as a hero—just like his ancestor, the Duke of Marlborough—and had finally found an appropriate adversary in Hitler. The only thing driving him now was the grand coalition against Hitler and the annihilation of Nazi Germany. Compromises were no longer part of that equation.

Bonhoeffer's entire body convulsed and shuddered at the sound of these massive, shocking words, and for several moments he felt like a little boy again watching his ball bounce away, irretrievably, down the street. But then, with a voice quaking with defiance, "Nevertheless, we *must* try to move things toward a different, more favorable conclusion. God will help us. He is on our side."

"You're sure about that?"

"Absolutely sure, yes. God does *not* abandon the righteous. Of that I am absolutely convinced."

"Well, I must say I envy you your trust." Visser 't Hooft had gotten up out of his chair and walked over to the book cabinet. He pulled out a slender volume. "Our friend William Paton—you perhaps already know that a year ago he established a group to outline the future peace—has just published a book, *The Church and the New Order in Europe. . . .*"

Bonhoeffer took the book and paged through it.

"I think it would be a good idea if you were to review the book—thoroughly—and correct some of the incorrect assumptions that British propaganda has been disseminating concerning the conditions in Germany. Not the least of which," he could not repress a laugh, "is this hope in a German 'workers' rebellion,' which the BBC is constantly trumpeting."

"The SS would annihilate any such attempt in a few, short, bloody hours." Bonhoeffer, too, could not repress a cynical laugh. Then he looked up again at Mont Blanc. "Hitler must disappear. His Gestapo must disappear. And then, after that has happened," he shut the book with a loud slap and laid it back on the table, "then we will create a new order according to the divine commandment. To that end, however, we need the assurance that the Allies will grant us a bit of time to catch our breath. . . ."

Because Bonhoeffer was still looking out the window, he did not notice the other man's slight, sad smile. Visser 't Hooft merely said softly, "Well, yes, wonderful! That's certainly an offer for all of Germany's adversaries. And I'll see to it that the right people in England and America hear about it. But for the moment, the ecumenical movement cannot really do more than that."

At the end of September, Bonhoeffer returned to Germany, unfortunately not really with a light heart, but at least guardedly optimistic. He wanted to stay a short while in Munich before going on to Berlin to deliver his report to his brother-in-law. At the main train station he took the tram to Munich's Schwabing district, to the house of Countess Kalckreuth. He could not help chuckling to himself at the thought of her.

Last winter, it was in a *considerable* state of excitement and anxiety that she had summoned him back to Munich from Ettal. The Gestapo had just paid her a visit. As it turned out, however, they had only wanted to let Bonhoeffer know that his registration requirement in Schlawe had been lifted.

The tram was filled above capacity. Bonhoeffer, lugging two suitcases, got to it just before it pulled away and managed to get the last free seat. He sat down, his face flushed, and took a moment to catch his breath. "Always a crazy mad rush, eh?" The person sitting next to him smirked, his round, good-natured red face exuding Bavarian affability. Bonhoeffer could only nod and return his cordial smile.

At the next tram stop, only a few people got off, while a whole new crowd got on. Bonhoeffer caught sight—more in profile, really—of an old man, slightly stooped, with snow white hair. He politely got up. "May I offer you my seat?" The old man looked more unnerved than grateful.

"Huh? A German offering his seat to that swine Jewboy?" The round-faced man sitting next to him stared at Bonhoeffer with angry eyes, with now not the slightest trace of any quaint Bavarian amiability. Only now did Bonhoeffer get a better look at the old man.

He was wearing a yellow Star of David on his overcoat.

This Nightmare Has Got to Come to an End

An overcoat with a yellow star also hung on the coat rack in the house on Marienburg Allee, and Bonhoeffer's ears perked up as he heard voices in the garden room. Ah! Visitors! Bonhoeffer recognized the voice of the elderly Frau Merseburger, one of his mother's close acquaintances.

He didn't particularly like the woman, was not particularly inclined to listen to her rather verbose prattling, so he resolved to sneak up to his attic room as inconspicuously as possible. But he stopped in mid-step despite himself, leaned over the stair railing, and listened.

"We're allowed to take fifty kilos of luggage, that's what it says in these instructions; we also have to list all our furniture and valuables— but what are we to take along?" he heard the elderly woman say. "Only clothes? Jewelry? And winter clothes already? We don't even know where they're taking us or how long the trip is supposed to last."

Bonhoeffer stood there, completely still, and stared at the yellow star over on the coat rack.

A lot had happened during the weeks Bonhoeffer had spent in Switzerland and during his several days of rest and relaxation in Wallis afterward. On September 1, a decree had been issued in Germany stipulating that all Jews—even baptized Jews—were required to wear a yellow star in public, and an unpleasant shudder had swept over Bonhoeffer.

A star with six points—the sign of the house of David, the house from which *Christ himself* came. Now Christians and Jews were under the same sign, just as in the photographs showing people with a star on their chest together with the "Aryan" Christians at the Lord's supper, and for several moments Bonhoeffer seriously considered wearing that yellow star himself.

But that would have been a mere boy's game. A childish, naive protest. It would have helped neither Frau Merseburger nor any of the others who had received that same letter telling them to be prepared to vacate their residences.

"Of course you can live here with us," Bonhoeffer heard his mother say. The other woman's voice became fretful. "I don't know if that's even allowed. What they're saying is that for now we're all going to be housed in the synagogue on Leventzow Street. They've already cleared it out. . . ."

Later Bonhoeffer himself did not really know what drew him to the neighborhood of the synagogue on this and the following nights. Hidden in a dark building entryway, he was intent on not letting anything escape his view. *Otherwise*, he thought, *I won't really understand what's going on.* And on the night of October 16, things did indeed begin to happen.

Cars pulled up, policemen climbed out, several people grouped between them, all wearing the yellow star. Jews. Carrying their luggage. They were led into the synagogue, almost cordially, in any event not roughly, no shouts, no whips. It all was taking place very quietly, very unobtrusively, and for precisely that reason Bonhoeffer felt a cold chill of dread wash over him. It was as if a procession of ghosts were shuffling into the nocturnal building, very orderly, in almost complete silence, according to some mysterious, incomprehensible choreography.

A procession into the realm of the dead, he thought. With utter bureaucratic correctness.

The next day, at about 7:00 in the morning, trucks drove up, then more toward noon, then yet more during the afternoon. And again no shouts, no whimpering, not even the slightest, most tepid gestures of protest. *They need to defend themselves*, Bonhoeffer thought. *Why the hell don't you defend yourselves?*

Germans, he thought almost instantaneously. Germans first, Jews second. A German doesn't defend himself when the authorities flex their muscles. Surely the authorities know what they're doing.

And he himself? Would at least *he* protest? Would at least *he* jump into those trucks and pull the people out and prevent the whole departure from taking place? Or at least *try*?

No. He would not. Nor would anyone else. And more than a few people strolled by on this fine day, completely normal citizens, Berliners, on their way to take care of daily errands.

Although some stopped and gawked, most hurried on by. "What're those people doing there?" blurted out a little boy. His mother quickly took his arm and hurried on down the street. And one older gentleman related how such things were done in 1914, during the great military call-up. "Well, there were certainly no trucks then. *We* had to go on foot. . . ."

In one of the trucks—it was already midday—Bonhoeffer saw a young girl wave to an old woman who was crouched down in another truck, probably the girl's mother or grandmother. She waved back. A farewell, perhaps forever. As naturally as if saying goodbye for summer vacation.

Bonhoeffer suddenly felt a burning sensation in his throat. Unable to stand it any longer, he rushed away, down the street in the opposite direction. But he could still see the images of all these people, shuffling, one foot after the other, completely passive, toward ruin. He started feeling queasy, leaned against a lightpost, then vomited in the street.

"Lousy drunk," a passerby snarled.

"It could have been me," said Friedrich Justus Perels, a jurist and an attorney for the Pastors' Emergency League during the 1930s, now assigned to the chancellery of Horst Holstein, the top lawyer for the Confessing Church, and himself a Jew—or a half-Jew, in any event "non-Aryan." He was the only person in the entire Confessing Church to whom Bonhoeffer had confided the truth about his identity as a double agent.

The two men were now sitting together and drafting a report concerning this transport removal of Berlin Jews—probably fifteen hundred during this first wave, and two more transports were to follow. Word had it that these people were to be transported in boxcars to the Polish town of Łódź, which the Germans now called "Litzmannstadt."

Bonhoeffer gathered up the densely written pages. "I'll take these over to my brother-in-law."

Hans von Dohnanyi leafed through the report and nodded. "Very good, Dietrich. We'll put this in the safe with the other materials."

"Which safe?"

"Didn't I tell you about the safe in our Zossen branch? Deep underground, in the bunker? The most secure place in all of Germany. The Gestapo won't find that very easily." In that safe Dohnanyi had stored not only all the materials concerning the previous coup attempts, but also, since the campaign in Poland, his perpetually growing "terror files" documenting all the misdeeds, abuses, and atrocities perpetrated by the National Socialist regime.

"But it doesn't belong in a safe, Hans. It needs to be broadcast from the highest building. Every German needs to hear about this, it needs to be broadcast as loudly and as publicly as possible so that even the slowest-witted person can understand what's really going on in this country."

"Dietrich, don't you think most of them have already long suspected it? But there's a war going one, and everyone has other concerns. Everyone thinks only of himself. So not a bad time at all, my *Führer*, to start implementing your plans for the Jews."

Dohnanyi stood at the window and looked down toward the Havel River. He and his family had moved into this house in Sakrow in August, primarily at the insistence of Christine, who had grown weary of the "eternal gypsy life." A beautiful, bright, airy house with generous space. The carpets were not quite as heavy as at home on Marienburg Allee, there were fewer pictures on the walls, and the furniture was not quite so ponderous and dark. Otherwise, however, there was not much difference between the two houses.

The same house, the same world, Bonhoeffer thought. "Little princes." That was how his brother-in-law had put it once.

And, indeed, that they were. Embedded in a caste that was sometimes a prison in its own right. But between its bars—this, too, Dohnanyi had remarked—people at least still knew what was proper. For example, that one did *not* transport people away like livestock in boxcars to some faraway destination in the East. . . .

"Hitler allegedly recently said something quite interesting in a discussion about the perpetual lack of unity among the Germans.

His lackey Goebbels was there and, of course, immediately spread the gossip further," Dohnanyi said from over at the window. "Hitler's opinion is that the only reason the Jews have managed to endure throughout the millennia is that *everyone* has hated them. It's that hatred that has fused them together. And now a similar hatred will rescue the Germans as well. They, too, will become internally united once they feel that all other nations hate them. And I fear," Dohnanyi's voice had become as soft as if he were speaking only to himself, "I fear Hitler will soon be very, very close to achieving this goal as well."

He laughed awkwardly and seemed to be waiting for a response. But Bonhoeffer was not in the mood for philosophical discussions. "But nothing is *forcing* us simply to accept that. We must at least protest loudly enough so that the entire world cannot *help* but hear us. Think about Count Galen!"

The Galen incident had been only a few months earlier. Rumors had been circulating about the systematic murder of the mentally ill and permanently handicapped, and Bonhoeffer had met in the house on Marienburg Allee with his father and Friedrich von Bodelschwingh, who had hastily traveled over from Bethel. The old gentleman had fretted about what to do if someone came to take away the people in *his* charge.

Karl Bonhoeffer had declared himself willing to supply any and all necessary medical attestations. But the real clap of thunder had come from the bishop of Münster, Count Galen, a clap so loud and powerful that, as a matter of fact, the euthanasia program—which had already begun—was broken off on orders from the very highest authorities.

"Yes, yes, our good lion in Münster! We should certainly give him his due . . . but neither should we overestimate him," Dohnanyi now sighed. "During a time when millions of soldiers are fighting at the front and many are also wondering whether they, too, should they be severely wounded, might be—well, might be 'eliminated' as a piece of 'life unworthy of life,' as that wonderful expression puts it—I think it's dawned on even Hitler himself that this entire idea of euthanasia is not exactly one that will strengthen troop morale. But now? With the Jews?"

He walked back into the room and sat down in one of the floral-patterned easy chairs, carefully crossing his legs. "There's still only one solution, namely, a coup, and that can come *only* from the armed forces. And just now, the preliminary signs for something like that are not at all so unfavorable. . . ."

"I've already heard that several times before." Bonhoeffer's words sounded angrier than he intended. But ever since the high military command had simply accepted this nonsense, this madness with the Russian campaign without a word of protest, his confidence in their will to mount any resistance—any at all—had plummeted to zero. Dohnanyi was more optimistic.

"Even our commander in chief, General of the Army Walter von Brauchitsch, who just a year ago had dismissed *any* attempts to move in this direction by insisting that 'words such as treason and conspiracy are *not* part of the Prussian vocabulary,' seems to have undergone a certain change of disposition since this 'commissar's command' was given. These days he doesn't seem quite as closed off to such considerations as earlier. Although, to be sure. . . ."

He once again looked out the window into the golden-brown autumnal foliage, then offered his brother-in-law a cigarette before taking one himself.

"We're dealing with military people here. Their job is to attain victory," he said while lighting the other man's cigarette. "They will not undertake anything *against* Hitler unless they are absolutely certain that *his* fall will *not* also immediately bring about military defeat. And such a signal can come only . . . from the other side. Especially from England, some sign that they are willing to negotiate with us and guarantee that Germany will remain intact—if they do that, then hardly a single high-ranking officer would remain on Hitler's side. Then, however . . ."

He leaned back in the chair and contentedly watched his carefully executed smoke rings dissipate in the air. "Then it will be time to open the safe and bring everything to light. That people may *finally* understand what a monster they have been freed from."

He laughed. "Do you remember Jürgen Fehling's production of *Richard III* in the State Theater? When Werner Krauss as Richard lay dead on the stage and from all sides there was singing and rejoicing to celebrate his death? 'The day is ours, the bloody dog is dead. . . .' I'm hoping to hear just such choruses soon, and not just in the theater."

"And until then?"

"Until then? Well . . ."

They smoked a while in silence. Somewhere in the distance they could hear what was probably a flock of wild geese, sounding their cries out during flight. "Unsettled journey, beware, beware, the world is full of murder there," Bonhoeffer hummed softly. Walter Flex's fearful, anxious poem from the trenches of the Great War, alongside the hymns of Paul Gerhardt and Heinrich Schütz, had always been his favorite song.

"And what will become of the Jews in the meantime?" he finally asked.

"I don't know either," Dohnanyi answered after a long pause. "The only thing we can do is be patient, hope that the grand coup will happen, and till then see whether we can at least be of some help in individual cases. I know it's a meager, paltry gesture, but it's better than doing nothing at all. . . ."

Bonhoeffer would find himself coming back to these words quite frequently during the next few months as he, with Dohnanyi's help, tried to protect Charlotte Friedenthal, the secretary of the Confessing Church, from imminent deportation. "Can't you add her to your list?" he finally asked his brother-in-law.

The reference was to "Operation 7," which Roeder would later discuss so exhaustively in his hearings with Bonhoeffer. Operation 7 was an attempt to get a group of at-risk Jews into Switzerland under the pretext of engaging them as a network of agents abroad in the service of military intelligence.

"No one but your or Canaris's friends," Bonhoeffer had said the first time he read the names on the list, first seven, then fourteen. "Who among all those people on the trucks had such a friend?"

Dohnanyi did not answer. But he did add Charlotte Friedenthal to his Operation 7 group. After finally arriving in Switzerland in the fall of 1942, she at first had to become accustomed again to *not* having to wear a yellow star on her coat.

What horrible times. Horrible. And Bonhoeffer finally could only think, *Enough; this nightmare has got to come to an end. All we need is a sign from the others, a sign that all they want is Hitler's fall, not Germany's destruction.* But, *Where is that sign? Who can give it to us?* He still felt bitterly disappointed at the utter lack of response to his criticism of William Paton's little book, *The Church and the New Order in Europe:* not even a response from Paton himself or from his "Work Group for Peace."

So, who, then, might give such a sign?

This question pursued him with numbing monotony, even into his dreams, accompanying him like a depressing, omnipresent shadow during his third trip to Switzerland in the spring of 1942. During that stay, Visser 't Hooft told him—more in passing, really—that the bishop of Chichester would soon be going to neutral Sweden for negotiations with the church there.

George Bell! Uncle Glocke!

This was a new idea. The bishop, with his considerable connections reaching even into the highest levels of the British government, could well be the one to provide deliverance. Yes, indeed.

He simply *had* to see and speak with Bell in Sweden. At any cost. *Bell* would be able to provide that sign. Bonhoeffer was absolutely sure of it.

PLEASE, PRAY FOR US!

"Ah, but I fear you overestimate me, my good friend!"

George Bell put on his brightest smile and simultaneously wondered how Bonhoeffer had succeeded in getting to Sweden so quickly. Truth be told, Bonhoeffer himself was astonished.

He had just been in Zurich, and today, suddenly, he was here in Sigtuna on Lake Mälaren, just north of Stockholm. Between the two he had been in Berlin with a slightly stunned Dohnanyi, whom Bonhoeffer had implored as never before, "I absolutely *must* get to Sweden, Hans! *Please,* let me make the journey. *Immediately!*"

At first, Dohnanyi had hesitated. "A conversation with the bishop, fine. But Schönfeld is already on his way to see him from the ecumenical movement."

"Schönfeld!?"

That name still left a slightly bitter taste in Bonhoeffer's mouth, for there had been years—actually the entire 1930s—when this Hans Schönfeld, a theologian and political economist, had been Bishop Heckel's most intimate associate in the Church Foreign Office, a party to Heckel's sycophantic, regime-toadying church policies.

In Geneva, where Schönfeld was now a member of the nascent World Council of Churches, Bonhoeffer had encountered him again— and had been caught up short, was almost speechless, in fact, to find he had become a resolute enemy of Hitler, with a double identity just like Canaris and Oster, like Bonhoeffer's brother-in-law, or even like Bonhoeffer himself. "We're all tightrope walkers." Bonhoeffer thought of Dohnanyi's words at the *Hamlet* performance at the State Theater.

But a remnant of mistrust still remained. *When all is said and done*, Bonhoeffer occasionally thought, *even Heckel himself may turn out to have been a member of the resistance. Of course, not until it's all over.*

So, this Schönfeld was now with Bell in Sweden and had apparently made a not inconsiderable impression on him. And yet now that Bonhoeffer was alone with Bell, the bishop looked rather pessimistic. "Peace negotiations with Germany? Well, fine, yes. But with whom there? Who *really* belongs to the German resistance? Indeed, does that resistance—please excuse me, Dietrich, this is not aimed at you personally—does it really even exist?"

Bonhoeffer had to name names. And he did so. Dohnanyi had given him explicit permission. He spoke about General Ludwig Beck, the chief of staff who had resigned after the Sudeten crisis and who was the real central figure of the resistance, and about the other central figure, Leipzig's former mayor, Carl Goerdeler. And he named generals, members of labor unions, church leaders, the former president of the Reich Bank and the former Reich minister of economics, Hjalmar Schacht. . . .

Bell frowned, "Him, too? Really?"

"Yes, I know, an opportunist. But it is *precisely* such inveterate opportunists who have the most accurate sense for when it's time to change flags again."

Bell nodded and simultaneously sighed deeply. "If only these men would give some sign that could convince the British that a resistance movement really exists, a movement that is something more than just a bunch of noble words. . . ."

"Like in Norway, I know."

Bonhoeffer had been there during the spring, just after Cathedral Provost Trondheim had received orders prohibiting all worship services. The response was that first all the bishops, then all the Norwegian pastors had resigned their offices. Then there were arrests, interrogations, hearings, and house searches.

Dohnanyi had summoned his brother-in-law to him. "Make it absolutely clear to this Norwegian Hitler, Quisling, and his minions that their aggressive church policies are doing nothing but putting German troops there at risk!" And then, leaning forward, he added in a whisper, "And at the same time encourage your Norwegian colleagues to persevere in their resistance!"

"I only wish," Bonhoeffer now said to Bell, "that our own Confessing Church had shown as much courage and determination as the Norwegian church."

"You were there alone?" Bell wanted to know.

"No. Helmuth von Moltke went along as well, from military intelligence. He's one of us. We almost became friends even though we didn't always have the same opinion."

"For example?"

"Well, Moltke opposes *any* removal of Hitler through violence."

"And you don't, my boy?"

A long silence followed, and Bell almost regretted asking the question. But then Bonhoeffer began speaking after all, very slowly, almost dragging his words out, and yet quite unequivocally. "I would first leave my church. One could not—would not be *permitted* to— put it into a position of having to cover what I might do. . . ."

"And what is it you might do?"

"Kill Hitler. With my own hands."

"You'd really do that?"

"Yes."

Bell had to repress a laugh. This man sitting across from him, so cultured and so well mannered in all his blond propriety and uprightness—this man, of all people, holding a dagger or a revolver or a bomb. *You, too, Brutus.* . . . No, the mere *idea* had something absolutely comical about it. And yet Bell's urge to laugh quickly dissipated. *My God,* he thought to himself—just as, a year earlier, Karl Barth had wondered—*what on earth has the monster Hitler turned this man into? And not just this man, but many others like him as well.*

Bonhoeffer himself was not a little unnerved by his own words. *Is such a man still Bonhoeffer?* he thought, *If he could kill another person, kill someone who was, after all, still a person just like himself? Is that still me?*

Yes. That was still him. That, too, was Bonhoeffer.

And now he spoke further while the seagulls screeched from out over Lake Mälaren, spoke about the letter he had received this past winter from a former Finkenwalde student in Russia.

From the middle of that Russian hell of impenetrable ice and snow, that student had written about the power of faith, and about the promise of the Sermon on the Mount, "blessed are the merciful." But he himself—Bonhoeffer could still see the bright, boyish face of this Erwin Sander, a face that sank into a frown whenever someone else suffered even the slightest injustice—he and his comrades had not been permitted to be merciful, had shot fifty prisoners to death "because we were on a march and were not able to take these prisoners along." Even women and children "suspected of supplying partisans with provisions are disposed of with a shot through the base of the skull," the rationale being that "these persons must be done away with in this manner because otherwise German soldiers would have to forfeit their lives."

That was exactly what Sander had written. Word for word.

Were these words merely meant for the censor? And the information actually contraband? Or did Sander really think that way? Sermon on the Mount here, shot to the base of the skull there? And if Bonhoeffer himself had been a soldier in that same situation, would he, too, have drawn his revolver just as did all the others? Would he really have . . . What horrible things war makes of human beings. . . .

"That's another reason we need peace," Bonhoeffer continued, "so that we can do penance for all the things we have done to others. That must be. For every single one of us, whether perpetrators or merely those who *tolerated* such horrific acts."

"Well, that's certainly not a position that will prompt much applause in Germany just now. Not even among your friends, I fear." Bell tried to smile. Bonhoeffer merely nodded. "No. I'm sure it won't." *I'm alone*, he thought. The perpetual outsider just like during the church struggle in the 1930s. The perpetual loner.

The screeching of seagulls over Lake Mälaren became louder and more boisterous. Bell stretched a bit. "What a splendid day here in May. We ought to take advantage of it for a short walk along the lake before the others arrive for tea, your colleague Schönfeld and the two Swedish church representatives. . . ." He stood up, softly laughing. "You and Schönfeld on a mission for the same cause—well, politics certainly creates strange bedfellows."

They strolled along the lake. Bell forced himself to speak in an empathically neutral, objective voice. "As I said before, first the German resistance must provide a clear, unequivocal signal. And time is getting short, Dietrich. There are increasing signs that Hitler has passed his zenith, not least because of America's entry into the war last year, and now the Germans—just as in the previous war—are *again* having to fight on two fronts."

"Word has it that this summer he'll be initiating a decisive assault in Russia and that then there will no longer even be an eastern front," Bonhoeffer countered.

"Yes, yes, the inexorably advancing Herr Hitler. I know. He intends to have brought Russia to its knees by next summer at the latest." Bell peered out across the lake so intensely one would have thought he was expecting to find the solution to all these problems out there amid the gentle haze. "Well, let's wait and see. In any event, our prime minister is diligently working on the alliance of all these countries against Germany. You no doubt already know what his 'Atlantic Charter' with the Americans calls for—no separate peace negotiations with the enemy. War until the enemy is completely defeated. . . ."

"Which will cost several million more people their lives, on both sides." Bonhoeffer thought of the increasing reports of former Finkenwalde students who had been killed in action. Erwin Sander, who had written of the horrific executions, would himself not survive Russia. And Bonhoeffer thought of the people wearing the yellow star. What would be *their* fate if peace did not come soon?

"I fear neither Hitler nor Churchill care about those millions."

"Then talk to him!" Bonhoeffer was almost shouting.

"Me? The 'German friend,' as they call me?"

Silence. Only the seagulls still screeched. Slowly, as if stunned, Bonhoeffer shook his head. "Each side is waiting for the other side to send a signal. It's always the *other* side that has to make the first move—and in the meantime entire nations are bleeding to death," he said softly amid the boisterous gulls.

Bell raised his arms in a gesture of helplessness.

This particular May 31 was sunny, clear, cloudless, and really wonderfully and uncommonly warm. Bonhoeffer would have preferred to tear off his clothes and leap directly into the water just as he had done in the Baltic during the days in Finkenwalde. But here, out in the broad expanse of the lake, perhaps a cramp or a heart attack would seize him, rendering him unable to save himself, and perhaps help would arrive too late, and perhaps he would sink down beneath the azure surface of Lake Mälaren. *Not a bad way to die*, he thought. Then he could just forget everything. Including his disappointment now.

Yes, Bonhoeffer was disappointed.

He could not really say what exactly he had expected. He vaguely suspected, however, that not even someone like Bell could really perform miracles. In the final analysis, were people of his ilk— conservative humanists—still even the right people for the task at hand? Were not others taking center stage now—people like England's

prime minister, this Churchill with his baby face, or Stalin, or Stalin's
foreign minister, Molotow, who had just signed a Soviet-British
"mutual assistance pact" in London?

Yes, no doubt about it, they were the ones with the real power. Not
someone like George Bell. All he could do now was talk about universal
Christian brotherhood, something which ultimately—"Well, let's
wait and see. Have just a little more patience, my friend!"—would be
victorious over everything else. Good old Uncle Glocke.

Bonhoeffer followed the flight of a seagull diving down to the water.
Words, words, words. Isn't that what Shakespeare's Hamlet himself says?
he thought. Yes, indeed. Words. *Universal Christian brotherhood.* He
let those words pass. Only much, much later would he encounter
them again.

Bell sensed his annoyance. He put his arm on Bonhoeffer's shoulder
in a fatherly gesture. "Don't be so hard on yourself, Dietrich. There are
still a few beautiful things in this world, for you as well. Isn't there a
tiny bit of space somewhere where you can get away from everything
and just be yourself?"

Klein-Krössin, Bonhoeffer thought. The estate of Frau Kleist-
Retzow. That would be good for him. The peace and quiet there.
Pomerania's stringent clarity. Perhaps do some work on his *Ethics.*
And maybe a reunion with the granddaughter there, Maria. She had
just finished secondary school, or so he had heard. She, too, might be
at Klein-Krössin just now.

Bell continued speaking. "Of course, I'll do whatever I can. And if
Churchill himself proves to be inaccessible, then perhaps I can speak
with his foreign minister, Anthony Eden. I know him quite well, a very
pleasant fellow. But I can't really do more than that. Or did you have
other suggestions?"

Bonhoeffer mumbled something, but the screeching of gulls
drowned out his words.

"Pardon me, what did you say?"

"Please, pray for us."

THE STRANGER IN THE TRAIN

That week in June had turned beautiful and clear and bright in Klein-Krössin. Frau Kleist-Retzow had given Bonhoeffer *thorough* instructions concerning what he *absolutely* must mention in his *Ethics*. And Maria had been there as well. Eighteen years old now, recently graduated, and even prettier than Bonhoeffer had remembered her.

It was terribly, terribly difficult for Bonhoeffer to leave all that behind, and he shuddered at the thought of his train trip from Berlin down to his "base" in Munich, in the middle of the night, in the pitch black train. These days, because a war was going on, trains were not allowed to have any lights on at night.

Nonetheless he was quite pleased at still having been able to secure a seat, and in first class at that, next to the window. He leaned back in the plush seat and would have liked to have smoked a cigarette, but at the mere sight of his cigarette case his fellow passengers in the packed compartment—only the seat directly across from him was empty and apparently reserved—had cleared their throats so indignantly that he quickly pocketed the cigarettes again.

Instead he now pulled out a pad and pen and decided to write a letter while there was still enough light. To his friend Eberhard, the only person to whom he could confide certain things.

"Dear Eberhard, you are to be the first to know. . . ."

That he was in love. Profoundly and seriously in love, as never before in his entire life. Of course, in love with Maria von Wedemeyer. He could hear Eberhard's voice, "But Dietrich, she's only eighteen. . . ." And he already thirty-six, Bonhoeffer added in thought. Twice as old. Nonetheless. Her and her alone could he envision as his wife.

To that point, women had never meant all that much to him. This or that occasional infatuation, fine. Then the relationship with his cousin Elisabeth. With her, highly intelligent as she was, he had always spoken just as he had with men. Otherwise he always had trouble talking with women. And he had hardly ever been able even to *imagine* one of them as a companion.

Nor had he ever really missed having such a companion. Certainly not in the almost monastic society of men at Finkenwalde—even though most of the seminarians could not help gawking at every even modestly pretty girl. Nor, certainly, had he missed such a companion in later years, when being tied to a wife and family would sooner have been a burden.

So what had happened in the meantime? Why were things different now? Why this idea of a wife named Maria? Bonhoeffer put his pad on his knees and reflected.

A man needs a woman to whom he can return home. No, not his words. He had merely read them somewhere. But they were probably right. Bonhoeffer, too, would like to be able to return home to someone, especially now—with all his restless traveling between Berlin and Switzerland and Munich and Sweden and wherever else— would like to have *one* place where someone would be waiting for him, someplace where he could take off his mask and just be himself.

With a wife. With Maria.

Or was this just sweet deception? Daydreams? Fantasies lasting sixty seconds and no longer? Would it not be better—certainly with respect to Maria as well—simply to forget the whole thing, to dispense with any notions of "future" in their relationship and just allow it to remain one, single, beautiful moment in time?

Bonhoeffer—with the world and God in perfect focus and yet touchingly naive with regard to the straightforward affairs of the heart—did not know the answer to that question himself. And it was precisely about *these* things, and about all his doubts, that he would have liked to ask his friend Eberhard, who had at least managed to become engaged once—thought it later fell apart—and whom Bonhoeffer had long suspected of being not all *that* inexperienced with women. Or at least *more* experienced than he himself, the older of the two.

Then it occurred to him that he actually should be writing this letter to Maria. But no. He decided it was too early. He went back to his writing pad, but it had already gotten too dark, and his handwriting became fuzzy before his straining eyes. He would have to finish the letter in Munich.

The train suddenly stopped with a lurch. Bonhoeffer could not see any station signs. "Do you have any idea where we are?" he asked one of his dozing fellow passengers. At just that moment, the compartment door swung open with a harsh, imperious clatter. "Excuse me!" It sounded like a military order, nasal, assertive, abrupt. A man stepped into the compartment, tall, in a long military trench coat. Apparently the person for whom the seat across from Bonhoeffer had been reserved.

He heaved his suitcase up into the luggage netting and hung his coat and hat on the wall hook. The man was wearing a uniform with a heavy leather belt. He sat down, a slender, severe shadow of a man. Silver runes glittered on his collar. Waffen SS, the military wing of the SS. No one said a word. But a blanket of anxiety descended on the other passengers, even more claustrophobic and suffocating than the stale air in the compartment.

The man did not seem to notice. He merely looked out the window, indifferently. Bonhoeffer assessed his profile. Not really an impressive head, too narrow, harsh. Bonhoeffer was reminded of one particular lawyer whom his brother-in-law had once inconspicuously pointed out to him. "Herr Freisler. The worst of them all." This man here resembled that Freisler a bit—at least to the extent Bonhoeffer could see in the dim light of the compartment.

The train clattered on through the advancing darkness of this warm, early summer evening. The man pulled out a cigarette case, bowed politely, and asked, "Would you like one?"

"I fear it would disturb some of our fellow passengers here."

"Not me!" A laugh. The man lit up a cigarette and began smoking. A member of the "master race." Someone accustomed to winning. To victory. "And today Germany belongs to us. . . ." No objections from the other passengers to the cigarette. Just submissive cowering. As if in protest, Bonhoeffer also lit up a cigarette. Outside, the gloomy German landscape raced by.

"Excuse me, but might I put a question to you?"

It was the man across from him. Surprisingly gentle and polite. "I don't mean to be importunate. . . ." He cleared his throat almost as if in embarrassment, almost as if he wanted to begin a confession. *Pater, peccavi . . .*

Bonhoeffer leaned over, quite in the posture of a father confessor, tilting his head slightly as if to listen better, his ear turned toward the man, and folded his hands in his lap.

"You're a pastor, aren't you?"

Bonhoeffer leaned back, a bit startled. "What do you mean?"

A quiet laugh. "My hobby. Guessing people's occupations. And I immediately guessed 'pastor' for you."

"Does that bother you?" Bonhoeffer spoke the question so sharply and quickly that he himself was almost taken aback. But the man showed no reaction. "You mean because of this?" In the semidarkness Bonhoeffer saw the man tap the SS runes on his collar. "A great many things can be reconciled with this. Including Christianity." He leaned forward almost as far as the compartment would allow, and whispered, "I'm referring to the right Christianity. Not 'German' Christianity."

The other man was a Christian? A member of the Confessing Church? Or more likely an agent provocateur? Bonhoeffer forced himself to be calm. They had sent this man to set him up, to bait him, he thought. *In vain, my friends! I'm as clever as you are.* The other man had gone back to smoking and gazing out into the darkness.

"Nothing has been able to take my faith away from me—not even my other faith, my faith in Adolf Hitler and in National Socialism. And my colleagues and comrades have come to accept that. They know I am unshakably loyal to the *Führer* and the Reich," he said after a lengthy pause. "And in the end, only those who *believe*, those who have *faith*, can endure—in their innermost hearts—what Germany's enemies . . ."

"Wicked enemies," Bonhoeffer concurred with artificial enthusiasm. *But* you, he thought, *are referring to Jews and Bolsheviks, whereas I am referring to Hitler, to Himmler, to the Gestapo. And, yes, to the SS.*

" . . . what these criminals are doing to our fatherland. Yes, *criminals*." He paused. Then, very softly, "Those who love Germany pray for that. What," he suddenly turned his head toward Bonhoeffer, "do *you* pray for, Herr Pastor?"

"Naturally, I, too, pray for Germany. What else would one pray for?" Bonhoeffer hastily responded, simultaneously thinking of his conversation with Visser 't Hooft concerning exactly the same question. In that conversation, he had responded that he was praying "for the defeat of my country, for I believe that is the only possibility of paying for all the suffering which my country has caused in the world."

Even Visser 't Hooft had involuntarily gaped at Bonhoeffer in astonishment at this answer. And this man here in the train would unquestionably have pulled out his pistol and shot Bonhoeffer on the spot. Instead, he offered Bonhoeffer his cigarette case again. "Come, have one, Herr Pastor! An English brand, imported through Sweden. Excellent."

Bonhoeffer let the man light his cigarette. In the glow of the lit match he could see the man smiling, like a wolf, Bonhoeffer thought. "Being in certain positions does have its advantages. One can almost forget the horrific, abominable things one witnesses—and must witness—over time; you, me, all of us, every day. . . ."

"We're silent witnesses of evil deeds," Bonhoeffer mumbled.

"Excuse me?"

"Oh, nothing," Bonhoeffer hastily replied, "just the first line of a poem, from the Baroque period, I think. . . ." They both leaned back, smoked, and were silent again.

No, it was not the first line of a Baroque poem. It was the first line of a rendering of accounts Bonhoeffer was anticipating writing this year for himself and for a few others—like Dohnanyi, Oster, and Eberhard—as both encouragement *and* admonition.

"We have been washed with many waters, we have learned the arts of pretence and equivocal speech," it would say. *And yet all these waters,* Bonhoeffer thought, *have not been able to cleanse us after all. The filth of these years will always be on our hands.*

He thought of Karl Barth. One evening there in Basel, Barth had invited him to see a movie, a film with Marlene Dietrich, whom Barth idolized like a pubescent boy—"the immortal one," as he called her, a "borderline case of creation history." Later, after the film, the two men had sat together in a bistro with a plate of cheese, Barth's other passion, and a glass of wine.

"I know what many people in Germany would say about me if they could see us sitting here now," he had said, pausing to eat a slice of cheese, his zeal betraying his hearty appetite. "That Barth! Spends the winter all cozied up in Basel, goes out to Marlene Dietrich movies, eats cheese—all while we here are kindly permitted to soil our hands for Herr Hitler. Here's to you, Bonhoeffer!"

He had raised his glass. "I'm genuinely sorry I could have doubted you. You, too, may well be soiling your hands. But you're doing so for the ultimate cause—*against* Herr Hitler."

For whom is this man across from me, here in the train, soiling his hands? Bonhoeffer now wondered. *And on behalf of what cause? Do you also press the barrel of your revolver into the back of the heads of women and children? Do you also beat to death conscientious objectors from the clergy in concentration camps? Or are you one of the elite, someone who has other people do the dirty work while you smoke your English cigarettes and try to guess the occupations of tortured inmates?*

The train bleated out a long, shrill whistle. Almost like a cry for help.

They arrived in Munich toward morning. The warmth of the sun had not yet dispelled the morning chill. Bonhoeffer stood shivering on the platform.

Suddenly the man from the compartment was standing next to him, his face, a bit fatigued from lack of sleep, was no longer quite so sharp and angular. He had lost the Freisler profile, and his smile was genuinely pleasant. "Let me wish you a pleasant stay in our 'capital city of the National Socialist movement,' Herr . . ."

"Bonhoeffer. Dietrich Bonhoeffer."

"Gerstein. Kurt Gerstein."

Poor Dietrich

Bonhoeffer watched the slender man disappear in the early morning Munich fog. He soon forgot the man's name and even the entire encounter in the train. He would never learn who this Kurt Gerstein really was.

A member of the SS *and* a member of the Confessing Church, Gerstein had not been lying. In fact, he had already been expelled from the party because of his church membership. Then he returned and was accepted into the Waffen SS. At the time of his encounter with Bonhoeffer in the train, he was division leader of the SS Institute of Hygiene with the task of securing the poisonous gas for the genocide that had been set into motion the previous January at the Wannsee Conference.

He had tried to alert other countries through their diplomats and the church. In vain. After the war—he surrendered voluntarily—he died a mysterious death in a French prison. Given his absolutely unshakable commitment to Christianity, friends dismissed any possibility of suicide. They sooner suspected that Gerstein had had information that might make things unpleasant for countries *other* than merely Germany.

In any event, one morning he was found hanged in his cell, at about the same time when—at the beginning of the Cold War and in their fight against their new enemy, the Communists—the American intelligence services were quite unabashedly beginning to use Bonhoeffer's former interrogator Manfred Roeder and his methods, which had so successfully exposed the resistance group Red Orchestra.

Gerstein's name was included on the monument in Paris to the victims of fascism, and Israel designated him one of the "Righteous among the Nations." Because of the double identity he maintained during National Socialism, historians have compared him with Dietrich Bonhoeffer.

Meanwhile, during this summer of 1942, Bonhoeffer himself was primarily concerned with seeing whether Bell would manage to talk with the British foreign minister, Anthony Eden, and whether—even if he did see him—anything would come of the meeting. Things seemed to go very well indeed at first. After seeing the initial documentation, Eden had written "very interesting" across the top.

"Very interesting" was also what he said now, sitting across from Bell in the Foreign Office and flashing a camera-ready smile more suitable for Hollywood than the British cabinet. Churchill, however, just happened to really like handsome Tony.

"I took the liberty of having some information gathered about your German informants." He leaned back in his chair with the casual salon elegance of an Oscar Wilde character and toyed with an oversized golden paperweight on his desk. "Highly honorable gentlemen, no doubt about it, particularly this Herr Bonhoeffer. No Venlo people."

The "Venlo incident" took place right at the beginning of the war. In the Dutch town of Venlo, two British secret agents had been lured into a trap by alleged members of the German resistance who were in fact Gestapo agents. Their purpose was to gather "proof" in the postwar trial against the alleged Bürgerbräu Keller assassin, Johann Georg Elser, that "perfidious Albion"—Britain—had been involved.

"Highly honorable," the minister repeated, "but is it enough to topple a Herr Hitler?"

Bell enumerated the names Bonhoeffer had mentioned to him, especially those of the generals. Eden nodded at each name and seemed impressed. Only after a lengthy pause did he ask—albeit with politely coquettish skepticism—"And it's only now, after willingly conducting his war for him—and without any opposition or objection—that all these important gentlemen have suddenly come upon the idea of getting rid of their *Führer*?"

Bell felt taken by surprise, not least because Eden's objection could not so easily be dismissed. "Better now than never," was the only thing he could stammer out, simultaneously annoyed at the banality of his own response. The other man politely ignored his embarrassment.

"Let us assume that Hitler could indeed be eliminated along with his power apparatus—the Gestapo and the SS," he said. "What then? Would all the conquered territories be vacated, and would a new, different Germany emerge that would *no longer* be a danger to everyone else?"

"Well, certainly not a Germany in which a democratic form of government could immediately be implemented. And my friend Bonhoeffer sees that as well. He has no illusions in that regard. A more workable idea would be the reestablishment of the monarchy, in the constitutional sense."

"The Germans are to get another emperor, another kaiser?" Eden raised his eyebrows incredulously.

"Had they only left the old one on his throne, we would doubtless never have had to deal with Herr Hitler." Bell felt more certain of himself again. "Germany first needs to be able to catch its breath. *Then* one could negotiate a peace that would be advantageous for both sides. . . ."

" . . . and negotiate for a Germany within the boundaries of, say, 1937? Without Czechoslovakia being occupied? And of course, also without Poland? A peaceful, civilized nation?" Eden added. Bell breathed a sigh of relief. The other man seemed much more open to these ideas than Bell had hoped.

"This peaceful, civilized Germany," Eden continued, "would be essentially the same Germany that has already *twice* driven Europe into war, the first time, I might add, quite without the help of Herr Hitler and the SS."

Eden's suddenly harsh tone startled Bell. The foreign minister then got up and stood with his hands on the edge of the desk facing Bell. "Of course. For a few years we might have a bit peace and calm with such a Germany. More tea, Bishop?"

Bell politely waved him off.

"For a few years," the minister repeated, then began to pace back and forth with lengthy steps, "but then the Germans will start feeling strong again, several million, combat-ready battle machines in the middle of Europe who have *already* successfully stormed Poland and France, who have *already* advanced far enough to see Moscow's onion domes shimmering on the horizon, and who, quite frankly, think it something of a surprise that they have *not* managed to invade England itself. Are you sure you won't have more tea? And please do have some of the cookies; my personal cook baked them."

Bell again politely declined. Neither the cookies nor the tea seemed particularly attractive at this point. Eden, by contrast, stuffed two cookies into his mouth at once. "She recently admitted to me," he continued, wiping some crumbs from his moustache, "that she's been having nightmares about SS boots stamping around London's streets. I had quite a time of it calming her down, you know, assuring her that things will never get that far. The bombs raining down on our rooftops *quite* take care of any need we might have of 'things German.'"

He laughed briefly, then looked up as coldly and harshly as otherwise only his lord and master Churchill could do. "The European continent has been destroyed. Thanks to Herr Hitler and the *same* gentlemen who are now so intent on getting rid of him. And for what purpose? Merely to begin the *same* game all over again, just next time without him and with even better prospects for success and victory?"

His voice crackled with sarcasm. "One either has the Germans by the throat or on their knees. Are you familiar with that saying, Bishop?"

Bell did not answer.

"I would suggest," his voice was clearly putting the final note on the conversation, "that we first see to it that we get them on their knees— and let them stay there a while. And no one is to prevent us from doing precisely that. Including some Herr . . ."

"Bonhoeffer?"

"Yes, Bonhoeffer." Eden folded his arms after the fashion of Napoleon. "And you, Bishop, shouldn't become *too* intensely engaged on behalf of such men. They mean well. And that is exactly what makes them dangerous."

At this moment, Bell visualized Bonhoeffer, his blue eyes reflecting his profound belief that this world was perhaps not so bad after all.

On the contrary. It is indeed that bad. Here as well as there. Everywhere, the only issue is power and gauging power. And who is better able to oppress whom. Bell felt his anger rising. "Surely you're not suggesting that the Germans who oppose Hitler are already thinking about the next war and that we, at least those of us trying to promote peace with them, are in fact assisting them in that next war?"

Bell spoke so vehemently that the minister was taken slightly aback. He waved his hand in a defensive gesture. "God forbid, friend! Yours and all the others' intentions are certainly honorable. I am certainly taking you on your word on that one. It's just that in times of war, we must be careful not to be shortsighted. . . ."

He hesitated. "No, we will no doubt *not* be meeting the Germans on the field of battle so soon again. But who's to say that future wars will still be fought on battlefields?"

Bell did not understand.

"Perhaps future wars will take place somewhere completely different," Eden continued, "for example, in the world market, where the Germans are generally considered quite skillful. Give them a soap box in the middle of the desert, and before you know it they're driving away in a Mercedes. Or at least in one of those—what are those little tin cans called that the *Führer* has given them?—in one of those *Volkswagens*. . . ."

The minister laughed once more, but then immediately turned serious again. "Being a match for one's adversary means first of all not underestimating him, in *any* respect, and means taking cover against him in plenty of time." Eden sighed with a well-practiced theatrical *denouement*. "Peace in the world. Let us pray for that! I, however, am a politician, not a man of God like you. You are permitted to believe in eternity. I have to think about the future. And it is in the *future*, is it not, that our beloved country must remain a world power."

Point well taken. Bell understood that this was the end of their conversation. He stood up, laboriously. "So I'm not really permitted to send any signal of hope to Germany?"

Eden merely shrugged. "Well, you know our good Winston! A big-game hunter. And he's not about to let anyone else shoot down the biggest prey he has yet encountered in his life, namely, this Hitler and his Germany, and he is *certainly* not going to let the Germans themselves do it." He laughed again. "He'd sooner do without whiskey and cigars."

Bell still did not give up. But although he made various other attempts in England and even spoke before the House of Lords, he found scant applause. The overall disposition toward such suggestions remained icy.

"There really is no more hope that the war might end in the way your brother-in-law would like," the bishop remarked despondently in a conversation with Gerhard Leibholz, who with Bell's help had obtained a lecture position at Oxford. "If Hitler really can be toppled only by the military, and the latter really are waiting for the offer of an honorable peace—then he should abandon this dream, and do so quickly."

"*Armer Dietrich*," Leibholz said softly. Poor Dietrich.

Bell nodded. "*Armer Dietrich.*"

It only occurred to them later that they had spoken German together.

TEGEL, SEPTEMBER 25, 1944

Although Paul von Hase had visited Dietrich hardly three months ago, the outside world around Tegel has changed so fundamentally that it seems like at least three *years*. That said, however, the world here *inside* Tegel has hardly changed at all. Here Bonhoeffer is still sitting in his cell, still waiting for his trial, still waiting for the sentence, or for any—*any*—sign of perhaps an unexpected turn of events.

Today, on this day in late September, he is waiting for Knobloch.

Two months ago Knobloch had rushed into his cell quite out of breath and excited, not even bothering to greet Bonhoeffer. "Quick, quick, Herr Pastor, come to the infirmary, quick, something's going on. . . ."

In the infirmary they and others had gathered around the radio, though this time not to listen to the *Peer Gynt Suite* or the *Missa Solemnis* conducted by Furtwängler.

This time the black box had spit out news flashes, incomplete, fragmentary. Knobloch had turned the dial until they could hear foreign stations as well, British, French stations. Bonhoeffer translated what he understood. Something about a coup attempt, an assassination attempt on the *Führer* at his headquarters, the "Wolf's Lair," in Eastern Pomerania.

That was July 20, 1944.

"Is he dead?" Bonhoeffer had asked hoarsely. The others around the radio had merely looked up briefly, Knobloch putting his finger to his lips with a "shhh!" Then more news fragments, contradictory, and finally the familiar voice, throaty, guttural, dripping with hatred: "A tiny clique of stupid, cowardly, criminal officers . . ."

Hitler had survived. This last serious coup attempt, too, had failed.

Bonhoeffer had stumbled back to his cell, stunned, dazed. *It's all over*, he had thought. This was the absolute end of all the hopes to which he had clung based on his uncle's whispered allusions. The only comfort now was that no one could implicate him or his brother-in-law—who was in the prison hospital with two lame legs—of having anything to do with the coup attempt.

In the final analysis, Bonhoeffer had thought that night, *Uncle Paul was absolutely correct. Here in prison we are indeed safer.*

Hitler's wheels of revenge had already begun rolling. A "July 20 Special Commission" was established with Ernst Kaltenbrunner at its head, and the list of names Bonhoeffer had so proudly enumerated for Bishop Bell in Sweden—the whole circle of illustrious conspirators—began to shrink. Shot to death, hanged, including Paul von Hase. And then the investigators had begun calling on members of military intelligence.

Oster had been arrested, then two days later, on July 23, Canaris as well. Although there was still no serious evidence of high treason against them, how long would that situation last?

"The air's getting thin, Herr Pastor." Those were Knobloch's words as he had stood before Bonhoeffer one morning in September. Bonhoeffer could only shrug and turn back to Dostoyevsky's *House of the Dead*, which he was currently reading. "I know; but what can I do about it?"

"Some things, Herr Pastor." And Knobloch had begun to speak about his parents' garden plot, and about how secure one was there. Several people were already hiding there among the allotment gardens, in the huts, Jews and Communists. "They're sitting there like in the bosom of Abraham. And our people are keeping watch." Probably Social Democrats like

Knobloch himself.

"And how am I to get there, to this 'bosom of Abraham'?" Bonhoeffer had laughed softly at the idea and taken it more as a joke. But Knobloch was serious.

"Simple. Through the gate. And I'll accompany you all legitimate-like, and if anyone stops us, I'll mumble something like 'orders of the *Führer*' or something. And then away we go to Mother's garden hut. Of course, I'm going to stay there too until this whole business is over. I mean, I don't want to end up under the hatchet either, you know what I'm sayin'?"

He had grinned broadly and trustingly. "Can you imagine how cozy and all we'll be there? And finally enough time to really talk about God and the world and all that, without the stench of the cells and all. . . ."

An absolutely insane plan.

But maybe that was precisely what Bonhoeffer had liked about it. That it really was completely, utterly crazy and unimaginable. Hadn't there already been a *great many* things in his life that a person could call completely unimaginable?

"First you'll go to my parents, no . . . ," Bonhoeffer hesitated, reconsidered, then, "no, not to my parents. We won't involve them in this. But you'll go to my sister and her husband, Rüdiger Schleicher. They live in the house next door and they'll give you money, and ration cards—after all, we'll need something to eat besides carrots and potatoes. And then also . . ."

Bonhoeffer had paused.

"What else, Herr Pastor? Everything else we need is already in the garden hut, really. . . ."

"Maybe the Schleichers can rummage up a jumpsuit or overalls, a blue one or something like that, like mechanics wear." Bonhoeffer had recently seen something like this during his time in the exercise yard. "After all, I can't just walk through the front gate in my prison garb. But senior guard Knobloch and mechanic Bonhoeffer. . . ." They had both laughed; Knobloch had nodded his approval. "Super idea, Herr Pastor!"

"And for heaven's sake don't call me 'Herr Pastor' just as we're leaving. We might as well just stay here in that case." They had laughed again.

So, today, on this September 25, Bonhoeffer is waiting for Knobloch to return from the Schleichers.

He finally arrives carrying a package. "Everything's here, Herr Pastor. Including the blue overalls. Heaven only knows how your brother-in-law found them so fast. . . ." Bonhoeffer nods and yet softly sighs. "But how long—really—will we be genuinely safe in the garden hut?" He dreads the thought of having to live in perpetual fear, of having to panic at *every* sound, *every* footstep.

We have to get completely out of Germany, he had thought the night before, *by absolutely any means necessary.* He thinks about the Swedish legation and its pastor, with whom the Confessing Church had always been on good terms. Maybe he can come up with passports for them.

"For me, too, Herr Pastor?"

"Of course. If you help me flee, you'll be in as much danger as I am."

Knobloch flashes a broad, satisfied grin. "The two of us up there in Sweden. I've always wanted to go there. And now even without 'Strength through Joy.'" Bonhoeffer smiles at Knobloch's reference to the state-controlled organization that has made leisure activities available to the "masses."

The next week, on October 1 ("Too conspicuous if I show up at your relatives' too often"), Knobloch returns to the Schleichers. And again Bonhoeffer waits.

A relationship of fate, he thinks, *like many others in my life—like that with Franz Hildebrandt or Eberhard.* There with colleagues from the same social standing, here with a prison guard and Social Democrat who has perhaps never even been *inside* a church. And why not? The world outside there is a different one now. Why should there not be completely different, completely new relationships and communities in the future?

When Knobloch arrives, Bonhoeffer senses he is a bit addled. "What's wrong?"

"I'm supposed to come back tomorrow, they said. They're all flustered and upset."

"Why? Did something happen?"

"The Gestapo must have been there, and one of your brothers, I think they said Klaus . . ."

"What's happened to him?"

"They've picked him up, or are going to pick him up, it wasn't really clear, everybody was just so upset and all, and your brother-in-law, Herr Schleicher, he mumbled something, sounded something like . . . like . . ."

Knobloch pauses, trying to remember. Then, hesitatingly, "Something like 'the safe has been opened.'"

The safe in the Zossen bunker. With all the documentation, all the lists of names, everything. All the Gestapo needs to do is check off one after the other. And it's doing exactly that, having been led there by a former driver in military intelligence— Kerstenhahn is his name.

So, now one can no longer say, "They have nothing concrete against us." Now they have everything. Or more exactly, they have something that is better and more thorough than even the most lengthy confession.

"But fine, I'll go back tomorrow. They'll all have calmed down again by then. . . ." Knobloch has walked over to the cell door again.

"*No!*" Knobloch, startled by Bonhoeffer's abrupt and harsh response, turns around.

Bonhoeffer stares straight ahead, then says very softly, "Or rather yes; *yes*, do go back! Tell my brother-in-law that our plan is *over*, it's *no more*, it's *over!*" The authorities would immediately return to the Schleichers. And the Gestapo would be merciless with the family of any fugitive co-conspirator, *merciless*. Better to stay here and take whatever fate hands out. And to do it alone.

Bonhoeffer avoids Knobloch's disappointed gaze, waiting to look up until he has closed the cell door behind him with a heavy clank. But he regrets nothing. He has always been able to rely on his family, and now they should be able to rely on him.

He stares at the piece of paper he's holding. A poem he had written a few days ago. He has sent a copy to Eberhard. Verses about his favorite character in the Bible, Moses, the Pharaonic prince of Hebrew lineage who, renouncing all his privileges, had wanted to lead his people to the promised land. He has called the poem "The Death of Moses."

> *On the mountain's summit now stands*
> *Moses, man of God and prophet old.*
>
> *Unwavering now his eyes behold*
> *the sacred, promised land below.*
>
> *For now, as gentle death draws near,*
> *the Lord himself has descended nigh*
>
> *to show from heights silent and clear,*
> *that future promised, now so near;*
>
> *the weary traveler he allows*
> *to greet in silent tranquility,*
>
> *and bless with his final breath*
> *his home, then peace in gentle death.*

Bonhoeffer then reads the next lines in a soft, almost silent voice:

> *From a distance now this land you'll see,*
> *though never there, never will you be.*

Are We Still of Any Use?

1942/43

*"It may be that judgment day
will dawn tomorrow.
In that case, we will gladly cease with our work
on behalf of a better future.
But not before."*
—Dietrich Bonhoeffer, Christmas 1942

"I Know That I Will Love Him"

Ursula Schleicher filled her glass again with wine punch, took a sip, and then looked over toward the chairs in the back corner of the winter garden. "Just look at our Dietrich," she smiled, nudging her husband, Rüdiger, "usually so ready and willing to entertain everyone in the room—but today the young Wedemeyer girl seems to be all the company he needs. They've been sitting together the entire evening already!" Rüdiger Schleicher also glanced over into the back corner, where Bonhoeffer was sitting next to Maria von Wedemeyer—perhaps a bit closer than was really necessary?

The family still had its little celebrations here in Grunewald, almost as if the outside world were not really plagued by the death and destruction they all knew was going on elsewhere. But tonight on Marienburg Allee the occasion was special. Hans-Walter, the Schleichers' only son, was scheduled to be sent to the front the next morning, and all the cheerfulness and merriment seemed markedly artificial and forced. Here, too, the shadow of war was omnipresent.

At the end of June 1942, Hitler's grand offensive in the East—"Operation Blue"—had commenced, an attempt to reinvigorate the now-crumbling euphoria following the lightning victories of the *Blitzkrieg* and the nation's high-riding hopes for the "great victory." And indeed, Liszt's *Préludes* were already being played on the radio before each new, triumphal "special bulletin."

Sevastopol: fallen. Voronezh: fallen. One hundred fifty thousand Soviet prisoners-of-war. Advance to the Caucasus, where German troops raised the Reich flag on the highest mountain, albeit much to the chagrin of Hitler, who prohibited such circus acts in the midst of the "greatest struggle of nations in history."

Then his orders to march on Stalingrad. That was to be the death blow to the Soviet power. Everyone was waiting for the special bulletin: "Stalingrad: defeated."

It never came. What came instead, and in increasing numbers, were lists of soldiers killed in action, with the added note "at Stalingrad." One of the soldiers on those lists was Hans von Wedemeyer, the estate owner in Pätzig in the Neumark region, Maria's father.

"He was a soldier, through and through. He hated Hitler and yet died in Hitler's war," Maria now said. Bonhoeffer could only shrug his shoulders helplessly. A young man walked by in a field gray uniform. Hans-Walter Schleicher. Bonhoeffer was especially fond of this nephew. He stood up.

"Well? Are you content to be going to the front?" He knew how anxious the young man was to join those his own age. "You'll be experiencing some horrible things, Hans-Walter, but remember that you're also taking along with you much that is good." Bonhoeffer put his hand on his nephew's shoulder for a brief moment. "All the experiences of the home you grew up in, your faith, and your ability to recognize what is truly beautiful in this world. Like music." The young man had inherited his uncle's musical inclinations.

"How old is he?" Maria asked as the young man walked away.

"He just turned eighteen."

"Eighteen. And my brother Maximilian just turned twenty-two." Maria pensively looked down at her hands folded in her lap. "My father at least had a chance to live his life, and to live it richly and well. But how on earth is it that young men like these, young men who have not even had a chance to *begin* their lives, have to be shot down at some faraway front during such a war?" She spoke very calmly, really more with curiosity and puzzlement, as if pondering one of life's many riddles.

Bonhoeffer, who was otherwise quick with a response to such questions, did not quite know what to say. And he certainly did not want to flee into banal platitudes in front of this clear-minded, bright young girl.

"It's really more a question of tradition. Young men have long been raised in this tradition—generation after generation," he began with some hesitation, not wanting to come down so hard on Maria while she was thinking about her father and worrying about her brother, and yet at the same time not wanting to betray his own position. "They rarely ask, and are rarely asked, whether they really *believe* in what they're dying for. That, too, is part of the tradition, though some people . . ."

He paused, sensing Maria's questioning gaze.

"Though some," he continued, a slight undertone of pride emerging, "some, that is, a very few, are able to fight only for that which they genuinely believe in. And they have it rather hard, my dear . . . Mm, Fräulein."

He still felt a bit awkward with this form of address—rather than simply "Maria" as earlier. But the young woman seemed to ignore it, merely nodding almost imperceptibly, as if encouraging him to continue.

Bonhoeffer now became more animated. "If they approve of the goal they're fighting for, then fine and well. But if they don't, if they oppose it, then they must find other fronts than the one out there. And then they have the right, perhaps even the obligation, to refuse to take up arms."

"Like you, Herr Pastor?" Maria in her own turn could not really dispense with addressing him as "Herr Pastor" even though he had repeatedly asked her to do so.

"I haven't refused military service; I . . . ," he began again earnestly, horrified at the thought that this girl here might view him as a coward or shirker. But this time she interrupted him. "My father did what he considered his duty. And you, Herr Pastor, do what you think is yours. And you are surely just as courageous a man. But tell me," she seemed to want to change the subject, "will we be seeing each other again at Grandmother's?"

Maria's grandmother had just had a cataract operation and was lying in the Franciscan Hospital in Berlin with bandages over her eyes. She had summoned her granddaughter to her bedside to read aloud to her until her eyesight returned. For all practical purposes, Bonhoeffer and Maria's paths could not help crossing there, and for his part Bonhoeffer could not help suspecting that it was no accident Maria's grandmother had arranged things precisely thus.

The next horrible news came at the end of October.

Maria's brother Maximilian had also been killed in action. Because Bonhoeffer had given Maximilian confirmation instruction, it would have been quite natural for him to be invited to the memorial service in Pätzig. Which was why he was all the more surprised to get a phone call from Maria's mother. "It is my wish, Herr Pastor, that for the time being you *not* come here. And please *refrain* as well from writing any more letters to Maria. . . ."

Bonhoeffer stared at the black telephone receiver for a while, stunned, long after he had actually hung it up. What in heaven's name was *that* supposed to mean?

He knew absolutely nothing of any vehement conversations between mother and daughter in Pätzig.

"And you believe you love him?"

"I know that I *will* love him."

What a daughter! Frau von Wedemeyer had almost laughed out loud at the response, a response that was *so* typical of Maria.

So, she did not love Bonhoeffer. But she knew with all the considerable assurance of her nineteen years that she *would* love him someday? A man almost twice her age, and without the *von* of German nobility in front of his name? And anyway, what did this man really *do*?

A pastor without a church, without a congregation, perpetually away on obscure trips abroad without anyone ever really learning the purpose. But Maria's mother knew instinctively that the most foolish *tactical* move would be to make the beloved man look bad in front of her daughter.

"Perhaps he is indeed a suitable man for you," she began cautiously, "but are you also a suitable woman for him? He loves his books, his academics. Could you countenance that, I mean, in the long run? You like so much to *laugh*, to dance, to have fun, you're a young girl who wants to *enjoy* this world. Can you imagine yourself at the side of a quiet scholar who wants to carry on 'erudite' discussions while you'd rather chat in Low German with the servants?"

She paused for effect, then affected a superior smile. "What would your husband say if—as was recently genuinely the case—you were to get up in the middle of the night, put on an evening gown, and prance about the house singing along with some sort of Negro music or other. . . ."

Maria blushed. Why had her mother had to come upon her at *exactly* that moment, of all times? Her mother now reached for her hand. "I'm not interested in forbidding you from doing anything, Maria, just in helping you choose the path that's best for *you*."

For one year—this was now her mother's suggestion—the two should not see each other. No letters, no conversations, and certainly no meetings during this period, a period that would moreover be long enough for Maria to possibly meet a different, younger, more attractive man.

That was Ruth von Wedemeyer's secret goal even though her words spoke of a different one. "The child needs to come to some sort of inner equipoise," she had told Bonhoeffer when he had come to Pätzig in November after all.

Bonhoeffer felt righteous anger welling up inside him. Who was he—a pastor, a doctor of theology, a professor—that he had to suffer this woman treating him like a schoolboy? *If she were a man*, he thought for a moment, *I'd give her a good piece of my mind.* But then he looked at this woman, dressed in widow's black, and he was overwhelmed with sympathy—as he was with all the women during this wretched war who were trying to be both father and mother to their children. And this sympathy smothered his anger.

I need to talk about all this with Eberhard, he thought during his return trip from Pätzig. *Maybe he can write to this lady and make it clear to her that I'm not one of those men young girls need to be protected against. Lucky friend!*

Eberhard, too, had fallen in love with a girl almost half his age, namely, Bonhoeffer's seventeen-year-old niece, Renate Schleicher, and *her* parents had had no great reservations or objections. When their engagement had been celebrated on the fourth Sunday of Advent, Bonhoeffer had observed the couple not without a little envy.

Why can't things ever be like that for me, without the inevitable problems and complications? Why do I always get a small tragedy delivered free of charge as well? he thought. Was fate—perhaps resentful of his privileged past as a little prince—now extracting its revenge?

"Seek not the favor of the gods!"

He had always thought this expression a bit of nonsense. He could never quite imagine a God who could begrudge his creations their happiness. Now, however, he wondered. Perhaps there was such a God after all. And perhaps Maria's mother was also right, whereas he—a bit plumpish, his hair already thinning, and, frankly, old compared to Maria—perhaps he was indeed not really a suitable partner for a girl not yet even twenty years old.

Well, then, who was he?

I am Bonhoeffer. And, who knows, perhaps Bonhoeffer is not even supposed to have a female companion. Perhaps he has been condemned to being alone and will simply have to bear the hand he's been dealt. He bravely smiled over toward the engaged couple.

The year came to an end. They celebrated New Year's Eve out with the Dohnanyis in Sakrow. Pancakes had been served, everyone had been guardedly cheerful, and toward midnight, as Bonhoeffer was gazing out into the dark garden, Dohnanyi came over carrying two glasses of champagne.

"You're thinking about your Maria, aren't you?"

"Well, yes, about her, too." Actually, he had been thinking about how absurd and petty problems such as his really were while elsewhere entire cities were perishing in firestorms and daily thousands of people were being mowed down on the battlefield.

"Have you ever actually *asked* her whether she loves you and wants to marry you?"

"No. Not yet. Not really." *I haven't yet gotten up the courage*, he almost added. But he didn't want to admit that even to his brother-in-law.

"Well, *ask* her. And then just do what Christine and I did." They, too, had initially become secretly engaged. But Bonhoeffer shook his head. "I'm too old for that sort of thing, Hans. I'm probably just going to have to accept that I won't be seeing Maria for an entire year. Unless I climb up on her balcony like in Shakespeare."

Dohnanyi laughed. "You, of all people, a Romeo? Ah, Dietrich! But I must say I'm genuinely happy you have at least found your Juliet."

Bonhoeffer, too, had to laugh. "But can you imagine Romeo and Juliet as a 'normal' married couple who buy furniture, argue over the color of the wallpaper, and decorate a nursery? Isn't it *precisely* their unhappy ending that lends them tragic grandeur?" He sighed. "Not that I take myself for a Shakespearean hero. But seriously, should someone like me even marry at all? Are any of us still of use in a normal life or a normal world?"

"Because 'we have been silent witnesses of evil deeds, we who have had to learn the arts of equivocation and pretense and who speak false words to false friends,' as you wrote in your essay?" Dohnanyi smiled. "By the way, thank you for sending me a copy. A wonderful Christmas present, that essay, 'After Ten Years.' . . ."

"Ah, just a few thoughts, really." Bonhoeffer waved him off.

"Dangerous thoughts that could cost all of us our heads. Eberhard," Dohnanyi laughed, "hid his copy beneath a tile on his roof. Let's hope the bombs don't 'extract' it any time soon."

Now Dohnanyi, too, looked out into the garden. "A very good description of these ten years during which we have at least *tried* to stand up to evil, and your question is certainly justified. Are we really good for *anything* now except treason and resistance? Will it *ever* be possible for us to say yes to a world again as naturally as we still could ten years ago?"

Outside, beyond the trees, the Havel River glittered in the moonlight. A half-moon peered down from the crystal-clear, cold night sky. An idyllic scene of almost dangerous harmony.

"The only thing left for us now is to take the narrow, almost imperceptible path, and to do so each day as if it were the last, and yet to live in faith and with a sense of responsibility as if a great, grand future still lay ahead of us." Dohnanyi had spoken these lines as softly and with as solemn an intonation as if he were reciting a poem. "It may be that judgment day will dawn tomorrow. In that case, we will gladly cease with our work on behalf of a better future. But not before."

"Well, I see you've learned my scribblings by heart!" Bonhoeffer was astonished.

"I didn't have to. I've quite mastered the lesson as well." He handed Dietrich the glass of champagne. "So, then, before the apocalypse crashes down on us, let us now quickly drink to Dr. Luther's apple tree and to his assertion that 'If I knew that tomorrow was the end of the world, I would *still* plant an apple tree today!'" Dohnanyi lifted his glass. "And to you, Dietrich! May judgment day tarry perhaps a *bit* longer that you might still have the opportunity to woo your Maria!"

And they did indeed drink to that prospect. And to the prospect that the coming year might not be quite so terrible.

O Queen! O Heaven! How Lovely Still Is Life!

As a matter of fact, however, that year, 1943, turned out to be much, much more terrible.

The battle for Stalingrad turned into precisely the catastrophe many had already seen coming in the fall. A defeated Sixth Army staggered into Soviet prisoner-of-war camps. That was the great turn in the war.

Soon thereafter a plane was shot down in Africa thought to be carrying Winston Churchill to a conference in Casablanca. In fact, it was carrying the British actor Leslie Howard, who a short time before, as Ashley in *Gone with the Wind*, had made hordes of teenage girls sob with grief.

Churchill had, however, in the meantime conferred with the American president Franklin D. Roosevelt in Casablanca. Between cigar puffs, they came to an agreement that there was to be no peace with Germany without unconditional surrender.

"Is that now the beginning of the end?"

Dohnanyi was sitting together with Oster, who had been promoted to major general the previous year. Oster had momentarily lost his familiar optimism, then quickly regained his confidence. "Perhaps this is also our chance. Perhaps now even the most inveterate procrastinators among us will finally comprehend that there is but one path now: to end the war now, when our armed forces are still able to make a halfway decent impression on the enemy."

"But are the armed forces genuinely able to do that now?"

"Not if Hitler drives them into the ground once and for all, and that is what the gentlemen in Casablanca are counting on. They, too, are no doubt familiar with Hitler's assertion that he has *never* quit until five minutes *past* twelve. But now?"

Oster leaned back in his chair. "Even though over a million German soldiers have been killed in action, there are still almost two million on active duty, one of the strongest and most feared armies in the world today. Even Churchill will stop and consider whether he *really* wants to fight to the last man with such an army."

Dohnanyi now performed his signature gesture, folding his hands beneath his chin and leaning his head forward like a hunting dog that has just picked up the scent. "Perhaps. But perhaps not. What needs to happen is for there no longer to *be* any Hitler in the first place. Hitler needs to be dead for our generals to abandon him. They *won't* do that as long as he's still alive and still their commander in chief."

"Exactly. And now the race begins. What will come more quickly, Hitler's fall—or that of Germany?"

Bonhoeffer had been more concerned with something else during these winter days. He had received a letter.

From Maria. She wrote that her mother was indeed still insisting on a year of separation and that she, Maria, did not really want to go against her mother's wishes in that regard. Nevertheless—or for precisely that reason—she was now giving him her irrevocable, unshakable yes. Forever.

So, there it stood. The yes that he himself had not even gotten up the courage to request.

Bonhoeffer felt ashamed. Maria was braver than he. Without his even having declared his own intentions to her, she had bet everything on a single card—and played it. And what if he had now said no? She would have been the girl who—shame of shames—had run after a man.

Courageous Maria! Completely unconcerned about reputation or convention!

His admiration for her now included an almost boyish feeling of giddiness that Bonhoeffer had, quite frankly, never experienced. He thought of his schooldays, when they had assigned roles to read Schiller's play *Don Carlos* aloud. His had been the role of Marquis Posa. "O queen! O heaven! How lovely still is life!"

Yes, life was lovely. Despite everything.

Bonhoeffer felt life and activity well up in him again. He wanted to act. To *do* something that peace might come soon and with it a life together with Maria. He wanted to start up with his trips abroad again, the secret assignments, perhaps to Switzerland, or to . . .

"Easy, Dietrich!" Dohnanyi tried to calm him down. "Yes, we can send you to the Balkans, for discussions with members of the ecumenical movement there. You can go ahead and apply for a visa."

The Balkans? What on earth was he supposed to do there? And again Bonhoeffer suspected that although his brother-in-law was indeed concerned with taking care of Bonhoeffer as one of his relatives, he did not particularly put much stock in Bonhoeffer's active participation in military intelligence.

"And if I were to travel to Rome?"

He asked the question so softly that Dohnanyi at first did not even understand it. But then he wrinkled his brow. "What do you expect to accomplish in Rome? Establish contacts through the Vatican with the

British the way our Josef Müller did three years ago? And then what? Ah, Dietrich!" He sighed. "You yourself have already seen how useless even the direct contact through George Bell turned out to be."

"No. Not contact with the British. With the Vatican itself."

"And ultimately with the pope himself?" Dohnanyi took off his glasses and began to clean them, now looking at his brother-in-law with his shortsighted eyes, skeptically, almost amused.

Bonhoeffer would not be deterred. "Think about the ruckus during the 1930s with the pope and his encyclical *With Burning Concern* and all the protests there against National Socialist policies! If the pope would *now* summon the Allies to conclude a peace with Germany as soon as Hitler is out of the way. . . ."

"Well, Dietrich, as you know, we have a *new* pope now."

Dohnanyi was referring to Eugenio Pacelli, the former nuncio of Berlin who had become Pius XII in 1939. "They call him the 'German pope,' and word has it that he would never take any action directly against Hitler, not least because he wants to use Hitler as a shield against the godless pagan Stalin if push ever comes to shove. . . ."

Bonhoeffer shook his head. "But still. If he can now hear from me what is happening to the Jews, for example . . ."

"Do you really think he hasn't known about all that for a long time now?" Dohnanyi breathed on his eyeglasses and continued to clean them. "As you know, we have connections everywhere, including with the nunciature here in Berlin. A man recently surfaced there, a member of the SS no less, who related utterly horrific, gruesome, completely incredible things that are allegedly happening to the Jews in the East."

"Nothing is incredible in that regard, Hans."

"Yes, I fear you're right. But this man—what was his name again?— anyway, he wanted this information to be funneled on directly to Rome, to the pope. . . ."

"And?"

"No reaction. Nothing. Silence. The pope is not responding at all." Dohnanyi put his glasses on again. "Ah, yes, now I remember the man's name. Gerstein . . ."

Bonhoeffer's ears perked up. Although the name seemed familiar to him, he could not immediately place it. Dohnanyi looked at his watch. "Oh, man, isn't today February 17? Goebbels is about to speak in the Sports Palace, no doubt to explain to us how Stalingrad is *actually* a great victory. We certainly don't want to miss *that.* . . ."

He turned the tuning knob on the radio until the all-too-familiar "advertising voice" of Herr Goebbels could be heard talking about how émigrés abroad were helplessly mocking their archenemy. His voice swelled with its customary, predictable pathos. "And I now ask you before those of our enemies who may be listening to us on their own radios. . . ."

The Net Closes In

On this February 17, 1943, the little man Goebbels enjoyed, with little doubt, his greatest day.

Five thousand worshipful faces looking up at him, five thousand voices shouting out a collective "*Heil!*" And he, standing there above them all, the *high priest* of the grand, brooding god Hitler who had withdrawn behind the clouds, sullen, grumbling, ruminating over the incomprehensible defeat at Stalingrad. Goebbels, the regime's premier "advertising executive," was truly in his element here. Nor did he shy away from the truth. No, indeed. He presented an "unadorned description of the situation." And he also mysteriously suggested that all previous sacrifices were absolutely *not* in vain, but that only "the future itself will provide the explanation!"

But for now—his thin arms stretched up into the air like spears and his eyes burning with a fire hardly less ardent than the "bonfire of the vanities" of the fanatical Florentine monk Savonarola—for now he was content to conjure in lurid colors the imminent onslaught of the Asian hordes against the venerable, almost two-thousand-year-old culture of the West, as whose highest representatives—obviously—he viewed himself and his *Führer*. At the latter notion Bonhoeffer, who had been listening intently enough, could not suppress a shrill, cynical laugh. Dohnanyi glanced up at him, half amused, half irritated. Then the two listened further.

The man up on the podium in the Sports Palace, an enormous banner behind him with the words "Total War—Quickest War," had in the meantime transitioned to his "ten questions to the German nation" and had just arrived at number four, the most crucial and grandiose of all. "Do you want *total* war? Do you, if necessary, want it even *more* total and *more* radical than we have *ever* imagined it?"

Again, the huge hall resounded with a single, fanatical, roaring *Yes!* And thus it continued, always with the same refrain, "*Führer*, give the orders! We will follow. . . ." and "German women, to *work!* German men, to *arms!* . . ."

Goebbels finally left the stage after evoking Theodor Körner's cry from the Wars of Liberation at the beginning of the nineteenth century—"Rise up now, O people; break forth now, O storm!" No one in the hall, however, caught the terrible irony that the very battle cry against Napoleonic *tyranny* had just been counterfeited into a cry *for* the tyrant Hitler.

In the anteroom, however, Minister Goebbels weighed himself. In four hours, he had lost seven pounds, and his hoarse voice was frayed by declamations and shouting. "I could have told that crowd out there to jump out a window—and they would have *done* it."

Well, not quite all of them. Nor was all the apparent "trust" in Hitler quite as sincere, grand, and unshakable as he had just demanded with his "fifth question to the German nation."

The next morning, two slender figures flitted through the main administration building of the University of Munich, a young woman and a young man. They were laying flyers on the steps and landings. Suddenly a voice boomed in the otherwise empty corridor. "Hey, you! What're you doin' there?"

It was the custodian.

The two figures disappeared out the door. The man picked up one of the flyers and read, his eyes getting ever wider. "The brilliant strategy of the corporal from the Great War has driven 330,000 German men into meaningless and irresponsible death and destruction. *Führer*, let us thank you. . . ." He dropped the flyer. "Hey, that stuff isn't allowed here." He snorted with indignant excitement. "Well, I'm gonna report that and pronto." Yes, indeed, being somebody important was a *good* feeling.

In a very short time, the students Hans and Sophie Scholl and the other members of the resistance group "White Rose" had been arrested and indicted. And Dohnanyi's old adversary Roland Freisler—the former leftist and "Bolshevik" who was now wearing the red robe of the president of the People's Court because, as Hitler put it at his appointment, he "deserved another chance"—was finally in a position to demonstrate that he was even *more* right-wing and *more* radical than anyone else in the regime.

By February the Scholl siblings had been found guilty, sentenced, and executed. By October, four other members of the White Rose had been executed as well.

Bonhoeffer put his hands behind his head and gazed into the blue spring sky. Young people being slaughtered on the battlefield. Young people being executed on the scaffold. Had the entire world turned into nothing more than a deathbed? Was *he* himself already lying in that bed as well? Was *his* head, too, already beneath the same guillotine blade that had severed the heads of the Scholls?

He forced himself to think about something else.

"We should be infinitely grateful to the Scholls, Hans. Now all the world knows that the entire German nation is not just a mass of roaring, bellowing yes-men like the five thousand in the Sports Palace. There are *other* Germans as well. The Scholls died for the honor of us all."

"Glorious honor, glorious death." Dohnanyi did not seem to be guided by emotions *quite* as sublime. "And as far as our own plans are concerned, we can now count on our friends in the Reich Central Security Office being *doubly* vigilant with regard to such activity," he continued. "Not a particularly good situation, Dietrich, believe me."

Bonhoeffer did not understand what Dohnanyi was getting at. "Look, I realize it was nothing but a pitiful, meager protest by a few students down in Munich. I also realize it was just a tiny group of outsiders and loners who had no real hope of accomplishing anything, ever. But after the assassination attempt in the Bürgerbräu Keller, you yourself said that someday such outsiders and loners might perhaps be our last hope."

"Of course." Dohnanyi fumbled through his pockets looking for a cigarette. Bonhoeffer gave him his own cigarette case. "But what," Dohnanyi said after taking the first, deep drag, "what did this Swabian carpenter, this Johann Georg Elser, *really* accomplish that night? Let me tell you."

After another long, greedy drag on the cigarette, he continued. "The security measures around Hitler were intensified to the point that since then, an assassination has for all practical purposes become impossible. One simply cannot get to Hitler. That's what Elser accomplished."

He paced back and forth, nervously, dragging ever more greedily on his cigarette. "Things don't look good for us, Dietrich. The days when Canaris and our dearly departed Heydrich—God have mercy on his wicked soul!—negotiated a ceasefire between military intelligence and the Central Security Office and these two weren't getting in each other's way so frightfully—those days are over. The police over on Prince Albrecht Street are getting ready to lower the boom on us. And I fear. . . ." He interrupted himself. "Do you have another cigarette, Dietrich?"

Bonhoeffer gave him one from his case. "You fear what, Hans?"

Dohnanyi flicked the lighter twice, then a third time. No flame. He let his hand sink to his side with the cigarette in it. "I fear they've found the perfect platform to lower that boom."

Dohnanyi was speaking even more truth than he himself could have suspected at the time. Certain developments had been set into motion a year ago.

In Prague, at one of the two main train stations, a small-time black marketeer had been apprehended doing a brisk business with American dollars and jewels. During the interrogation he had stammered out some names of people behind the scenes, including the honorary Portuguese consul in Munich, Adolf Wilhelm Schmidhuber, and his secretary, Heinrich Wilhelm Ickradt. Both men were also members of the Munich branch of military intelligence, where Schmidhuber was something like Bonhoeffer's "supervising officer"—even though he had not really done much "supervising" in that capacity.

But Bonhoeffer was genuinely fond of the merry descendant of a Bavarian brewery dynasty. Dohnanyi, too, valued the black-haired rogue and generously overlooked Schmidhuber's inclination—one he hardly concealed—to pursue all sorts of activities well outside the sphere of legality. For it was precisely through such activity that this Schmidhuber had garnered for military intelligence the reputation among its enemies for being Germany's most effective and well-oiled entity as far as self-sufficiency was concerned. A person with Schmidhuber's merry personality could only laugh at this "honor," as did Dohnanyi. Oster, who was more skeptical about such things, could not.

Now, however, things got very serious.

Schmidhuber was arrested at the end of October 1942. His interrogator was Franz Xaver Sonderegger from the Gestapo, who would later reappear at Roeder's side at both Bonhoeffer's and Dohnanyi's arrest. A very skillful and capable man, this Sonderegger. Schmidhuber, when asked about his black-market money activities, quickly stumbled over his own words and became hopelessly entangled in contradictions. He finally started talking about money he had been asked to make available for Herr Dohnanyi, who, he claimed, needed the money for agents smuggled into Switzerland. Fourteen people, and yes, all of them were Jews.

Sonderegger's ears perked up.

Schmidhuber, never the strongest or toughest person in any case, nor—certainly—the brightest, now babbled on, increasingly compliant toward his interrogator, for he now thought his former friends in military intelligence had betrayed him. In a fit of vengeance, he now provided a plethora of allusions to a clique of generals who were planning something like a coup soon and intended to negotiate peace with the enemy.

Even at the beginning of the war, Schmidhuber now maintained, contacts had been made with the British by way of the Vatican for just this purpose. Then later contacts through the Protestant church in Sweden. And then he started naming names. Josef Müller. Bonhoeffer. And, with increasing frequency, Dohnanyi, the "old conservative" who allegedly thought the war was lost and was already making plans for a "start-up government" during the postwar period whose first action would be a ceasefire.

Well, well, Sonderegger thought. The office of military intelligence nothing but a resistance nest full of conspirators and traitors, and corrupt to boot, neck-deep in illegal money exchange and nepotism. . . .

Sonderegger was certain that this time he had a fairly big fish on the line, ultimately perhaps even a fish by the name of Canaris. First, however, he had to focus on the smaller fish.

"What," Sonderegger leaned over to a Gestapo colleague, "is this Dohnanyi doing wheeling and dealing such enormous sums of money? Schmidhuber claims he smuggled no less than a hundred thousand dollars into Switzerland for Dohnanyi, and jewels as well, all for this handful of Jews who are allegedly working as agents for us."

"And allegedly with our authorization, so I hear."

"Well, that's possible enough. But that much money? What can this Dokhnanyi—or whatever his name is—what can he be thinking?"

"I think he pronounces it 'Doh–nan–yee.'"

"No matter. Anyway he's Hungarian or something. But why did he recruit this particular pastor with a botched career, of all people, to be secret agent, this Dietrich Bonhoeffer, even securing a military deferral for him?"

"Bonhoeffer's his brother-in-law."

"Ahh. . . ."

A thick file was sent on to the head of the SS and chief of the German police, Heinrich Himmler. Sonderegger already saw himself on the highest rung of the ladder of success. Peculiarly, however, Himmler reacted rather coolly.

"We really shouldn't make too much of this, don't you agree? Let's just treat it as no more than a money-laundering operation and leave it at that," he remarked to General Wilhelm Keitel, head of the High

Military Command, an officer so blindly dedicated to Hitler that in the officer canteens he was mocked as "General *Lackey*-tel." "And above all, as far as I'm concerned they need to quit bothering Canaris, a very bright man . . . and who knows what need we may have of him later?"

Himmler, too, thought the war was already lost. He, too, was keeping an eye out for confederates who might be of some use to him during the inevitable negotiations with the Allies.

The "Cash Fund Deposit Affair," as it became known, a file of no less than sixty pages, was withdrawn from the jurisdiction of the Gestapo and transferred to that of the armed forces, albeit with the assistance of the ever-valiant Sonderegger. He in his own turn now joined the new investigative official, Manfred Roeder, a senior prosecutor for the military high court who was still bathed in the glow of his success at having liquidated the Berlin resistance group Red Orchestra.

All this took place during the first days of April 1943. In the middle of March, Dohnanyi could not have known anything about these developments. He sensed only that a net was inexorably, inescapably closing in on him and all the other conspirators. "Unless something happens we aren't anticipating."

"What else can happen, Hans?"

"Oh, nothing. Just a thought. Something can always happen. Even quite suddenly."

Dohnanyi wiped his brow nervously and forced himself to act with a kind of hectic cheerfulness. "So, now, yes, let's think about what we can do to make your father's big day as grand as possible; let's be sure to. . . ." He stopped in mid-sentence, as if he had just thought of something completely unexpected, and then stared off into space for a brief moment. "My God, what a gift—to live to be seventy-five years old—in *this* day and *this* age and *this* world."

The Next Celebration Will Be Your Wedding

"No, no, no, not at all. That's funeral music. We need a birthday cantata!" Bonhoeffer sat at the piano in the Schleichers' house rehearsing "Praise Ye the Lord" with all the family members who would be attending his father's seventy-fifth birthday celebration. He looked reproachfully at the singers, then turned to Dohnanyi. "And what's with you, Hans? Why are you missing *every* cue?"

His brother-in-law did not answer. Instead he looked for the umpteenth time at his watch on this Sunday morning. "Why is your husband so nervous?" Ursula Schleicher whispered to her sister Christine. "Things are about to happen," Christine whispered back.

"What things?"

The maidservant entered the room and cut off Christine's response. "Telephone, Herr Dohnanyi. Apparently something quite important." Dohnanyi rushed out past the girl and into the library and grabbed the phone roughly.

"Yes?" He listened, then went rigid, his face pale. "*Again?* Nothing?" With exaggerated hesitation, as if in slow motion, he hung up the phone. In front of him, the rows of books on the library shelves turned into a brownish golden blur.

"There *must* be some power or other that's protecting the man. There *must* be. Heaven or hell, one or the other, but *some* power is protecting him. Despite everything." That was the one, recurring thought on which he monotonously focused now.

It was March 21, 1943, Veterans Memorial Day, and word had it that Hitler would spend this day laying a wreath at the Berlin armory on Unter den Linden and then viewing weapons captured from the Red Army. "We won't get a chance so soon again to get *this* close to him when he's *this* exposed," was the reasoning among members of the resistance.

"A person could get very, very close to him this time. But we need to find someone willing to risk his own life," was the assessment of Rudolph von Gersdorff, a military intelligence officer on the eastern front who was just now on leave in Berlin.

"And so, who should that be?"

"Me."

A lengthy pause followed this crisp, brief word. Then someone finally asked, "And how? With a revolver? But we know Hitler always wears a bulletproof vest. Even his hats are said to be bulletproof."

Gersdorff seemed to have considered that possibility as well. "We need to get some explosives. Set the timer for ten minutes. He'll need at least that long for the ceremony in the armory. I'll wrap the explosives around my body."

"But *you'll* never survive!"

"Am I intending to survive?"

So, today, on March 21, Dohnanyi walked over to the library window and looked over at his in-laws' house next door. Security, prosperity, solid values. That's what these houses expressed, their clear, orderly facades perpetually standing sentinel against disorder. But conspiracy and treason just did not seem to flourish in this world here with its dulled brass signage on the front gates and the gently crunching gravel walks in the front gardens.

Not this time. Nor two weeks earlier. When Dohnanyi and his superior, Canaris, had flown from Königsberg to Smolensk, where Hitler was paying a visit to the front. And there . . .

Dohnanyi now heard loud laughter coming from the adjacent room. *Eberhard! You good lad*, Dohnanyi thought.

Two weeks ago, Eberhard had not the slightest idea what he really had in the car when, at Dohnanyi's request, he had driven Dohnanyi from Berlin to Königsberg in Karl Bonhoeffer's limousine. The trunk had contained some explosive cargo; in fact, a suitcase with a bomb of the sort made only in England. Dohnanyi had secured the material through channels in military intelligence, and now its purpose was to cleanse the country of its *Führer* during Hitler's flight high above the city of Minsk.

That had been March 13.

Everything went as planned. Dohnanyi had delivered the suitcase to his coconspirator Fabian von Schlabrendorff, who in turn had given it to an officer in Hitler's entourage. "Could you be so kind as to take this suitcase back to Germany? It has two bottles of cognac for a very dear friend." The officer merely nodded. Schlabrendorff watched as he disappeared—with the suitcase—into the waiting Condor airplane.

A few hours later, the plane landed in East Prussia with an unscathed

Hitler on board. The bomb had failed to explode—probably because of the unanticipated drop in temperature.

But this time, Dohnanyi thought on the morning of March 21, *it simply* must *work*. He was almost gleeful when being driven to the house on Marienburg Allee that day. "Stay here," he had told the chauffeur. "I may be needing you again soon." Inside the house, the birthday cantata rehearsal had begun. In the meantime, Gersdorff was waiting at the entrance to the armory, the explosives wrapped around his body. Again, everything was going according to plan.

Hitler arrived for a quiet ceremony for fallen heroes and wreath-laying in the armory courtyard out front. When Hitler turned toward the entrance, Gersdorff raised his right arm in a Hitler salute while his left hand inconspicuously fumbled on his belt. Hitler, staring straight ahead, had merely gestured absently with his forearm in response. The timer was ticking. . . .

One minute . . . two. . . .

Footsteps, boots, echoed loudly. The *Führer* was returning already! After only two minutes! Gersdorff again raised his arm in salute and stared as Hitler disappeared in the distance. Only five more minutes, now four. . . .

Gersdorff rushed into a washroom and disarmed the bomb. Then immediately looked for the nearest telephone to put the code through. "No success." Dohnanyi now returned to the others, ignoring their curious gazes. He put his arm around Christine, who looked up at him with anxious, questioning eyes. "Shall we continue with the rehearsal? Let me apologize, I really wasn't very good earlier." And to Christine, very softly, "It didn't work. Again."

On March 31, the Bonhoeffer house radiated in all its glory in a way it had not done in a long, long time, with the seventy-five-year-old Karl Bonhoeffer in the middle of it all. And indeed, *everyone* had come to the celebration, even the elderly Ferdinand Sauerbruch, Bonhoeffer's friend and superior in the Charité Hospital. Full of curiosity, he leaned over a rather impressive-looking document. "Well, what have we here? You've been awarded the Goethe Medal, Karl? And, my, my, I see Hitler himself signed it. . . ."

"Yes, him of all people," the elder Bonhoeffer grumbled. Sauerbruch slapped him on the back, laughing. "Well, just keep to Goethe! He'll abide. We'll soon enough forget the other one." The cantata commenced—"Praise ye the Lord. . . ."

"So, were you satisfied with our performance, O harsh maestro?" Dohnanyi had come over to the piano, where Bonhoeffer was still sitting—albeit with a somewhat absent expression on his face, lost in thought, his hands still lying limp on the piano keys, as if unwilling to separate themselves from the sounds. "Satisfied? Well, with all of you, certainly. But," he leaned back, "with everything else?"

He started to say something, hesitated a moment, then looked up at Dohnanyi. "In the future, will we still be able to *praise* some 'Lord' who rules everything so magnificently?"

"Dietrich!"

Dohnanyi was almost horrified. He might have expected such a statement from someone else, indeed, even from the birthday boy, Karl Bonhoeffer himself, but certainly not from his brother-in-law.

Bonhoeffer continued with an unusually fatigued voice. "The world is completely shot up, decimated, ravaged, millions have been murdered, cut down. So, do we really want to make the Lord 'up there' responsible for it by praising him like this? Is it not . . . well, *blasphemous* to claim we can see *his* kingdom here on earth amid all this chaos and misery and violence, and a *magnificent* kingdom at that?"

The house was filled with a merry cacophony of laughter, voices, chattering, and the clinking of glasses in endless toasts. Bonhoeffer didn't seem to notice any of it. "There *is* a God, and there is also grace and mercy and love of one's neighbor. But at some point we must cease *fleeing*, cease straying into the cozy, comfortable notion—the cozy, comfortable *alibi*—of some gentle, benevolent father who *really* does love us if we are but pious and devout and obedient and behave properly. . . ."

He interrupted himself and broke into a flat, almost sad smile. "That's how I imagined him when I was a child, when Mama let me look through her picture Bible with all the illustrations by Schnorr von Carolsfeld. As an old man with a long beard—who's even kindly toward chimney sweeps. . . ."

"Chimney sweeps? How does that fit in?" Dohnanyi laughed.

"I don't even know myself anymore. Just one of those things kids think of. But I fear God doesn't love chimney sweeps or anyone else among us who's responsible for turning his world into what we have here now. We're going to have to start getting along *without* his love, going to have to start keeping our faith in him *without* his benevolent deeds. Or," he looked straight at his brother-in-law, "do *you* still believe in the precious God of our childhood?"

"I do believe in him," Dohnanyi answered calmly, "and I have no intention of not praising him for having governed everything so magnificently. Otherwise," he sighed, "I could not have endured all this here, these past few years."

He smiled. "By the way, I spoke with Canaris about your trip to Rome. You'll be able to set off next month. Perhaps you really will reach the Vatican after all, you—Don Quixote!"

Bonhoeffer had fairly leapt up in excitement at this announcement. Before he could answer, however, his father walked up to them both, though this time not at all with a gloomy look on his face, but rather quite bright and contented. "What a wonderful celebration all of you have given me! Indeed, indeed, it seems we Bonhoeffers still know a thing or two about celebrations! And the next celebration, Dietrich, will be your wedding!"

He put his arms around both men's shoulders and smiled broadly. "It's easy to grow old when a person has sons and sons-in-law as splendid as you two."

Five days later, on April 5, Bonhoeffer and Dohnanyi were arrested.

SCHÖNBERG, LOW SUNDAY (APRIL 8) 1945

An utterly cloudless sky. Radiant sunshine. Like in August. Bonhoeffer gratefully stretches out toward its beneficent warmth. *They can take everything else away from us, but not this,* he thinks, sitting down on the small bench in front of the school. What, by the way, is the name of this place anyway?

Ah, yes, Schönberg. North of Passau. Four days ago they were in Regensburg. Then the truck had broken down on the road that runs along the Danube River and they had had to transfer to a bus. The driver had also given some village girls a lift. They talked about a film—a propaganda film encouraging the population to stand fast—that had been made nearby, even as the American artillery could be heard just off in the distance.

So, this band of prisoners has been here in Schönberg since the day before yesterday, just below the town of Zwiesel with its famous glassware. Green fields all around. The setting could not be more tranquil, more peaceful. Bonhoeffer closes his eyes.

Six months to the day since the door to his cell in Tegel was opened with a harsh clank. "Get up! You! Get ready! You're being transferred!"—"What? Why?"—"As a member of the intelligence service you're no longer under military jurisdiction. You're being transferred over to the Reich Central Security Office on Prince Albrecht Street."

That had been on October 8, 1944.

Bonhoeffer had gathered his things together and then realized that his mood—imperceptibly—had turned into a strange, tender sort of melancholy. The cell had become more "home" to him than he had ever really admitted to himself. It had become almost as familiar, almost as much his "world" as a second parental home. He stopped for a brief moment and reflected. He realized, not without considerable surprise even to himself, that here, in a way, he had been born a second time. Indeed, it was here that he first really became . . . Bonhoeffer.

Knobloch was standing out in the corridor, a pained look on his face. *A real friend*, Bonhoeffer had thought. Bonhoeffer had asked him whether he might open a few cells and allow him to say good-bye to fellow prisoners. A final embrace. One of the prisoners later recounted that "Bonhoeffer's eyes were genuinely luminous."

Then Bonhoeffer had been assigned a new cell. This time in a basement. Narrower, darker than the earlier one. And the prisoners in the surrounding cells had familiar names. Canaris, Oster, Josef Müller, Friedrich Justus Perels—he, too, the man with whom Bonhoeffer had worked out a plan for reorganizing the church after the war and with whom he had composed a pulpit proclamation for the first worship service after peace had arrived. "We summon everyone to personal confession. . . ."

A different Gestapo prison held his brother Klaus, his brother-in-law Rüdiger, and his friend Eberhard, whose only sin was being Schleicher's son-in-law. The others were in even deeper trouble. The Zossen files spelled out with painful clarity precisely which position each individual was to occupy after Hitler's fall.

More hearings. More interrogations. Conducted now not by smooth Manfred Roeder, but by the considerably gruffer Sonderegger. As it turned out, however, he had not been a complete monster, at least not toward Bonhoeffer, even though he did—at least at the beginning—make some threats involving torture and alluded to drawing Bonhoeffer's family into things. "Surely you wouldn't want your lovely fiancée to be incarcerated as well, would you?" But Bonhoeffer had remained steadfast.

With the heightened instinct of a hunted animal, he had sensed that the Zossen files did not really contain much about him. So he had dug in his heels and played the somewhat naive, guileless pastor, and Sonderegger had eventually seemed to take the bait, becoming almost friendly, offering cigarettes, even promising to provide some reading materials should the pastor so desire. Bonhoeffer had asked for some works by Johann Heinrich Pestalozzi, the Swiss educational reformer, and Plutarch. Sonderegger had passed this wish on to Bonhoeffer's father.

Bonhoeffer still has the Plutarch volume with him here in Schönberg. It's upstairs in the sleeping room on the second floor with the colorful beds. An almost comfortable, cozy room.

And down here on the bench, too, it's quite nice. Bonhoeffer squints into the crystal-clear blue sky.

The sky had been just as clear and just as blue back on February 3, when rumors began circulating about four new death sentences passed down by the horrific judge Roland Freisler against Klaus Bonhoeffer, Rüdiger Schleicher, Perels, and the lawyer Hans John. Were they still alive? Had they already been executed? This regime worked quickly and thoroughly, that much everyone had learned.

Then, on February 3, that clear blue sky was suddenly pierced by waves of American planes, dropping bomb after bomb after bomb. The building on Prince Albrecht Street alone had been hit eight times. The prisoners had screamed, gone berserk, wept, the cellar walls had shaken like the sides of a sailing ship in the midst of a hurricane. Outside, on the street, people had rushed into the bomb shelters in the subway tunnels. One of them wore the uniform of a military staff physician.

The bombing had ended. From the Zoological Garden eastward, Berlin was one, flaming, smoking landscape of ruins and decimation. It had been the heaviest bombardment of the capital to date.

The man in the uniform, Rüdiger Schleicher's brother Rolf, had just arrived from Stuttgart. He hurried on to the People's Court, hoping he might still do something for his condemned brother. Right at the building's entrance, an officer had caught him by the arm. "You're a doctor? Come, quickly. *Quickly.* There's a severely wounded man here, somebody very, *very* high up on the totem pole, it seems. . . ."

Schleicher had knelt over the lifeless body. *Roland Freisler.* "The scoundrel is dead," Rolf Schleicher had later said to his sister-in-law Ursula. Yes. Freisler's death *could* be what might save her husband and the others.

On that morning of February 3, two other, elderly people had also climbed up out of the subway station on Potsdam Square. "Well, aren't we a sight?" Karl Bonhoeffer remarked to his wife, a package under his arm, "as black as chimney sweeps! How Dietrich would laugh!"

"Yes, I believe he would." Paula Bonhoeffer, too, laughed. They had hoped finally to see their son again.

On this particular day, however, they had gone back home and then returned to the prison on Prince Albrecht Street on February 7, leaving the package and a letter as a birthday present—Bonhoeffer had turned thirty-nine on February 4. But they did not seen him again. That afternoon he and several other prisoners had been transported to the concentration camp Buchenwald.

"May I introduce you to Payne Best?" That had been in the washroom in Buchenwald. Bonhoeffer's cellmate, Friedrich von Rabenau, a general and theologian, had introduced the two men as elegantly as if they had been in a sophisticated British social club.

Bonhoeffer had shaken the captain's hand; Payne Best was one of the two British Secret Service officers whom the German security service had lured into a trap in Venlo in 1940. "And this is Wassily Kokorin, an air force officer in the Red Army." A Russian. "And one of Molotow's nephews," Rabenau had whispered. Bonhoeffer had also shaken Kokorin's hand. Kokorin would later teach him a few words in Russian just as Bonhoeffer would familiarize Kokorin with a few points of church history.

But first, half naked and bending over the sink, he had spoken with Payne Best, asking him whether after July 20 his countrymen in England now finally believed there was a different, better Germany. "I don't really know the answer to that myself." Neither man had heard Churchill's commentary on the assassination attempt against Hitler, to wit, "murderers tried to murder another murderer; that's all."

Buchenwald was considered the "concentration camp for prominent persons." But "prominent persons" were no safer from bombs than were ordinary prisoners. The Communist leader Ernst Thälmann had already been killed during one air raid—Bonhoeffer recalled the Thälmann-enthusiasm of his Wedding confirmation student, Teddy, so many years before— though whether by the bombs or as a result of "precautionary liquidation" no one could really say. And again, the sound of American artillery was getting very, very close.

So, now yet another departure. Away from Schönberg. But to where?

"To Flossenbürg," they had been told. Everyone had shuddered. Flossenbürg, in the Upper Palatinate Forest, was known as the worst of all the German concentration camps, a camp where probably sixty thousand prisoners were crammed together in housing for sixteen thousand. In reality, it was no longer really a prison at all, but merely an execution factory. *I wonder whether they'll shoot me there or hang me*, Bonhoeffer had conjectured. And to his own astonishment, the notion left him quite calm, with an almost neutral, objective curiosity.

But no! Not to Flossenbürg after all!

The truck, an ancient vehicle powered by a wood-burning generator, had chugged along at scarcely twenty miles an hour in a different direction. The prisoners had breathed a sigh of relief. The worst seemed to have been avoided.

They won't shoot me to death! They won't hang me! Bonhoeffer had rejoiced to himself. And only then did he notice how completely, totally he had made closure with everything. He had gazed out at the passing springtime scenery with hungry eyes, rejoicing in the sight of every tree, every meadow, every brook, and could think of nothing but, *I'm alive! I'm permitted to stay alive!*

His euphoria had ignited the others. They, too, laughed and joked with relieved faces—and it all had intensified when they reached Regensburg the next evening, where they were to stay before continuing on to Schönberg.

In the Regensburg city prison they had encountered people who shared the same fate as they—members of renowned families and people with respected names, names like Hammerstein and

Stauffenberg who were now being incarcerated after the manner of "guilt by kinship."

Lively greetings were exchanged, the laughter and shouts recalling more a class reunion than a prison corridor. Indeed, an outsider might have thought these people had already been liberated. A new tone had emerged among the prisoners, almost imperious. They were intent on not putting up with rudeness from the guards now, even demanded better food. "What? Vegetable soup again? And no bread?"

Princes, Bonhoeffer had thought while spooning his soup. And that's also what he's thinking now, sitting here on the bench in front of the schoolhouse in Schönberg, the sun on his face and the world around him more peaceful than he can remember. The war will be over soon, maybe even in a few hours, and they're already preparing to take over things yet again—these privileged sons of privileged houses.

But he himself has no desire now to be a prince in this world. That's over for him. Once and for all. Just someone in shirtsleeves, like everyone else. That's how he'll be after this war. He'll help create a new church just like the one he and Perels had sketched out, an independent church, free, liberated from all the previous petrified bureaucracy and *certainly* from the lackeys and opportunists fawning around the throne of the powerful in their frumpy bishops' gowns.

That new church—Bonhoeffer can already envision it—is to be young and courageous and completely independent of the state, and supported solely by believers themselves, just like the American model. . . .

America. New York. Worship services in Harlem. He hears stamping feet, clapping hands, lilting voices singing "Oh, when the saints. . . ."

That is how faith must be. Spontaneous. Sensuously immediate, direct. It is *this* faith that will build its own church. And Bonhoeffer is resolutely intent on participating in that project. One person among many. Not special anymore.

"Dietrich!"

The voice is right next to him, and with a heavy Russian accent. Wassily, his dark eyes presenting a request. "It's Sunday, the . . . how do you call this Sunday?"

"Low Sunday."

"The others much would like to have worship service. . . ."

"Most of them are Catholic. So it's not really possible."

"And if I, a *pagan*, ask you so to do?"

Bonhoeffer laughs, stands up from the bench, and calls to the others. Payne Best is the first. "In exchange, I'll even let you use my electric razor later." He's the only one here with access to such a luxury item.

They all stand in front of the schoolhouse, in the sunshine. Bonhoeffer prays, speaks. His text is Isaiah 53:5. "And by his wounds we are healed." Several men in civilian clothing are walking up in the background.

"Prisoner Bonhoeffer? Come with us."

The other prisoners cringe. Bonhoeffer remains calm. "Surely there's time for me to fetch a couple of things, isn't there?"

Upstairs in the bedroom, he picks up the volume of Plutarch, writes his name in the front and in the back. At least this trace of him, this evidence of his existence, will remain behind. Downstairs he walks over to Best. "I told you, I believe, that I'm acquainted with the bishop of Chichester. . . ."

Best nods.

"If you ever see him again, please deliver this message to him. . . ."

Bonhoeffer looks up into the blue sky. "Tell him . . . that this, now, here, is probably the end. But for me it is the beginning of life. And also . . ."

He hesitates. Imagines that he hears Bell's voice back on the shores of Lake Mälaren, then suddenly recalls—with painful precision—what in his profound disappointment at the time he had allowed simply to pass by, to flutter off without really perceiving it properly.

Forgive me, Uncle Glocke—Uncle Bell—for not really having taken you seriously back then, he now thinks to himself, but then says to Best, "Tell him that back in Sigtuna—he'll know what I'm talking about—that he was right about the *inevitable* victory of a global Christian fellowship. Yes; he was right. That victory will come. I *know* it will."

Carrying his few possessions under his arm, including a volume of Goethe, he gets into the waiting car.

~

Are You Bonhoeffer?

1948

"And the Lord said,
'If I find at Sodom fifty righteous
in the city, I will forgive
the whole place for their sake.'"
—Genesis 18:26

The Happiest of Men, Perhaps

Karl Bonhoeffer, now eighty years old, was sitting at his desk and rereading the letter for the third, maybe even the fourth time. He was having trouble comprehending what it said.

Somebody had written—but who? Ah, yes, a pastor from Bielefeld—so, a pastor from Bielefeld had written that people would probably be wanting to name some streets after Dietrich Bonhoeffer, and he—Bonhoeffer's father—really should protest, should object to the idea. Why? Because this sort of honor belonged only to those who had been martyred for their faith—not to people like his son, who had died, quite frankly, for not entirely unproblematic political reasons.

Karl Bonhoeffer put the letter—with its stiffly opinionated handwriting—back on the desk and looked out into the approaching dusk.

He had lost two sons and two sons-in-law. Unlike his son Walter, who was killed in action during World War I, these men were despicably, wretchedly slaughtered. Dietrich and Hans von Dohnanyi

had been hanged; Klaus and Rüdiger Schleicher shot in the back out
on a field in the middle of the night near the Lehrter Train Station in
Berlin—during the very last days of the war, the Russian army already
positioned literally before the gates of Berlin. Other murdered victims
included Friedrich Justus Perels and Hans John.

Martyrs? Or simply victims? Did it even matter?

And now these very same men were to be treacherously murdered
yet again, silenced in the literal sense of the word, by churchmen such
as this one here. Even while the war was still going on and Dietrich
was still alive, these clerics had refused to include him in their Sunday
intercessory prayers because he was merely a "political" prisoner.
And on the first anniversary of July 20, the name Bonhoeffer was not
among the many that were read from the pulpit that day.

Karl Bonhoeffer was having a difficult time understanding all this.

With some effort, he got up, walked over to the radio, and turned
the dials. Just to listen to something else, to think about something
else. Anything else. On one station he could hear a nasal tenor voice
singing about Capri and the red sun—one of the hit tunes of this
period. Karl Bonhoeffer quickly turned it off.

It was in front of this radio that he and Paula Bonhoeffer had sat
on July 27, 1945. As in the earlier days of Goebbels's propaganda,
they had listened to the BBC as well. But there was no news this day.
Instead, there was a pealing of bells, and a chorus singing a chorale.
Then the bishop of Chichester spoke about his murdered friend,
Dietrich Bonhoeffer.

It was a memorial service for him, and there were more people
in the Holy Trinity Church on London's King Square than on any
other day since the very first day after the announcement of peace.
Besides Bell, Franz Hildebrandt had spoken as well. The BBC had
initially been reluctant to broadcast the service, but it was through
that broadcast that Bonhoeffer's parents had first learned for certain
what they had hitherto only suspected and feared, namely, that their
son was dead.

Only later did the details surrounding his death also become
known.

Actually, things had looked rather promising at first. Although Bonhoeffer had disappeared from Berlin itself, word had it that he was still alive, having been taken first to Buchenwald and from there to somewhere in southern Germany. One rumor even had it that he was already free. So Maria set out to find him.

Then April 5, 1945, had come.

The "*Führer's* circle" met at noon in the Reich chancellery. Ernst Kaltenbrunner, head of the Reich Central Security Office, handed Hitler a bulging dossier with carefully marked passages. "This, my *Führer*, was found almost by accident in yet another safe. These are Admiral Canaris's diaries."

Hitler took the dossier with trembling fingers and, still shaking, put on his glasses (whose existence were being kept top secret) and began to read, mumbling each individual word through bloodless lips. His lower lip twitched, and a narrow stream of spittle ran down from the corner of his mouth. The other men present at the meeting stared at this quivering pile of flesh struggling with the fitful cramps of Parkinson's disease, a man who looked years, even decades older than he actually was.

Indeed, this man sitting before them was far, far removed from the incisive demagogue of his younger years, or even the imperial, stone-faced, Caesar-like *Führer* of his later period. This man now was little more than a burned-out wreck, a mass of withered, collapsing human parts.

And yet this pile of wrecked parts could *still* spit out death and ruin and hatred, just as he did now with a slavering, barking, gurgling harangue against his enemies. Contempt and malice dripped from his words—*So* this *is the* real *reason why* he, *the* greatest *commander of* all *time, the* greatest *genius, had not conquered the* entire *world: Treason! Treason* and nothing but *treason. All around him. Treason!*

And finally, stammering and slobbering: "*Destroy them! Destroy all of them! Immediately! Mercilessly! Ruthlessly! Now!*" SS officer Kaltenbrunner came to rigid attention and clicked his heels in acknowledgment.

This Kaltenbrunner was a cultured man, an educated man, a lawyer. He did not just turn his murderous hordes loose, though that doubtless would have been easier and, at least for those affected, more merciful, since it all would have happened very quickly. But the Germans were intent on not making such things easy for themselves. Even *crimes* must be committed in an *orderly* fashion.

Hence a special court was hastily convened. SS Colonel Walter Huppenkothen was the "official" prosecutor, and the SS judge Otto Thorbeck was summoned to Flossenbürg from Nuremberg. Because no car could be found, he had to travel there on a freight train and then cover the last stretch on bicycle. Initially, however, on April 6, there was a stop in the concentration camp Sachsenhausen.

There, in the prison infirmary, only half conscious and apparently sedated with morphine, lay Hans von Dohnanyi. He was hardly cognizant of any of the court procedures, the guilty verdict, or, really, much of anything connected with the farce constituting these "legal proceedings"—nor, probably, even of how he was then carried out to the execution wall on a gurney and not shot to death but hanged. That was probably on April 9, 1945, though the exact date could never be ascertained. The "special court" had long since moved on.

Huppenkothen arrived in Flossenbürg on April 7. The prisoners were summoned. Canaris, Oster, the former intelligence captain Ludwig Gehre, the former senior military judge Karl Sack.

But where was Bonhoeffer?

Members of the SS stormed through the camp, yelling at prisoners, including Fabian von Schlabrendorff, Dohnanyi's co-perpetrator at the Smolensk airport who was later also drawn into the events of July 20; and Josef Müller, who miraculously escaped all this senseless murder and ultimately, together with Schlabrendorff, was liberated by the Americans. "Are you Bonhoeffer?"

No. None of them was Bonhoeffer. Bonhoeffer was not there.

He was still in Schönberg, enjoying the sunshine. Perhaps, just perhaps this moment was the first tiny move toward the freedom for which he had been so ardently yearning. And on the way there, near the town of Weiden, where the road split off left toward Flossenbürg, their truck—still the same limping, putrid vehicle powered by a wood stove—had suddenly been stopped, and two prisoners ordered out, Josef Müller and Ludwig Gehre, the latter of whom the henchmen had probably thought was Bonhoeffer. The truck had then journeyed on without them. To the right, away from Flossenbürg.

A slip-up—nothing more, and quickly remedied—in the otherwise well-oiled bureaucracy of annihilation run by the National Socialists. "Prisoner Bonhoeffer! Come with us!" Huppenkothen's henchmen had appeared in front of the Schönberg schoolhouse. Soon thereafter, Bonhoeffer arrived in Flossenbürg. The trial could begin.

That was April 8, 1945.

But, no, no farce this time. Instead there was an orderly trial consisting of orderly legal proceedings. At least that is what Herr Huppenkothen and Herr Thorbeck could not emphasize strongly enough later, in the 1950s, when *they* themselves were on trial. And with the convenient assistance of a former military judge from the National Socialist period, they were indeed acquitted, since they had—as the court put it—followed orderly, correct legal procedure. On the other hand, the sentence against Bonhoeffer and those who shared his fate was not annulled until 1996. As the commentator Curt Riess once remarked, Hitler could *certainly* rely on his lawyers. Including after the war, and including in Bonhoeffer's case.

There were, it might be pointed out, no defense lawyers in that case, nor any court reporter, nor, strictly speaking, even any qualified judges, since none of the accused was really subject to SS jurisdiction in the first place. Although Huppenkothen and Thorbeck did acknowledge this, they were quick to point out that the entire day was filled with interrogations and hearings. That is, these prisoners—if it please the court—*certainly* had ample opportunity to defend themselves at length. So Huppenkothen's explanation.

Just their bad luck that their sentence had already been determined long before the trial ever got started. Death by hanging. For all five.

Early in the morning on April 9, the time had come. The snarling and barking of dogs had startled the other prisoners awake. The courtyard was bathed in cold, harsh light. The condemned had to undress in the shower cell, completely. Then they were herded over to the gallows, naked, one after the other. Bonhoeffer is said to have been the most composed of them all, even speaking a final prayer. Then he, too, had climbed the stairs, with complete calm.

At least that was the recollection of an SS camp doctor regarding the last moments of this "unusually likable" man. Later, however, doubt was cast on his testimony because he could not have been in position to view the execution. Others maintained that the execution had taken much longer, and was allegedly much more agonizing.

Bonhoeffer's father, however, was not particularly interested in hearing about such details.

"Hanged on the gallows, naked," was all Karl Bonhoeffer registered. Naked. Precisely this particular bit of information had something peculiarly comforting about it. You came into the world naked, and you left it naked. The corpse was then burned. Not a trace was left.

Bonhoeffer's father reached over to the bookshelf and pulled out the volume of Goethe, the only thing his parents had received back from among Dietrich's final possessions. The elderly man passed his hand over it.

He wanted to weep. But everything inside him was dark and silent. "I wish I had your God, Dietrich," he thought, "then I could be angry with him, and curse him, and could turn my back on him. But like this?" His despair dissipated into empty space, without echo.

But the letter from Bielefeld was still lying on his desk, this summons to prevent his son from being remembered by having a street named after him "because," as the letter writer had written, "we do not particularly want to have the names of our colleagues who died for their faith to be mentioned together with political martyrs."

What a world.

This world, this Germany in 1948, the last year Karl Bonhoeffer was alive, was at this time still permeated by the smoke and haze of war, still littered with its ruins, and there were those who were whispering, darkly, secretly, that probably fifty years—at least—would have to pass before all this here could *ever* be a Germany as it had been earlier.

But this Germany recovered with almost unnerving rapidity, and returnees such as Gerhard Leibholz, who became a supreme court judge in Karlsruhe in 1951, found before them a country that between 1933 and 1945 must have been one, long, malevolent nightmare from which people had finally been awakened. "All of you had it good over there in England; you have no idea what we went through here in Germany." That, too, Leibholz occasionally heard.

The Nazis seemed to have descended on this land as if from the Mongolian steppes, murdering, burning, destroying, and the inhabitants had timidly, fearfully cowered beneath their swords. And then—the horde had retreated, without a trace, and everyone quickly set about rebuilding the burned houses more beautifully than ever, each with its own lacquered furniture, refrigerator, and fluorescent light over the kidney-shaped coffee table.

There were, to be sure, laments enough for the victims—Jews and others—especially on public days of remembrance and other memorial days. The resistance fighters especially were stylized into austere, heroic "men and women of July 20." And it was all done with a certain earnest solemnity and with a touching, lofty feeling, as if one had just seen Christians burned at the stake in ancient Rome.

Signs in streetcars admonished passengers to observe the courtesy of yielding their seats to handicapped veterans. And people were glad to do so. But if perchance someone remarked that he had been in a concentration camp, fellow passengers became uncomfortable. Did anyone know why he had been sent there? What had he done? Might he even have been a—Communist? *That* was the greatest fear during the otherwise so merry, self-assured 1950s, when people like Konrad Adenauer were garnering new respect for Germany abroad and people like Ludwig Erhard were setting the wheels of the "economic miracle" in motion.

Films such as *Canaris* or *The Devil's General* played to packed houses, devout, reverent dramas about the lives of tragic heroes who had perished because of the nobility of their character. The public, millions strong, had no trouble acknowledging these larger-than-life heroes. "Well, if *they* were not able to do anything to stop evil, then how could *we* ever have done anything?" Though also, "Well, you know, we, *too*, were a *little* bit like them, always ready to sacrifice, and with noble hearts as well. . . ."

People began to look for icons, for guiding lights. And they found them. In the jungle doctor Albert Schweitzer. In the girl Anne Frank. And finally also in Dietrich Bonhoeffer.

Bonhoeffer was recognized as one of the righteous persons for whose sake the Lord had ultimately not entirely destroyed Sodom-Germany. "But someone like Bonhoeffer is hardly enough," was the petty reasoning of ill-willed critics who did not find the glorious struggle of the Confessing Church during the Nazi period *quite* as glorious as the Confessing Church itself did. For most people, however, one Bonhoeffer was indeed enough.

And in a larger sense, people were no longer so disinclined toward those who had been in the resistance, not even abroad, where, cognizant of the Soviet threat, people began considering the Germans as possible allies as early as 1946. Indeed, Winston Churchill himself had fairly startled his own listeners in the British House of Commons with his assertion that there had indeed been an opposition in Germany, and even though it had become ever weaker through the liquidation of its members and the nerve-wracking international policies of the time, it nonetheless was to be reckoned as one of the noblest, grandest efforts ever witnessed in the entire political history of the world.

And this noble and grand effort included Dietrich Bonhoeffer.

That very inclusion, however, only began very quietly and very gradually. First, some of his books and poems were published. Then, in 1951, his *Letters and Papers from Prison* appeared. Its editor was Eberhard Bethge, who had sealed his friend's letters in a lead container and hidden them in his garden. Ultimately no one would exert such effort on behalf of Bonhoeffer's memory as he.

"I always have a bad conscience when I think of Dietrich," he once told Maria, who in the meantime had become his daughter's godparent.

He had spoken these words to her in 1976 in Geneva, at an international symposium on the occasion of Bonhoeffer's seventieth birthday. The host was the Bonhoeffer Committee, an organization founded three years earlier that would ultimately become the Bonhoeffer Society. Maria, too, had attended the conference.

She had emigrated to America in 1948 and made an impressive career for herself as a mathematician and computer specialist, the latter at a time when people in Germany could hardly even spell the word. Her private life, however—two failed marriages—was less impressive. She now sat opposite Eberhard in Geneva, still beautiful, still clear, still strong, and still with that dark, penetrating gaze.

"A bad conscience? Why? Because you survived and he didn't?" she asked. He nodded. "Whenever I publish one of his works or write about him, I always have the feeling I need to return to him a piece of the life that was taken from him."

"Well, yes, a short life; but a full—and fulfilled—life." Maria smiled and looked even more beautiful. "I read your book about him. A very good book. The best."

"You could write an even better one, Maria. When will you finally do that? Or at least publish the letters you two exchanged during your engagement."

"Ah, Eberhard." She rested her head in her hand.

"There are just so many rumors now about your relationship." Eberhard became animated. "Like why he fell in love with you and you with him. People are saying it was nothing more than teenage infatuation for you, and dull convention for him—since, after all, a pastor needs to be married to keep people from talking. But your correspondence, your letters" —Eberhard had been permitted to read a few—"your letters clearly show that you loved each other. Quite simply."

"Nothing was 'quite simple' with Dietrich." She laughed. "I think I fell in love with him when I once revealed to him that I wanted to study *mathematics* some day. . . ."

She broke off, giving in to gentle recollection. "I remember the day exactly. It was when we saw each other again when Grandmama was in the hospital. He invited me to a restaurant afterward, one allegedly belonging to Hitler's brother or half-brother. I can still hear him say,

'But don't let that spoil your appetite, dear Fräulein.' . . ." She let the taste of the word *Fräulein* linger for a moment, relishing the memory. "That really is how he addressed me then. . . ."

Just now, here in Geneva, she seemed to be entirely with Bonhoeffer, the same young girl she was back then. "He had already been to America. That's what impressed me the most. I had never met anyone who had been to America. . . ."

Eberhard politely cleared his throat. "And you told him you wanted to study mathematics?"

"Yes. Mathematics. And yet he didn't laugh at the idea. He took me completely seriously."

"And you? Did you also take him seriously?"

"Not like all you others did. All of you admired and esteemed him *so* highly. I really didn't. Later, yes, certainly. But at first I was just genuinely fond of him, even of his awkwardness, all his little vanities, the way he couldn't even tie his tie correctly. . . ."

"No, Dietrich really never could do that." Eberhard laughed. Maria's smile had taken on an unexpectedly motherly appearance. "Even as a very young girl, I always had the feeling that I needed to protect him. There was always something so precious about him, something so exquisite, like a prince from a fairy tale, something so . . ."

She hesitated. Then very softly, "Something so special." Then a lengthy silence, permeated by memories of this peculiar, remarkable man. A man who had been smart and yet sometimes quite foolish, modest and yet sometimes quite haughty. A man who even in his very last days on this earth had still acted like a manor lord, overseeing broad, expansive fields in the setting sun, nodding modestly, smiling, as if he and he alone had dominion over all this magnificence. And yet also a man just like the rest of us, searching, doubting, lost.

Everyone who knew him probably has 'his own' Bonhoeffer, Eberhard thought. After a pause, he finally said, "You know, he once wrote me—by the way, it was the very first letter in which he mentioned your name, Maria—that he wasn't really a *religious* person at all. Can you imagine? I have to admit I was flabbergasted at first, to say the least. . . ."

"But he was right," Maria continued the thought. "He probably genuinely wasn't religious. He *wanted* to have faith. But having faith was difficult for him. What he *wanted* was to be a child—naive—but he wasn't. Or maybe—maybe he was in death, in his very, very last moments." Again laughter, but with a note of sadness. "For him—to whom fate had been *so* generous—perhaps that was the final gift."

Eberhard nodded.

"Strange," Maria continued, "somehow thinking about his end doesn't disturb me. Not even the idea that his ashes were strewn to the four winds. That way he doesn't belong to anyone, not even to us. Only to himself. Free. Even in death."

She went on chatting, almost as if at a cocktail party. "And when I think of those last weeks of his life, I really see myself first—trundling around the country looking for him, lugging a suitcase with winter clothes. *Winter* clothes. I have no idea why I was thinking he needed winter things. Do you remember how *hot-natured* he was? He would have collapsed from heat exhaustion in all that woolen clothing. . . ."

They both laughed.

"And yet—my search for him, my *desperate* wish during this one, single week, finally to be with him, to have him with me, wholly, completely, not separated by prison walls—I think *that* was my marriage with him, more intensive, more passionate than any 'real' marriage could ever have been. And I think my two other 'real' marriages . . . ran aground on just that memory. Who has a chance up against the shadow of a dead person? And especially against Dietrich's shadow?"

"And have you ever considered how a 'real' marriage between you two might have ended up?"

"*Difficult.*"

Again they both laughed.

It was late afternoon. The final rays of the sun danced through the room. They heard voices and footsteps. "Time to get back to the others." Maria had gotten up. "You'll have to come visit me sometime soon in America, Eberhard. I have a beautiful house, on stilts, almost out in the surf. Whenever I have visitors, I open the door to the veranda and say, 'If it please, may I introduce you to . . . *my* ocean. . . .'"

Eberhard did not answer. He had remained seated and was scraping the toe of his shoe over the red and blue pattern of the Persian carpet.

"He once told me something very strange. Back when things were getting increasingly dicey at Finkenwalde. I asked him what sense it made anymore, all the effort, all the trouble, whether one ought not just go ahead and give up...."

"And? What did he say?"

"'I'm like Sisyphus,' he said, 'condemned to push the same stone up the same slope, forever, for eternity. That's my fate.'"

Eberhard paused, as if still startled at Bonhoeffer's answer. "And then he laughed, quite contentedly, as if *exactly* this prospect pleased him very greatly indeed."

"Dietrich as Sisyphus. Doing for the sake of doing. Otherwise Sisyphus is not really Sisyphus."

"Nor Dietrich Dietrich," Eberhard concurred.

"No, probably not. It was probably only by taking the very path he did that Dietrich could really become Bonhoeffer. And you know, I almost think he always knew that."

Maria looked over at Eberhard with a darkly serious gaze. "The French existentialist Albert Camus—you know, the one who had that absurd car accident even though he had already redeemed his train ticket?—he wrote a long essay on this same topic, very interesting. You really should read it...."

"Yes, I'm familiar with it."

Maria had sat down again. "Then you also know that Camus viewed Sisyphus as the prototype of modern human beings—of all of us. The fate of Sisyphus really symbolizes the absurdity of *all* human existence."

"I'm wondering if Dietrich would have seen it that way as well."

"Maybe. I think that without his faith, this life of ours—this existence of ours—would surely have seemed absurd to him, and ultimately probably even faith itself would have seemed absurd."

Again a lengthy silence. Again memories of Bonhoeffer. Finally Maria said, "And yet Camus also believes that no other human being has ever been as happy as Sisyphus...."

She paused, reflecting. The afternoon sunlight shone fully in her face. "Dietrich happy. The happiest of us all, perhaps."

She looks ill, Eberhard thought. Beautiful, but ill. The very next year, he learned that Maria had died over there in the United States. Cancer. Before the end, however, she had given permission for her correspondence with Bonhoeffer during their engagement to be published. "But with a proper commentary, please. I was still a very, very young girl back when I wrote these letters. But I have remained at Dietrich's side my whole life, even till today. That needs to be said in a book like that." She was only fifty-three years old.

Eberhard, on the other hand, lived to be very old indeed. Old enough to see how not only streets, but even hospitals, schools, and dormitories were named after his friend—and, of course, churches, even one in London, where, two years before Eberhard himself died, the transfiguration of Bonhoeffer reached its high point.

For in 1998, Bonhoeffer's statue was unveiled in the Gothic niche over the west portal of London's Westminster Abbey as one of the ten martyrs of the twentieth century, between the civil rights leader Martin Luther King Jr. and Maximilian Kolbe, the latter of whom died of starvation in Auschwitz. Bonhoeffer is depicted with his glasses, to be sure, but also in quite the impressive Lutheran fashion in his flowing robes and holding a Bible.

The archbishop of Canterbury spoke. The queen was present as well. Two people from his circle of friends, however, were not there, though they should have been. One was slender and dark, the other bright and pinkish. The slender, dark man would have nudged the other and whispered, "Our Dietrich! The old adversary! And behold, he's managed to become a saint after all." The other man would have recalled the last words that Payne Best had delivered to him: "For me it is the beginning of life."

But Franz Hildebrandt, who never retuned to Germany, had died in 1984, and George Bell back in 1958.

In Germany itself, the Bonhoeffer cult continued on. And anyone who wanted to send good wishes for baptism or confirmation would often choose a greeting card with the verses:

> *By benevolent powers wondrously sheltered,*
> *we, confident, await what may come.*
> *With us God abides, evening and morn,*
> *more surely still with each dawning day.*

Those were the last four lines from Bonhoeffer's very last poem, a poem he included in his final letter to his father as a New Year's greeting in 1945 and dedicated to Maria and his mother. And it was this poem, written in Bonhoeffer's perpetually poor, almost illegible handwriting, that Karl Bonhoeffer now pulled out on this late autumn day in 1948. He read the first stanza half out loud to himself.

> *Quietly, loyally surrounded by benevolent powers,*
> *safeguarded and comforted most wondrously,*
> *these days would I live with you*
> *and with you pass into the new year.*

He thought of a conversation he once had with his son. Dietrich was still a university student at the time. They were talking about Dietrich's favorite poet, Paul Gerhardt. Karl Bonhoeffer, an inveterate and sober agnostic, had made a bit of affectionate fun at the simplicity and directness of some of Gerhardt's stanzas as well as at their—well, at their *exuberance*. "The gold'n sun full of joy and bliss. . . ."

His son had remained quite composed. "Well, Father, let's not forget when that was written. Just after the Thirty Years' War, in the middle of a shattered, decimated country where people hardly *had* anything left besides the 'gold'n sun,'" he had said, then continued, "But is it not quite wondrous that someone still had the strength and faith to *praise* that sunshine *despite* all the other horrors around him?"

And these lines here?

Written between the walls of a Gestapo cellar, virtually in sight of the gallows. And yet "*By benevolent powers wondrously sheltered. . . .*"

The wind rattled against the windows. An early autumn storm huffed impatiently outside the house. Karl Bonhoeffer thought he should probably close the shutters. He looked over toward the garden gate and thought he saw someone coming toward the house, his hat drawn down over his forehead, hands pushed deep into the pockets of his trenchcoat, ambling with the slightly rolling gait so typical of Dietrich.

His father thought he saw the stranger lift up his head in the gentle twilight of the autumn afternoon.

Karl Bonhoeffer looked into the blue eyes behind the glasses, saw the broad forehead, the powerful nose. And he saw Dietrich's smile, a smile some called haughty, others yearning.

By Benevolent Powers Wondrously Sheltered

Quietly, loyally surrounded by benevolent powers,
safeguarded and comforted most wondrously,
these days would I live with you
and with you pass into the new year.

The old year would yet torment our hearts,
the burdens of our dark days yet oppress us,
hence grant, O Lord, to our souls most distressed
the healing comfort you have prepared for us.

And though the heavy, bitter cup of
suffering you might extend
filled even to the brim,
yet would we accept it without flinching
from your gracious, loving hand.

But should you grant us joy once more
in this world and its radiant sun,
then the past let us gratefully recall
and to you entirely our lives devote.

May warmly and brightly glow the candles
you have brought into our darkness today;
if it be possible, bring us together again.
We are sure: your light illuminates our night.

When silence profound now spreads itself around us,
may we yet hear that full voice
of the world unseen around us,
the hymn of praise sung by all your children.

By benevolent powers wondrously sheltered,
we, confident, await what may come.
With us God abides, evening and morn,
more surely still with each dawning day.

—Dietrich Bonhoeffer (end of 1944)

Chronology

1906   Dietrich Bonhoeffer born in Breslau on February 4

1912   Family moves to Berlin

1923   Graduates from secondary school (*Gymnasium*), begins
            university studies in Tübingen

1924   Journey to Rome. University studies in Berlin

1927   Attains doctorate (dissertation: *Sanctorum Communio*)

1927/28   Assistant pastor in Barcelona

1930   Qualifies for university lecturing (*Habilitation*)
            (*Act and Being*)

1930/31   Fellowship year at Union Theological Seminary in New York

1931   Private lecturer in Berlin, student chaplain, assistant
            pastor in Prenzlauer Berg, youth secretary with the
            ecumenical movement

1933/34   Pastor in London, attends ecumenical conference in Fanø

1935   Director of preachers' seminary in Finkenwalde

1936/37   Forbidden from teaching; seminary closed down;
            publishes *Discipleship*

1937/39   Works in the illegal "collective pastorates"

1939   Brief stay in America, returns in July

1940/41   Agent for military intelligence, first journey to Switzerland

1942   Journeys to Norway and Sweden (conversation with
            Bishop Bell)

1943   Engagement to Maria von Wedemeyer, arrest on April 5,
            incarcerated in the Tegel military prison

1944   October, transferred to Gestapo prison

1945   Transferred to Buchenwald concentration camp, then to
            Schönberg and to the Flossenbürg concentration camp.
            Executed on April 9

For Further Reading

By Dietrich Bonhoeffer

Conspiracy and Imprisonment: 1940–1945. Dietrich Bonhoeffer Works, volume 16. Edited by Mark S. Brocker, translated by Lisa E. Dahill. Minneapolis: Fortress Press, 2006.

Dietrich Bonhoeffer: Witness to Jesus Christ. The Making of Modern Theology series. Edited by John de Gruchy. Minneapolis: Fortress Press, 1990.

Letters and Papers from Prison. Edited by Eberhard Bethge. New York: Simon & Schuster, 1997.

Love Letters from Cell 92: The Correspondence between Dietrich Bonhoeffer and Maria von Wedemeyer, 1943-45. Edited by Ruth-Alice von Bismarck and Ulrich Kabitz, postscript by Eberhard Bethge, translated by John Brownjohn. Nashville: Abingdon Press, 1995.

Testament to Freedom. Edited by Geffrey B. Kelly and F. Burton Nelson. San Francisco: HarperSanFrancisco, 1995.

Wondrously Sheltered. Minneapolis: Augsburg Books, 2006.

About Dietrich Bonhoeffer

Bethge, Eberhard. *Dietrich Bonhoeffer: A Biography.* Revised Edition. Revised and Edited by Victoria J. Barnett. Minneapolis: Fortress Press, 2000.

Bethge, Renate, and Christian Gremmels, editors. *Dietrich Bonhoeffer: A Life in Pictures.* Centenary Edition. Translated by Brian McNeil. Minneapolis: Fortress Press, 2006.

About the Church Struggle in Nazi Germany

Barnett, Victoria J. *Bystanders: Conscience and Complicity during the Holocaust.* Wesport, Conn.: Greenwood Press, 1999.

Ericksen, Robert P., and Susannah Heschel, editors. *Betrayal: German Churches and the Holocaust.* Minneapolis: Fortress Press, 1999.

Haynes, Stephen R. *The Bonhoeffer Phenomenon: Portraits of a Protestant Saint.* Minneapolis: Fortress Press, 2004.

Index of Names

Paul Barz was born in 1943 in what at the time was called Leslau, Włocławek (Poland), on the Vistula River. After finishing secondary school (*Gymnasium*) in Hamburg, he apprenticed with a publisher and then worked as an editor with the periodical *Westermanns Monatshefte* until 1981. Since then he has worked as a freelance writer and journalist living in Wentorf near Hamburg, regularly contributing to *Welt am Sonntag*, the *Hamburger Abendblatt*, the *Westdeutsche Zeitung*, and as a writer for stage and radio. He has dealt extensively with the topic of "resistance and the Third Reich," including in various radio plays, most recently *Titelverteidigung* (Title defense) (for the Westdeutscher Rundfunk, 2005) and the play *La Paloma Ade*, which premiered in Hamburg in 2003 and dealt with the political entanglements of the actor Hans Albers.

His recent publications include: *Theodor Storm: Wanderer gegen Zeit und Welt* (Theodor Storm: Wanderer against Time and World), *Die Gegenspieler: Friedrich Barbarossa und Heinrich der Löwe* (The Opponents: Friedrich Barbarossa and Henry the Lion), and *Mozart: Prinz und Papageno* (Mozart: Prince and Papageno).